BUSINESS TAX AND LAW GUIDE

ALLIED DUNBAR

BUSINESS TAX AND LAW GUIDE

by

W I Sinclair, FCA,

A Partner in Kidsons

and

John McMullen, MA (Cantab), MIPM, Solicitor

Longman

© Allied Dunbar Financial Services Ltd 1988

ISBN 0-85121-462-2

Published by
Longman Professional and Business Communications Division
Longman Group UK Limited
21-27 Lamb's Conduit Street, London WC1N 3NJ

Associated Offices

Australia   Longman Cheshire Pty Ltd, Longman House, Kings Gardens, 91-97 Coventry Street, South Melbourne, Victoria 3205

Hong Kong   Longman Group (Far East) Limited Cornwall House, 18th Floor, Taikoo Trading Estate, Tong Chong Street, Quarry Bay

Malaysia   Longman Malaysia Sdn Bhd No 3 Jalan Kilang A, Off Jalan Penchala, Petaling Jaya, Selangor, Malaysia

Singapore   Longman Singapore Publishers (Pte) Ltd 25 First Lok Yang Road, Singapore 2262

USA   Longman Group (USA) Inc 500 North Dearborn Street, Chicago, Illinois 60610

British Library Cataloguing-in-Publication Data

A CIP catalogue record for this book is available from the British Library.

Printed in Great Britain by Biddles Ltd, Guildford, Surrey

Abbreviations

s	Section
Sch	Schedule
FA	Finance Act
TA	Income and Corporation Taxes Act 1988
CA	Companies Act
CGTA	Capital Gains Tax Act 1979
IHTA	Inheritance Tax Act 1984 (previously Capital Transfer Tax Act 1984)
VATA	Value Added Tax Act 1983
EP(C)A	Employment Protection (Consolidation) Act 1978
EPA	Employment Protection Act 1975

The authors

WALTER SINCLAIR qualified as a chartered accountant in 1959 and has remained in the profession since, first in general practice and then concentrating on taxation. He is now a taxation partner with Kidsons.

His interest in taxation led to writing on the subject and his authorship of *The Allied Dunbar Tax Guide* dates from its inception, as the *Hambro Tax Guide* 16 years ago.

Walter Sinclair is also the joint author of *The Allied Dunbar Capital Taxes and Estate Planning Guide*, now in its third edition. In addition, he contributes to a wide range of publications, including *The Times* and *The Daily Telegraph*, as well as being general editor of the *International Employment Tax Handbook*.

JOHN McMULLEN is a solicitor in private practice where he advises on Labour Law and Company Law. He is a member of the Institute of Personnel Management and a member of the Law Society's Standing Committee on Employment Law.

He has published articles in a number of legal journals, is a consultant editor of *The Company Lawyer*, and is the author of *Business Transfers and Employee Rights* (Butterworths, 1987).

Introduction

This book is a new companion volume to *The Allied Dunbar Tax Guide* and deals particularly with tax and law related to businesses. Thus, the book is designed to be of use to sole proprietors, partnerships and limited companies, covering not only those engaged in trading activities, but also the professions.

Insurance and pensions are of particular interest to businessmen and so two chapters deal with this area. One relates to general insurance and the other to life assurance and pensions.

The book has been designed as a general guide for both the professional and non-professional user. However, since the book concisely covers a very wide field, it has been necessary to omit some of the exceptions and qualifications with which the law abounds.

Obviously, the coverage of legal topics in a book of this size has also had to be selective. The book concentrates on key aspects of business law and no reference has been made, for example, to areas such as land law, employers' liability for accidents under health and safety legislation, and intellectual property law. Thus, if a particular problem is not fully covered by this book, you should look at a more detailed textbook or consult a specialist, such as a solicitor or accountant. Furthermore, if you are looking at a specific legal case or transaction of any complexity, you should seek appropriate professional advice.

For ease of reference, there is a full contents table and index. Also a glossary explains technical words and should be referred to if necessary. A particular feature is that all indexing and cross-referencing uses chapter and topic numbers. Thus 7.6 means the 6th-numbered topic in chapter 7.

This edition is based on the law as at 29 February 1988 and in particular contains tax law relating to 1987-88. However, a separate chapter lists the relevant changes announced in the March 1988 Budget, giving the proposals relating to the 1988-89 tax year. We are grateful to the Kidsons' Budget Team for their work on this chapter.

We acknowledge, with thanks, the very valuable assistance given to us in connection with this book by our respective colleagues, including Messrs KGS Stockings, ATII and G Wilson, FCA of Kidsons and VJ Jerrard, LLB and DC Vessey, BSc of Allied Dunbar Life Assurance plc. Our special thanks are extended to Vince Jerrard for contributing the chapter on Pensions and Life Assurance and to Mrs Gill Clark of Eagle Star Insurance, for writing the chapter on General Insurance.

29 February 1988

WI Sinclair

John McMullen

Contents

The Budget — 15 March 1988

by KIDSONS, CHARTERED ACCOUNTANTS

The main Budget changes are given below and should be referred to for events and periods after 5 April 1988 (sometimes from 15 March 1988). However, it must be emphasised that at the time of writing, the Finance Bill is still awaited and this will not become law until it receives Royal Assent in late July or early August. Thus, the proposals summarized below may be modified.

The 1988 Budget has made radical changes — income tax rates are drastically cut, as is inheritance tax. At the same time, capital gains tax is to be charged at income tax rates, so that the distinction between revenue profits and capital gains is much less important. This all has a profound effect on tax planning. For example, tax savings by incorporation are reduced (4.34).

INCOME TAX

Tax rate band changes

Reference
2.4

The basic rate has been reduced to 25% and all higher rates above 40% have been abolished.

The rate bands of income tax for 1988/89 are:—

Taxable income £	Slice £	Rate %	Total tax £
19,300	19,300	25	4,825
over 19,300		40	

Tax allowances

2.5

	1988/89 £
Single person	2,605
Married man	4,095
Wife's earned income relief (maximum)	2,605

Age allowance — single	(aged 65–79)	3,180
	(age 80 and over)	3,310
— married	(age 65–79)	5,035
	(age 80 and over)	5,205
— income limit		10.600
Additional personal allowance for children		1,490
Housekeeper	.	—
Dependent relative allowance — single woman		—
— other claimants		—
Daughter's or son's services		—
Widow's bereavement		1,490
Blind person's allowance		540

Basic rate   2.4

The basic rate of income tax is reduced to 25% with effect from 6 April 1988. Consequential adjustments arising from this change affect payment of annuities, interest and other annual payments including deeds of covenant, advance corporation tax and tax credits and the construction industry tax deduction scheme. The overall rate for discretionary and accumulation trusts will be 35%. MIRAS loans will be affected, producing a small increase in the net interest payable.

Car benefits   9.13

The scale benefits assessable for 1988–89 on directors and 'higher-paid' employees are to be doubled.

A Car scales: (cars under 4 years old)

		1988/89 £
Cylinder capacity	Up to 1400cc	1,050
	1401 — 2000cc	1,400
	more than 2000cc	2,200

Cars with original market value over £19,250

	£19,251–£29,000	2,900
	Over £29,000	4,600

B Car fuel scales:

Cylinder capacity	Up to 1400cc	480
	1401 — 2000cc	600
	more than 2000cc	900

Independent taxation of husband and wife   3.10

The Chancellor has announced a completely new system for taxing married couples, sweeping away a structure which has been in place for nearly two centuries. It will take effect from 6 April 1990.

The basic principle of the new system is that husband and wife will be taxed completely independently — the two incomes will no longer be added together. Each partner will pay their own tax, and be independent of the other. Thus married women will have the right to complete privacy and independence, for the first time.

As now, most taxpayers will not receive tax returns. When one is needed for a married woman's income, it will be sent to her direct, and many will welcome the opportunity to handle their own tax affairs for the first time. If a married woman wants to ask her husband to continue to fill in the tax return, she can of course do so, but she will have to sign it herself.

Each will be entitled to a single person's relief and tax rates. This means that with the 1988–89 rates, each will have £2,605 free of tax, paying 25% on the next £19,300 of income and 40% on the excess. (Couples of 65 and over will each have the single person's age allowance.)

Similarly, husband and wife will each have a full capital gains tax exemption (£5,000 for 1988–89) and pay the appropriate rate on gains above that.

There will also be an extra allowance, known as the married couple's allowance amounting to £1,490. This will normally go to the husband but if he has insufficient income, it will be wholly or partly transferable to the wife. For couples over 65, this allowance is £1,855 and from age 80, it becomes £1,895. Of course, these reliefs are simply for illustrative purposes and by 1990–91, they can be expected to be higher.

Mortgage interest relief   2.6

At present, mortgage interest relief is available on a loan of up to £30,000 to buy a home. But two single people sharing a home can get relief on loans up to £30,000 each, whereas a married couple share a single ration of relief.

For new mortgages, taken out from August 1988, the £30,000 limit on relief will apply to the house or flat, irrespective of whether there are one or more borrowers, married or single, living there. This puts unmarried couples on the same footing as married couples and eliminates the tax penalty on marriage.

At present, relief is allowable within the limit on the interest on loans applied to the purchase or improvement of a property used as the only or main residence for a dependent relative or former or separated spouse of the borrower.

It is proposed to abolish this relief where a loan is applied for this purpose on or after 6 April 1988. Relief will continue for the life of existing loans which already qualify under the present law. Relief will still be available to the relative or spouse where they pay the interest and have an interest in the property.

At the same time, it is proposed to abolish the equivalent capital gains tax relief for homes provided free for a dependent relative. This change will apply for disposals on or after 6 April 1988. Relief will continue to be available where a home would have qualified for the relief on a disposal before 6 April.

It is proposed to abolish relief on new loans for home improvements made on or after 6 April 1988. Relief will continue for existing eligible improvement loans.

Covenants   2.6

With the exception of covenants to charities, new covenants (made on or after 15 March 1988) will be taken out of the tax system altogether. The payers will not get tax relief, and the recipients will not have to pay tax on the money they receive.

People who already have covenants will continue to get tax relief for as long as the covenant lasts.

For the parents of students, tax relief will no longer be available on new covenants. But to provide broad compensation, there will be a new lower parental contribution scale for new students.

Maintenance   2.6

People receiving maintenance payments under new Court Orders or agreements from 15 March 1988 will not have to pay tax on them. A man maintaining his ex-wife (or vice versa) will get tax relief on the payments he mades, up to a limit equal to the difference between the married allowance and the single allowance (£1,490 for 1988–89).

Forestry

With effect from 15 March 1988 commercial woodlands will be wholly removed from the scope of income tax and corporation tax. This means that:

(a)   expenditure for the cost of planting and maintaining the trees will not be allowed as a tax deduction against other income; and

(b)   the proceeds from the sale of trees will not be charged to tax.

(c)   Tax relief under the existing rules will continue to be available until 5 April 1993 for those who are already 'occupiers' (typically owners or tenants) of commercial woodlands.

(d)   This relief will also be available until 5 April 1993 for those who become occupiers as a result of commitments entered into or applications for grants received by the Forestry Commission before 15 March 1988.

Redundancy payments   9.26, 10.29

The exemption from tax for redundancy and certain other lump sum payments on termination of employment is increased from £25,000 to £30,000 with effect from 6 April 1988. The additional top slicing tax relief on lump sums in excess of the exemption is abolished.

Pensions   11.9

The start date for personal pensions is confirmed as 1 July 1988 and the present retirement annuities tax regime will be extended until then.

The tax charge on refunds of employee pension contributions is 20% (previously 10%) with effect from 6 April 1988.

Assessments   2.47

Legislation is being introduced with effect from 1988/89 in order to remove any doubt concerning the Revenue's long-standing practice of making estimated assessments on income from overseas, income from letting property furnished, and interest not paid under the composite rate arrangements on a 'current year basis'.

BUSINESS TAXATION

Corporation tax   4.2

The full rate of corporation tax for the year ending 31 March 1989
is confirmed at 35% but the small companies rate is to be reduced
to 25%. The profit limits for the small companies rate remain as
before £100,000 and £500,000 but the marginal relief fraction will
become 1/40th. The marginal rate of corporation tax on profits
falling between £100,000 and £500,000 now becomes 37.5%.

ACT   4.8

The rate of advance corporation tax on dividends paid on or after
6 April 1988 will be payable at the rate of 25/75ths of the dividend.
The tax credit will similarly be 25/75ths of the dividend and will
satisfy the new basic rate liability of the shareholder.

Capital allowances   2.17

A number of technical changes to the capital allowance rules are
being introduced. Two of the changes deal with the
consequences of separate legislation for the existing reliefs for
property let on assured tenancy terms and for safety expenditure
on sports grounds.

Business entertainment   2.9

All entertainment and gifts after Budget Day (other than small
trade gifts below £10) provided by a business, whether to UK or
overseas customers, will be disallowable for tax purposes.
Previously the cost of entertaining overseas customers was tax
deductible.

Business expansion scheme   4.31

The BES is being extended to investment in companies engaged in
letting residential property on new-style assured tenancy terms.
To improve the targeting of BES there is to be a ceiling on the total
amount of investment in a company which can qualify for tax
relief in any 12 month period. A ceiling of £500,000 is proposed
except for ship chartering and private rented housing where the
ceiling will be £5 million. Investors in approved BES funds are to
get tax relief by reference to the closing date of the fund rather
than the date the fund invests the money.

Arrangements for taxing Lloyd's members

The present system is complex and costly to administer. With effect from the 1986 account it is intended that both underwriting profits and investment income will be charged to tax under Case I of Schedule D as income of the member's trade. Agents will be required to make a payment on account of the basic rate tax and members will be assessed on their aggregate syndicate profit at the basic and higher rates six months later. Capital gains from premium trust funds will not be affected.

Company residence rules   4.26

The Chancellor proposes to abolish the present requirement for Treasury consent to company migration, to introduce a simple test of company residence (the country of incorporation) and to provide for a tax charge on unrealised gains when companies migrate.

Top-slicing reliefs

The 'top-slicing' relief which applies to income tax charged on premiums for leases of land or buildings and certain similar payments is withdrawn. In addition, the 'top-slicing' relief given by extra statutory concession which may apply when two professional firms merge and one has to change its accounting basis to conform with the other, is ceasing. Both changes take effect for the tax year 1988/89.

CAPITAL GAINS TAX

Rebasing   6.8

As from 6 April 1988 capital gains and capital losses will be relevant only insofar as they have arisen since 31 March 1982, which is already the date from which indexation relief is available. Assets held on that date will need to be revalued as at 31 March 1982. Transitional rules will ensure that this does not produce gains or losses higher than those which would have arisen under the present rules. Where there would otherwise be a gain under one regime and a loss under the other, there will be neither a gain nor a loss for capital gains tax purposes.

Rates of tax   6.2

Individuals will pay capital gains tax at rates equivalent to the rates which would apply if their gains were treated as the top-slice of their income — 25% and/or 40% (1987/88 — 30%). This change will also apply to syndicate gains made by Lloyd's Underwriters.

Companies will generally continue to pay corporation tax at normal rates, but life insurance companies will continue to pay corporation tax at 30% on gains attributable to policyholders.

Annual exemption   6.4

The annual exemption for individuals, personal representatives and certain special trusts will be: £5,000 (1987/88 — £6,600) and for most trusts, £2,500 (1987/88 — £3,300) from 6 April 1988.

Losses   6.12

Realised capital losses brought forward from 1987/88 will remain available for offset against gains of future years. Their amount will be as computed under the old regime.

Married couples

The change to computing capital gains tax by reference to income effectively means that for 1988/89 and 1989/90 tax will be computed at the rates applicable as if the gains were investment income of the husband.

Separate taxation

With the proposed introduction of separate taxation of husbands and wives, from 6 April 1990 each spouse will be entitled to a separate annual exemption and their liabilities will be calculated solely by reference to their own income.

Retirement relief   6.26

The basic exemption for capital gains on qualifying disposals of business interests or family company shares by a proprietor or shareholder aged 60 or retiring younger on ill-health grounds will remain at £125,000. However a new 50% relief is to be introduced for gains on such disposals in the range £125,000 — £500,000, where the disposal is after 5 April 1988.

Anti-avoidance

Provisions are to be introduced with effect from 15 March 1988 in order to prevent groups of companies or associated companies from creating large artificial capital losses by the application of the indexation provisions to inter-company loans.

Share exchanges 6.18

An anomaly is to be corrected, to prevent double taxation of gains or double relief for losses arising following share exchanges within groups of companies.

INHERITANCE TAX

Tax rates 7.7

The threshold for liability is increased from £90,000 to £110,000. Above this figure tax is charged at 40% (20% for lifetime charges). These changes apply to transfers on or after 15 March 1988.

New bands £	% Rate of tax in band	Old bands £
0 — 110,000	NIL	0 — 90,000
—	30	90,001 — 140,000
110,001 upwards	40	140,001 — 220,000
—	50	220,001 — 330,000
—	60	330,001 upwards

The tax saving on an estate of £330,000 is £14,000.

Political parties 7.10

The £100,000 limit on gifts to political parties is abolished from 15 March 1988.

TAX COMPLIANCE

New measures

Various new measures are to be introduced based on the recommendations of the Keith Committee. Some have immediate effect, but others must wait until 1992.

Notification of liability 2.47

The present maximum penalty of £100 for failure to notify liability to tax is to be increased to 100% of the tax due. This is in line with the maximum penalty for non-fraudulent submission of incorrect returns and applies to 1988/89 liabilities. The new rules will make it clear that there is an obligation to notify the Inland Revenue of each new source of income which could give rise to additional tax liability. Because of the time permitted for submission of returns, this penalty will in effect commence from 6 April 1990.

Information powers

The powers of the Inland Revenue to obtain information, to assist in ensuring that taxpayers are duly assessed, are to be strengthened with effect from the date in July or August 1988, when the Finance Bill receives the Royal Assent. The new powers will enable information to be obtained about payments made by Government Departments and other public authorities for services, grants or subsidies from public or EC funds and the identity of business licence holders. The Department of National Savings will be required to divulge information about named taxpayers. Where the Inland Revenue can satisfy a Special Commissioner that a serious loss of tax has occurred, it will be possible for them to obtain information about taxpayers whom they are unable to name. This could require promoters of unsuccessful tax avoidance schemes to divulge the identity of all participants.

VALUE ADDED TAX

Registration   8.2

As from 16 March 1988 the registration limit is increased from £21,300 to £22,100 annual turnover. The single quarterly registration limit is increased from £7,250 to £7,500. From 1 June 1988 the limits for cancelling registration on the basis of expected future turnover will be increased from £20,300 to £21,100 annually. Restrictions on businesses wishing to register voluntarily will be removed.

Entertainment   8.13

As from 1 August 1988 VAT will not be recoverable on the entertaining of overseas customers.

Penalties   8.4

The flat rate 30% penalty for late registration only applies after 15 March 1988 where there is an 18 months delay. For delayed registration of less than nine months the penalty will be 10% and for delays of between nine and 18 months the penalty will be 20%. A new penalty (in addition to that already proposed for 1989) will apply to persons who persistently underdeclare or overclaim tax. The penalty (15% of the tax) will not be automatic and will only be used when a person has underdeclared or overclaimed tax twice within two years and a written warning has been issued.

STAMP AND CAPITAL DUTIES

Capital duty   5.22

The 1% Capital Duty hitherto payable on formation of a company or on increasing a company's capital is abolished from 16 March 1988.

Unit trusts

The ¼% Unit Trust Instrument Duty hitherto payable on all property put into a unit trust is abolished from 16 March 1988.

NATIONAL INSURANCE CONTRIBUTIONS 1988/89

Class 1 (Employed)
Not contracted out:

Levels of weekly earnings	Employee	Employer
£41.00—69.99	5.00%	5.00%
£70.00—104.99	7.00%	7.00%
£105.00—154.99	9.00%	9.00%
£155.00—305.00	9.00%	10.45%
Over £305.00	No further liability	10.45%

Contracted out:

Levels of weekly earnings	Employee		Employer	
	On first £41.00	Remainder	On first £41.00	Remainder
£41.00—69.99	5.00%	3.00%	5.00%	1.20%
£70.00—104.99	7.00%	5.00%	7.00%	3.20%
£105.00—154.99	9.00%	7.00%	9.00%	5.20%
£155.00—305.00	9.00%	7.00%	10.45%	6.65%
Over £305.00	No further liability			6.65% on £305.00 10.45% on balance

Class 2 (Self-employed) Flat rate per week	£4.05
Lower earnings limit	£2,250.00 p.a.

Class 3 (Non-employed) Voluntary flat rate per week	£3.95

Class 4 (Self-employed) On assessable profits between £4,750 and £15,860	6.30%

1 Making a choice between different forms of trading vehicle

1.1 Introduction

The following is a summary of the main considerations which might influence your choice of trading format. The discussion which follows is based mainly on English Law. In relation to partnerships in particular, Scottish Law has certain rules which might differ slightly from the rules set out here.

1.2 Choosing a format

There are various modes of carrying on business. The choice of which one to adopt should always be carefully considered. Very often tax considerations will be highly relevant and, in some cases, be the main reason for the adoption of a particular type of trading vehicle (chapter 4). That aspect in particular should always be carefully considered with your accountant or other financial adviser (4.33).

In this chapter, three common vehicles are discussed, namely the sole trader, the partnership and the limited company. There are other forms that can be used, such as a limited partnership, a workers' cooperative, a company limited by guarantee, an unlimited company or, indeed, an unincorporated association (such as a club or society) but these tend to be rarer and some of them include organisations set up otherwise than solely with a view to profit. This of course contrasts with the main aim of the sole trader, a partnership or a limited company, which is usually the making of profit.

1.3 Sole traders

This is possibly the simplest form in which you can trade. It requires little or no formality in itself (although, as in the case of a partnership or company or any trading vehicle, there may be inevitable formalities such as income taxation administration, consumer credit obligations, value added tax administration and employment obligations that affect all businesses). An individual sole trader can freely contract with any other person or, indeed, another company and can employ people. He or she can, of course, also incur liabilities, and the individual is personally liable on all contracts made. Commonly, if overdraft facilities are required from a bank, individual guarantees may be required and the individual's personal assets will be required to secure such a loan.

Despite the advantages that controlling your own business can give you, sole responsibility without being able to share this with others, and unlimited liability are two major drawbacks to being 'your own boss'. The ultimate consequences of unlimited liability in the event of business failure are described at 1.8.

1.4   Partnerships

A partnership is defined by the Partnership Act 1890 as being the relationship which subsists between persons carrying on a business in common with a view of profit. The definition of partnership is more fully described in chapter 5.

1.5   Terms implied in partnerships by the Partnership Act 1890

The Partnership Act 1890 implies certain rules into a partnership agreement. For example, every partner is the agent of the firm and can bind the others; every partner is liable jointly with the others for the firm's debts; unless the contrary is agreed all partners share equally in the profits and capital of the firm (and also its losses); a partnership is determinable at will on retirement and no new partner can be introduced without the others' consent. These rules and others are set out in detail in chapter 5.

1.6   The importance of an express partnership agreement

It can be seen that there are rules that will be implied into a partnership relationship in the absence of a provision to the contrary which may prove inconvenient. For example, it is inconvenient for a partner to be able to leave the partnership at will, to cause an automatic dissolution by his death, or for the partnership shares of the profits and contribution to capital to be fixed equally by statute, and for the powers of the partners to be fixed by statute. And you might want to fix your own rules as to continuing share of profits throughout illness, provision for holidays, remuneration of the partners, pursuit of private interests apart from the partnership business, and so forth. Much of this problem can be solved by use of an express partnership agreement (chapter 5).

1.7   The liability of partners for a firm's debts

One of the main drawbacks of a partnership is the fact that the partners can be jointly liable for the partnership's debts. For this reason, some partnerships convert themselves into limited companies to obtain the benefit of limited liability. Some partnerships, such as firms of solicitors and accountants, are, to this date, prohibited by their professional associations from so doing (although this may change in the future).

One exception to the rule about personal liability of partners is the case of a limited partnership which may be set up under the Limited Partnerships Act 1907. If a partnership is set up under this Act, it is possible for one or more partners to have limited liability for the partnership's debts. The limit of that liability would be by agreement with the other partners. However, such a partnership, to exist, must still have one or more general partners who are liable for the firm's debts on an unlimited basis.

Further, the status of a limited partner is lost if there is any participation in the management of the partnership firm by the limited partner. Having regard to the fact that limited liability may be achieved by use of the limited liability company, the limited partnership is comparatively rare. It is thought that, probably, only about 700 of these limited partnerships exist.

1.8   Personal insolvency

The most drastic consequence of business failure either as a sole trader (1.3) or as a member of a partnership is personal insolvency as a result of unlimited liability. The consequences of this cannot be underestimated.

Personal insolvency, or bankruptcy arises as a result of an individual's inability to discharge his debts.

Sometimes bankruptcy can be avoided by making a voluntary arrangement with your creditors with the assistance of an insolvency practitioner. In such a case, with the assistance and approval of the court, a settlement or set of proposals for partial discharge of debts may be binding on creditors if a three-quarters majority of creditors in value voting on the matter agree and, if so, the scheme is then binding on all other creditors.

But, otherwise, you can be made bankrupt by a creditor's (or your own) petition. Often this occurs after a statutory demand which you are not able to comply with.

If a bankruptcy order is made you become an undischarged bankrupt and are deprived of ownership of your property. You lose control over administration of your affairs and purported dispositions of your property are void.

Your trustee in bankruptcy may also be able to avoid or adjust certain transactions, such as transactions at an undervalue and preferences, which took place before your bankruptcy. Preferences are transactions which put people in a better position after your insolvency than they would have been in had the transaction not taken place. The time limits are:

(1) in the case of transactions at an undervalue: within five years of presentation of a petition of bankruptcy;
(2) if the transaction was not at an undervalue but entered into with an associate (an associate includes a spouse or other fairly close relation): two years;
(3) if the transaction was neither with an associate nor at an undervalue: six months.

For a preference to apply, the debtor must have been influenced by a desire to put the creditor into the better position in which he now finds himself. This is presumed unless proved to the contrary where associates are concerned. In most (though not all) cases, it must also be shown that the debtor was insolvent at the relevant time, and this may be presumed unless disproved in the case of dealings with an associate.

These provisions are obviously designed to control transfers of property to others (say a relation) close to the bankruptcy to avoid that property being taken by creditors. There are also rules against transactions defrauding creditors.

Bankruptcy commences on the day a bankruptcy order is made and continues until the order is discharged. In summary administrations, the time of discharge is two years, in other cases three years, and in criminal or repeated bankruptcy, five years (with the permission of the court).

An undischarged bankrupt cannot be a company director unless the court consents and, generally, the consequences of bankruptcy are traumatic.

1.9 The limited liability company

Because of the circumstances set out in 1.8 and for other reasons, the limited company is an extremely popular form of trading vehicle. There are approximately 860,000 companies incorporated at the Companies Registry. The vast majority of these are private limited companies.

A company must be registered under CA 1985 or have been registered already under one of the Companies Acts which preceded this Act. Many companies are incorporated under CA 1948 or earlier Companies Acts such as CA 1929 or 1908. Any new company would now be incorporated under CA 1985.

1.10 Forming companies

More formalities are necessary to incorporate a company than, for example, to form a partnership and these are discussed more fully in chapter 5. This can be one of the drawbacks of companies when compared with partnerships.

1.11 Private and public companies

The basic division between types of limited companies is between private companies and public companies. Briefly, a public company is a company which may offer its shares to the public, which uses the suffix 'public limited company' or 'plc' and which has to meet certain minimum capital requirements (such as a minimum issued share capital of £50,000, a quarter of which must be paid up).

A public company is generally also subject to more stringent requirements in CA 1985 and, if a listed company, to detailed Stock Exchange rules. In practice, public limited companies are much more substantial than the minimum figure of capital mentioned above indicates. A private company is a company which is not a public company; and it cannot offer its shares to the public.

1.12 Limited liability of shareholders of companies

Being a member of a limited company gives you the advantage of limited liability. The leading case illustrating this is *Salomon v Salomon & Co Ltd* (1897), where a promoter who had carried on the business of a leather merchant and wholesale boot manufacturer transferred his business to a newly formed limited company. The nominal capital of the company was £40,000 and Salomon took £20,000 worth of shares in part payment of the price of the business transferred. A further £10,000 of the purchase price was secured by debentures. The company went into liquidation with many trade creditors unpaid. Salomon took priority over them in respect of the £10,000 secured by debentures (see chapter 5). The trade creditors attempted to say that the company's debts were really Salomon's. Not so. The House of Lords held that the new company was a separate legal entity from Salomon and his liability was limited to the amount that he had subscribed for his shares, a sum he had, in fact, already paid.

Since then, the principle of separate corporate personality has been reinforced by many decisions, thus leaving the liability of members separate from the liability of the company. Occasionally, the courts 'lift the veil' of incorporation, look inside the company and treat the company's debts as the members' debts. These instances are very rare indeed, such as in the case of enemy activity, fraud, some revenue cases, some unusual cases involving groups of companies, and certain other highly exceptional examples. There are also some instances where, under statute, members or directors can be personally liable and these are discussed in chapter 5. Again, they are the exception rather than the rule. Limited liability must be one of the primary motives, apart from tax (4.33), for a businessman to incorporate his previously unincorporated business.

1.13   Advantages and disadvantages of incorporation compared with partnership

Having discussed the basic format of partnerships and sole traders and companies, perhaps it is now appropriate to set out a checklist which shows both the advantages and disadvantages of incorporating a previously unincorporated business and also the specific differences between companies and partnerships. This list ignores tax considerations, which, in themselves, may be a primary or even decisive motive for transferring an unincorporated business into a limited company form (4.33). Some relevant considerations will be as follows:

(1) As a company is a separate legal person from its members the debts and liabilities of a company are those of the company and not the members (contrast a partnership where the partners may be jointly liable, and, in Scotland, also severally liable). Although partners can be sued in the firm name this does not detract from the principle that, at the end of the day, if the partnership firm is unable to meet a claim, the partners are jointly (and, in Scotland, severally) liable themselves. One exception is in the case of a limited partnership under the Limited Partnerships Act 1907 (1.7).

(2) As a company is a separate legal person, it enjoys perpetual succession. Thus, a company is not affected by the death or

retirement of any of its proprietors. The company continues notwithstanding these events. Under the Partnership Act 1890, a partnership is dissolved *automatically* by death or retirement of one of the partners. Also, if a shareholder of a company dies, his or her share does not have to be bought out by the other members. It can simply pass to the personal representatives of the deceased member.

(3) Shares in a limited company can be transferred to any other person. This is not the case in a partnership where the partners may resist the introduction of a new partner without their consent.

(4) The property of a company belongs to the company and there is no need to change the deeds of title when the members change (eg by death or sale of shares). This contrasts with a partnership, in which case the property will be vested in the names of the partners. Any change in the composition of the partners may necessitate a change in the deeds of title.

(5) Each partner may take part in the management of a partnership. In a company, unless a member is a director, he may not take part in the management of a company. Membership of a company does not necessarily carry with it management rights.

(6) In principle, a member may mortgage his share in a company. This cannot take place in a partnership and, also, in principle, the partners may dissolve a partnership if any partner charges his share.

(7) A company can contract with its members (for example, enter into contracts of employment with its members and directors) but a partnership cannot.

(8) A company may have greater versatility in borrowing powers than a partnership, in the sense that it can issue certain specialised forms of security for loans, such as debentures and floating charges. A floating charge may not be issued by a partnership or a sole trader since a floating charge involves, in practice, a charge over moveable chattels. A floating charge over moveable chattels is not possible in the case of an individual or partnership and chattels can only be mortgaged by an individual or a partnership through a bill of sale under the Bill of Sale Acts 1878 and 1882. This would require each chattel to be specified which, in reality, is not practicable. The floating charge is further described at 5.20.

(9) There are fewer formalities to be observed in relation to a partnership than in relation to a company. There are no documents required to be sent to a registry, such as in the case of companies, where, for example, the Memorandum & Articles, statement of first directors and secretary, forms in relation to the issue of shares, certificate in relation to compliance with formation regulations, and statements of registered office are required to be prepared and filed with the Companies Registry.

(10) There is no limit to the number of members of a company, whereas partnerships are limited to 20 members (although certain

(professional) firms are allowed to exceed 20 members (eg solicitors and accountants)).

(11) There is less publicity in relation to a partnership in that the partnership deed, if any, is not required to be registered on any public register and the firm's accounts are not made public. By contrast, a company has to register its Memorandum & Articles (see chapter 5) and also many other documents during the life of the company, such as its annual returns and accounts and special resolutions and records of certain transactions and meetings and has to publish accounts.

(12) There are continuing expenses in the case of companies which are not necessarily applicable to partnerships, such as the requirement of an audit and the making of annual returns.

(13) Certain rules in company law do not apply to partnership law, such as the *ultra vires* doctrine (5.24), and the various special duties imposed on directors by statute (see, in detail, chapter 5).

(14) A company is subject to stringent capital requirements if a public company and must still observe certain rules as to capital even if a private company. A partnership may trade more or less as if it were an individual.

Some of these rules can be altered by agreement in the Articles of a company or the partnership deed as the case may be, and the distinction between companies and partnerships blurred. For example, you will often see that in smaller private companies the right freely to transfer shares to outsiders is restricted, thus making the position with regard to transmission of shares more analogous to partnerships in that context.

1.14   Conclusion

There are certainly advantages and disadvantages either way to be considered in choosing between the corporate and non-corporate form. Apart from the taxation considerations involved, a significant advantage of incorporation is limited liability. Choosing the partnership and sole trader form has advantages, by contrast, in lack of formality and expense and, also, freedom from the considerable restrictions and regulations contained in CA 1985 and elsewhere. As always, specialist advice is needed on which trading form is most appropriate, at whatever particular stage of a firm's evolution.

2 Tax on business income

2.1 Introduction — The taxation of income

If you trade as an individual or in partnership, your taxable income will be liable to income tax at a basic rate of 2̶5̶% and various higher rates from 40% t̶o̶ 6̶0̶% (2.4). These rates apply for the tax year 1987–88 (ending 5 April 1988). In arriving at your taxable income certain deductions are appropriate such as capital allowances (2.17), charges on income (2.6) and personal reliefs (2.5).

The capital gains of individuals and partnerships are considered later (chapter 6). The rate is generally 30% subject to certain reliefs. Both the income and capital gains of companies are subject to corporation tax (chapter 4). The rate is 35%, subject to a small companies rate of 2̶5̶% which applies where profits are sufficiently low (4.3).

The income of companies etc, partnerships and individuals is taxable according to a system of schedules and cases as follows.

2.2 Table: Classes of income

Schedule A
Income from land and buildings. This includes rents and lease premiums.

Schedule B
This applies to woodlands managed on a commercial basis and the 'assessable value' is taxed.

Schedule C
This covers income from government securities payable in the UK; also overseas public revenue dividends paid through a banker, etc here.

Schedule D
This is the main schedule applicable to the income connected with businesses. It is divided into separate categories as follows:

Case I   Trades (2.7).

Case II	Professions and vocations (2.7).
Case III	Interest, annuities and other annual payments received. This is now restricted on account of the 'composite rate' scheme applying to much bank and building society interest.
Cases IV & V	Income from certain investments, possessions and businesses overseas.
Case VI	This is a 'sweeping-up' case applying to miscellaneous profits not covered by any of the other cases of Schedule D.

Schedule E
This schedule applies to directors' remuneration as well as wages and salaries earned by other employees. It comprises:

Case I	The work is done in the UK and the employee is resident here.
Case II	Generally this case applies to a non-resident working in the UK.
Case III	The work is done wholly abroad by a UK resident but the salary is sent here during the course of the overseas employment. However, this case does not apply if the income is already taxed under Case I or Case II of Schedule E.

Schedule F
This schedule covers distributions made by companies including in particular dividends (4.8).

2.3 Income tax rates and personal reliefs

The 1987–88 rates of income tax and personal reliefs are given below. The 1988–89 figures are given in the 1988 Budget Notes. For further details, reference should be made to the *Allied Dunbar Tax Guide*.

2.4 Table: Basic and higher rates for 1987–88

Taxable Income £	Slice £	Rate %	Tax on Slice £	Total Tax £
17,900	17,900	27	4,833	4,833
20,400	2,500	40	1,000	5,833
25,400	5,000	45	2,250	8,083
33,300	7,900	50	3,950	12,033
41,200	7,900	55	4,345	16,378
Excess over 41,200		60		

2.5   Table: Personal reliefs — 1987–88

Personal allowances	1987–88 £
Single	2,425
Married	3,795
Wife's earnings (maximum)	2,425
Single parent addition	1,370
Age allowance	
Single (age 65–79)	2,960
(age 80 and over)	3,070
Married (age 65–79)	4,675
(age 80 and over)	4,845
Income limit	9,800
Dependent relative relief	
Single woman claimant	145
Other claimants	100
Housekeeper relief	100
Daughter's/son's services	55
Widow's bereavement allowance	1,370
Blind person's allowance	
Single	540
Married	1,080

2.6   Deductions from income

As well as personal reliefs (2.5) you are able to make various other deductions in arriving at your taxable income. The following are some examples:

(1)   One half of your Class IV National Insurance contributions.
(2)   Business losses and capital allowances.
(3)   Allowable retirement annuity premiums.
(4)   Parts of certain transfers to reserve made by Lloyd's Underwriters or other approved underwriters.
(5)   Donations to charity under Deeds of Covenant which are capable of exceeding three years. This normally entails four annual payments.
(6)   Loan interest payments are allowable in certain circumstances including:

(a) On the first £30,000 of your mortgage on your main residence (see also 1988 Budget changes as supplied in the Budget Notes).

(b) On property which you let out for at least half of the year (only relievable against your lettings income).

(c) For buying plant and machinery for use in your partnership. (Relief is given for three years after the tax year when the loan is taken out.)

(d) On money which you borrow for acquiring ordinary shares in a close company or lending money for its business. (Not applicable to a close investment company. You must either own 5% of the shares or own some shares and work for the company for much of your time.)

(e) For buying a partnership share or lending it money for its business.

(f) For paying inheritance tax. (Interest unrelieved in the year of payment can be spread forward or backward.)

(7) Generally, allowable mortgage interest is payable under the deduction of basic rate income tax, as are various other *charges on income.* The following are examples and are deductible from your income:

(a) Payments under Court Order for alimony or maintenance.

(b) Annual payments to retiring partners or their widows in accordance with partnership agreements.

(c) Certain annual payments made concerning the purchase of a business, such payments being made to the former owner or his widow or dependants.

2.7 Trades, professions and vocations

As mentioned above (2.2), profits from trades are assessed under Schedule D Case I whilst those from professions and vocations are taxed under Case II of Schedule D. The remainder of this chapter deals with the position concerning individuals and most of the general rules apply also to partnerships and companies. However, there are certain special rules which apply to partnerships (chapter 3) and companies (chapter 4).

For tax purposes, trade includes manufacturing, retailing, wholesaling and trading ventures in general. It may also encompass certain isolated transactions according to the rules (2.8).

A profession is an occupation requiring special intellectual skills. This is sometimes coupled with manual skills. Examples of those engaged in professions are doctors and dentists, solicitors, barristers, accountants and architects.

A definition of vocation is the way that a person passes his life; for example an author, actor, singer, composer or dancer.

2.8 Indications of trading

Normally, there will be no doubt that you are carrying on a trade (or profession or vocation) assessable under Schedule D, Case I or II. However, other activities might constitute trading and the following are indications:

(1) Dealing in property is likely to be treated as trading.
(2) Possessing expert business knowledge in connection with a transaction which you carry out will make it more likely that you are treated as trading.
(3) Repeating the same transaction is often evidence of trading.
(4) Should you buy an asset, work on it and then sell it, this might be treated as trading, for example buying a ship, converting it and then selling it.
(5) Isolated transactions in assets which produce income are not normally regarded as trading. Capital gains tax would generally apply.
(6) Regular buying and selling normally constitutes trading. However, purchases and sales of shares by an individual are not usually treated as trading, capital gains tax then applying.
(7) Where there are isolated purchases and sales of works of art, this is not normally regarded as trading since the works of art are owned to be admired rather than for commercial purposes.
(8) An isolated transaction might be held to be trading if its very nature is commercial. An example is a single purchase and sale of a quantity of unmatured whisky.

2.9 Computing the assessable profits for Schedule D Cases I and II

Normally, you will have annual accounts prepared for your business or profession. These will include a profit and loss account or an income and expenditure account. These accounts should generally be drawn up to the same date every year but need not coincide with the tax year (ending on 5 April). The profit shown by your accounts forms the basis of your assessment under Case I or Case II of Schedule D. However, adjustment to your profit (or loss) should be made as follows:

(1) Add any non-deductible expenses (see below) charged in your accounts.
(2) Deduct any profits included in your accounts which are not taxable under Cases I and II of Schedule D because they are non-taxable or liable to tax under other cases or schedules. Examples are: interest receivable taxed under Schedule D Case III, capital profits liable to

capital gains tax, rents receivable taxed under Schedule A, interest received net having been taxed at source, and dividends.

(3) Deduct amounts previously put to reserve and now recredited in your accounts (unless the original amounts were not allowed against your taxable profits).

(4) Deduct any allowable expenses not already charged.

(5) Add any trading profits not already included.

(6) Exclude government grants towards specified capital expenditure or compensation for loss of capital assets. Also, generally exclude regional development grants under the Industrial Development Act 1982 and certain grants to assist industry in Northern Ireland. However, often these items can be added to the costs of the assets for capital gains tax purposes.

(7) Add entertaining expenses (unless concerning overseas customers and their agents prior to 16 March 1988 (see the 1988 Budget Notes) or your own staff).

(8) Add fines for illegalities and connected legal costs.

(9) Add charitable donations unless wholly for business purposes. (Non-close companies are allowed donations up to 3% of their dividends.)

(10) Add political donations.

(11) Add the cost of acquiring capital assets (plant and machinery, buildings, motor vehicles etc). Capital allowances are frequently available.

(12) Add private or domestic expenses of yourself or your family.

(13) Add a proportion of expenses containing some private element. Should a private house be used for business purposes, the proportion deductible is not normally allowed to exceed 2/3rds of the rent and other costs.

(14) Where you own or partly own a business, your drawings are not deductible.

2.10 Example: Schedule D Case I computation

Jack Box trades on his own account in a manufacturing business. His accounts for the year to 30 June 1987 show a net profit of £40,000 including the following:

Expenses	£
Depreciation — Motor car	3,000
— Plant and machinery	6,000
Legal expenses re: debt collection	500
Bad debts provision (5% x sales debtors)	2,000
Entertaining expenses — UK customers	1,000
— Overseas customers	500
Loss on sale of motor car	1,500
Non-business charitable donations	100
Legal expenses re: new lease	400

Income	£
Bank deposit interest	300
General bad debts provision no longer required	500

Ignoring capital allowances compute Jack Box's adjusted Case I profit.

Jack Box Schedule D Case I computation based on accounts for year ended 30 June 1987:

	£	£
Net profit per accounts		40,000
Less:		
Bank deposit interest	300	
Bad debts provision no longer required	500	800
		39,200
Add: Disallowable expenses:		
Depreciation (£3,000 + £6,000)	9,000	
General bad debts provision	2,000	
Legal expenses re: new lease	400	
Charitable donations	100	
Entertaining UK customers	1,000	
Loss on sale of motor car (capital)	1,500	14,000
Adjusted profit		£53,200

2.11   Stock and work in progress

In preparing business accounts, stock and work in progress is normally valued at each accounting date. The profits are augmented or decreased by the excess or deficit of the closing stock and work in progress compared with the opening position. Thus, if the closing stock is valued on a more generous basis than the opening stock, the profits shown by the accounts will be higher than the true amount.

Your stock and work in progress is the amount of unsold raw materials, finished goods and work in hand that was owned at the end of the accounts period. The Inland Revenue pay special attention to the manner in which businesses value their stock and normally insist that, for tax purposes, the opening and closing stocks are valued on an identical basis. Normally, each item in stock is valued at the lower of its cost or net realizable value. The exact cost for each item may or may not include an addition for expenses, depending on the exact basis adopted. The general rule to ascertain cost is that identical items are identified on the basis that the earliest purchases were sold or used first (FIFO). The method chosen must be used consistently. 'Net realizable value' is the estimated proceeds from disposing of the stock in the ordinary course of business at balance sheet date. This is after allowing for all expenses in connection with the disposal.

For a period of about nine years up to 12 March 1984, generous stock relief was available in arriving at the taxable profits of businesses. This applied to individuals, partnerships and companies. Since the relief does not apply after 12 March 1984, however, no further mention is made here and if details are required, reference should be made to the *Allied Dunbar Tax Guide.*

2.12 Basis of assessment

Having computed your assessable profits from a business or profession, the question remains, for which tax year are they assessable? Assessments under Cases I and II of Schedule D are normally based on the profits of the accounts year ending in the preceding tax year. Thus if a business prepares accounts to 30 September each year, its 1988–89 Schedule D Case I assessment will be based on the profits for the year to 30 September 1987 (ending in the preceding tax year 1987–88).

Obviously, when you first start your business, you will have no previous year on which to be taxed. Therefore, special rules apply to the opening years of assessment. Similarly, there are separate rules for closing years and where you change your accounting date.

2.13 Opening years

(1) For the first tax year of a business, profession or vocation, you will be assessed on the profits from the starting date until the next 5 April. This may involve taking a proportion of your profit for a longer period. Thus if your business started on 6 July 1987 and makes up its accounts to 5 July 1988 showing a profit of £24,000 for that year, the assessment for 1987–88 will be based on the period from 6 July 1987 to 5 April 1988, giving 24,000 × 9/12 = £18,000.

(2) Your assessment for the second tax year would normally be based on the profits for the first complete 12 months. Thus, in the above example, your 1988–89 assessment will be based on the profits for the first complete year, which ends on 5 July 1988, giving £24,000.

(3) The third year's assessment is generally based on the preceding year. Thus in the example above, your 1988–89 assessment would be £24,000 (the profits for the accounts year ending in the preceding tax year).

(4) You will have the option to elect that the assessments for both the second and third tax years (but not only one of these) should be based on the actual profits for those years (see example 2.14). This election must be made to the Inspector of Taxes within seven years of the end of the second year of assessment.

(5) Special rules cover commencements following certain partnership changes (3.6).

2.14 Example: Schedule D Cases I and II — Assessments for opening years

Jack Box started in business on his own account on 1 July 1985 and prepared accounts for an 18 month period to 31 December 1986 producing an adjusted profit of £27,000. He selected 31 December as his regular accounting date and his adjusted profit for the year to 31 December 1987 was £9,000 and for 1988 it was £7,200. What are Jack's Schedule D Case I assessments based on those profits?

Jack Box — Schedule D Case I assessments

Tax year	Basis	Base period	Calculations	Assessment
1985–86	Actual	1.7.85–5.4.86	£27,000×9-1/6/18	£13,750
1986–87	First year	1.7.85–30.6.86	£27,000×12/18	£18,000
1987–88	Preceding year	1.1.86–31.12.86	£27,000×12/18	£18,000
1988–89	Preceding year	1.1.87–31.12.87		£ 9,000
1989–90	Preceding year	1.1.88–31.12.88		£ 7,200

The assessments for Jack's second and third tax years total £36,000 (£18,000 + £18,000). Jack Box can effect a saving by electing that his assessments for those years should be on the actual profits made in 1986–87 and 1987–88 as follows:

1986–87	6.4.86–31.12.86	£27,000×8-5/6/18	£13,250
	1.1.87–5.4.87	£ 9,000×3-1/6/12	£ 2,375
			£15,625
1987–88	6.4.87–31.12.87	£ 9,000×8-5/6/12	£ 6,625
	1.1.88–5.4.88	£ 7,200×3-1/6/12	£ 1,900	£ 8,525

The reduction in the aggregate assessments for 1986–87 and 1987–88 is £11,850 (£36,000 − (£15,625 + £8,525)).

2.15 Closing years

(1) If you permanently cease your trade, profession or vocation, your last year is assessed on an actual basis. That is to say, your assessment under Schedule D Case I or II is based on the actual profits from the previous 6 April until the date when your business ceases.

(2) The Inland Revenue has the right to make additional assessments in respect of the two tax years prior to the year in which cessation takes place. These are known as the two penultimate years.

(3) The Revenue has the option of increasing your assessments for the two penultimate tax years to the actual profits for those years. This is illustrated in the following example.

2.16   Example: Schedule D Cases I and II — Assessments for closing years

---

Jack Box ceases to trade on 31 July 1988 having made adjusted profits as follows:

Year ended 31 July 1985	£25,000
Year ended 31 July 1986	£18,000
Year ended 31 July 1987	£36,000
Year ended 31 July 1988	£27,000

What are Jack's final assessments on these profits?

Before it was known that Jack was ceasing to trade, his assessments would be as follows:

Tax year	Basis	Base period	Schedule D Case I Assessment
1986–87	Preceding year	Year to 31.7.85	£25,000
1987–88	Preceding year	Year to 31.7.86	£18,000
Total for 1986–87 and 1987–88			£43,000

When cessation on 31.7.88 is notified to the Revenue they will adjust the assessments for 1986–87 and 1987–88 as follows:

			£	£
1986–87				
Actual	6.4.86–31.7.86	£18,000 × 3-5/6/12	5,750	
	1.8.86–5.4.87	£36,000 × 8-1/6/12	24,500	30,250
1987–88				
Actual	6.4.87–31.7.87	£36,000 × 3-5/6/12	11,500	
	1.8.87–5.4.88	£27,000 × 8-1/6/12	18,375	29,875
Revised total for 1986–87 and 1987–88				60,125
Less: Already assessed				43,000
Additional assessments 1986–87 and 1987–88				£17,125
1988–89				
Actual	6.4.88–31.7.88	£27,000 × 3-5/6/12		£ 8,625

2.17   Capital allowances

Although you are not normally allowed to deduct from your taxable profits the cost or depreciation of capital assets, you are generally allowed to deduct capital allowances. These are based on the cost of certain assets which you use in your business or profession including:

(1)   Plant and machinery (2.19).
(2)   Industrial buildings (2.30).

(3) Agricultural and forestry buildings, etc (2.32).
(4) Hotel buildings, etc (2.33).
(5) Scientific research expenditure (2.34).
(6) Patents and know-how (2.35).
(7) Mines, oil wells etc (2.36) and dredging (2.36).

2.18 Base period

Capital allowances are computed with reference to the assets purchased and those used in your annual business accounts period. This is known as the base period. You must take the date when the expenditure was incurred, which is generally when the obligation to pay becomes unconditional. An exception is where part of the capital expenditure is payable more than four months later, in which case you take the date when that part is payable.

Having found the total capital allowances for a given tax year, they are deducted from the Schedule D Case I or Case II assessment for that year. For example if your business makes up its accounts to 31 December, then its Schedule D Case I assessment for 1988–89 will be based on its accounts for the year to 31 December 1987. In the same way, its 1988–89 capital allowances will be based on the year to 31 December 1987.

Base periods of less than one year might arise in the opening or closing years of the business. Also, one base period might apply to two tax years. In that case, the additions during the base period must be allocated to the earlier tax year in order to calculate the allowances. Should there be a gap between base periods, this added to the second base period unless this marks a cessation of trading. In that case, you must add the gap to the first period.

2.19 Capital allowances on plant and machinery

In general, the main category of business assets attracting capital allowances is plant and machinery. This includes furniture, fittings, office equipment, motor vehicles, the thermal insulation of industrial buildings and making certain buildings comply with fire regulations.

The main allowance available is a 25% writing-down allowance each year (2.21). There are special rules relating to motor vehicles (2.27) and plant which you lease out (2.29). When plant is sold, balancing charges and allowances might arise (2.22). First year allowances applied to expenditure before 1 April, 1986 but not subsequently (see below).

The main allowance available is a 25% writing-down allowance each year (2.21). There are special rules relating to motor vehicles (2.27) and plant which you lease out (2.29). When plant is sold, balancing charges and allowances might arise (2.22). First year allowances applied to expenditure before 1 April, 1986 but not subsequently (see below).

2.20   First year allowance

For expenditure prior to 1 April 1986, a most important allowance was available, which is noted here for completeness. Known as first year allowance, it applied at a rate of 100% on expenditure prior to 14 March 1984. After 13 March 1984 and before 1 April 1985, the rate was 75% with 50% applying for expenditure after 31 March 1985 and before 1 April 1986. In general, first year allowance did not apply in respect of motor cars.

2.21   Writing down allowance

Each asset is put into a 'pool' at cost price and a writing down allowance of 25% is given on the balance. (If you obtained any first year allowance, this was deducted from the cost in arriving at the 'pool' figure.) You have the option of taking less than 25% in any year, if you so wish.

Before 1 April 1986, writing down allowance was not normally given in respect of the first year. Expenditure after 31 March 1986 in general qualifies for no first year allowance, and writing down allowance runs from the first year.

Where the base period relative to the expenditure is less than a year, the rate of writing down allowance is proportionately reduced. For example, if the base period for your business is only six months for a given year of assessment, then any writing down allowances for that period would be at the rate of $12\frac{1}{2}\%$ ($25\% \times 6/12$).

2.22   Sales of plant and machinery — Balancing allowances and charges

When you sell an item of plant from your 'pool', you simply deduct the sale proceeds from the 'pool' balance. However, should the proceeds exceed the original cost of the plant, you only deduct the cost. Where the sale proceeds exceed your 'pool' balance, the excess is a balancing charge which is added to your assessment for the year.

Balancing allowances normally only occur in the event of a cessation. If you permanently cease to trade during a period, you receive a 'balancing allowance' equal to the remainder of your 'pool', consisting of expenditure less allowances already obtained, less its disposal value.

2.23 Example: Capital allowances on plant and machinery

Jack Box has been carrying on a manufacturing business for many years and makes up his accounts to 31 December each year. At 31 December 1984 the capital allowances written down value of his plant, etc was £5,250. He purchased the following new plant:

Date	Description	Cost
		£
on 1 April 1985	Machinery	6,000
on 30 June 1986	Machinery	7,400
on 30 September 1987	Office furniture	1,500

No other additions were made before 31 December 1987.

During the year to 31 December 1985 Jack Box sold machinery costing £1,000 for £450.

Compute his capital allowances for 1986–87, 1987–88 and 1988–89.

		'Pool'	Total allowances
		£	£
Balance brought forward		5,250	
1986–87 (base period year to 31 December 1985) Additions:			
1 April 1985	6,000		
First year allowance 50%	3,000	3,000	3,000
Sale proceeds		(450)	
		7,800	
Writing down allowance 25% × £4,800		(1,200)	1,200
Balance forward		6,600	£4,200
1987–88 (base period year to 31 December 1986) Additions:			
30 June 1986		7,400	
		14,000	
Writing down allowance 25% × £14,000		(3,500)	£3,500
Balance forward		10,500	
1988–89 (base period year to 31 December 1987) Additions:			
30 September 1987		1,500	
		12,000	

Writing down allowance		
25% × £12,000	(£3,000)	£3,000
Balance carried forward	£9,000	

2.24   Fixtures — Entitlement to capital allowances

Special rules apply to clarify who is entitled to capital allowances where machinery or plant is installed in a building and becomes a fixture. The plant may be treated as belonging to you, for capital allowances purposes, even though you are not the owner.

Under the rules, which in general apply after 11 July 1984, if you lease a piece of equipment and it becomes a fixture at a building, you only obtain capital allowances if you make a joint election with the lessee. If you pay to be granted a lease which includes a fixture on which the lessor would otherwise obtain capital allowances, you can jointly elect that you receive the allowances.

2.25   Short-life assets

Regarding short-life plant and machinery which you buy for your trade after 31 March 1986, you can elect to have the writing down allowances calculated separately from your 'pool'. This is known as de-pooling. The election must be made within two years of the year of acquisition and does not normally apply to assets leased to non-traders, or to cars or ships.

Selling the assets gives rise to a balancing charge or allowance. However, if the machinery or plant has not been sold within five years, it must be transferred to your pool at its tax written down value.

2.26   Example: Short-life assets — De-pooling

Jack Box makes up his business accounts to 31 December and buys plant for £1,000 on 30 June 1987, for which he makes a de-pooling election. The plant is sold for £100 on 15 May 1991. The capital allowances computations are as follows:

Year ended 31 December		£
1987	Cost	1,000
	25% writing down allowance	250
		750
1988		188
		£
		562
1989		

		141
1990		421
		105
		316
1991	Sale proceeds	100
	Balancing allowance	£216

Note: If the plant had not been disposed of by 31 December 1991, the written down value would be transferred to the general plant pool.

2.27 Motor vehicles

If you buy a car for use in your business, you obtain the 25% writing down allowance. However, special rules apply to cars costing over £8,000; in this case your allowance for any year is restricted to 25% × £8,000, ie £2,000. Each car costing more than £8,000 must be treated as a separate 'pool'. When any such car is sold, it gives rise to its own balancing allowance or balancing charge. Cars costing no more than £8,000 are all put into a separate pool. (This pool also includes assets acquired before 1 April 1986 which you lease out and which did not qualify for first year allowance).

Where your car is leased through your business and its equivalent retail cost price exceeds £8,000, the rental deduction from your taxable business profits is correspondingly restricted. To find the actual deductible rental, you multiply the true rental by $\frac{£8,000 + RP - 8,000}{2}$ and you divide by RP, the retail price of the car when new.

2.28 Hire purchase

The acquisition of plant or machinery on hire purchase entitles you to full capital allowances as soon as you bring it into use in your business. Allowances are given on the capital proportion of the total instalments. The interest proportion is allowed against your business profits in the year that the respective instalments are paid. For example, suppose that the cash cost of a machine is £5,000, but you buy it under a hire purchase agreement and are paying a total of £7,400 over three years. You get capital allowances on £5,000 as soon as you start to use the machine, ie 25% writing down allowance. You would also deduct the interest of £2,400 from your profits for the three years during which you pay off the instalments (ie about £800 each year).

2.29   Machinery for leasing

In general, you now obtain 25% writing down allowance on machinery which you buy for leasing out. However, the rate is restricted to 10% if you lease the assets to non-residents. Similarly, writing down allowances of only 10% are available where ships or aircraft are let on charter to non-residents.

2.30   Industrial buildings

The cost of new industrial buildings that are used in your business qualifies for writing down allowance at 4% of the original cost. Examples of qualifying buildings are factories, warehouses and some repair shops. If any of the expenditure was incurred before 6 November 1962, the allowance is only 2% of the original cost.

Expenditure incurred prior to 1 April 1986 attracted initial allowances as follows:

Expenditure incurred before 11 March 1981	50%
14 March 1984	75%
1 April 1985	50%
1 April 1986	25%

In general, initial allowances are no longer available, apart from expenditure in Enterprise Zones (2.31).

Note that up to 25% of the capital cost of an industrial building is allowed to relate to a non-qualifying use without restricting the allowances.

The sale of an industrial building will give rise to a balancing charge or allowance. This is computed by comparing the sale proceeds with the balance of original cost, less initial allowances and writing down allowances obtained. This applies even if you had ceased to use the building for industrial purposes. You must disregard any excess of the proceeds compared with the original cost. However, this may give rise to a capital gain.

2.31   Enterprise zones

Enterprise zones are designated by the Government. One of their attractions is that expenditure on industrial and commercial buildings qualifies for 100% initial allowance. Unusually, for this purpose, shops and offices are included and also integral plant and machinery. You are able to claim less than the full initial allowance, in which case 25% writing down allowance (straight line) is obtained on the original expenditure until it is used up.

2.32   Agricultural buildings

As the owner or tenant of farm or forestry land, you obtain allowance for expenditure on certain constructions on the land. These include farm or forestry buildings, farmhouses, cottages, fences, etc. The allowance consists of a writing-down allowance on your original expenditure. For expenditure between 11 April 1978 and 1 April 1986, there was an initial allowance of up to 20% and the balance was eligible for writing down allowance of 10% of the original cost for each year including the first. There is no initial allowance for expenditure after 1 April 1986, and only 4% writing down allowance applies.

In general, expenditure after 31 March 1986, which attracts a 4% writing down allowance is written off over a 25 year period. However, if within that time you sell or demolish the building, you have the right to elect for a balancing allowance or charge to be made. This election must be made within two years after the end of the relevant year of assessment.

Where the expenditure is on a farmhouse, the maximum allowance is generally limited to one-third of the total cost to take account of personal benefit.

2.33   Hotel buildings

Prior to 1 April 1986, there was an initial allowance of 20% on the cost of constructing or improving certain hotel buildings. Also, in every year there was a 4% writing down allowance based on the original cost. Subsequently, only the 4% writing down allowance applies. Special rates apply in enterprise zones (2.31). These include 100% initial allowance.

Among conditions for obtaining the allowance, the hotel must have at least ten bedrooms for letting to the public. Also breakfast, together with an evening meal must be offered as normal facilities. Furthermore, the hotel must be open for at least four months in the season, which extends from April to October inclusive.

2.34   Scientific research allowance

If you incur capital expenditure on scientific research for the purposes of your trade, this is wholly allowed in the year when it arises. Also, any revenue expenditure will be allowed as a charge against your taxable profits. This applies if it is related to your trade or is medical research concerning the welfare of your employees. After 31 March 1985, the 100% allowance does not apply to the cost of land and houses.

2.35   Patent rights (and know-how)

Expenditure which you incur after 31 March 1986 on patents for use in your business and 'know-how' obtains a 25% writing down allowance. Previous expenditure is treated differently, depending on whether it relates to patents or 'know-how'. However, costs in connection with creating and registering your own patents are treated as deductible revenue expenses in any event.

Expenditure prior to 1 April 1986 on patents obtained a writing down allowance of 1/17th of the expenditure for each of the 17 years starting with when you made the purchase. A sale may give rise to a balancing charge or allowance. However, where the proceeds exceed the original cost, you are assessed to income tax under Case VI of Schedule D on the excess, normally spread over six years or the remainder of the patent if less. Payments prior to 1 April 1986 to obtain 'know-how' for your business or profession carry a writing down allowance of 1/6th of the expenditure for each of the first six years.

Regarding 'know-how' used in your business which you sell, the proceeds are taxed as trading receipts. However, if you cease to trade within the six years, you are allowed to charge the balance of your 'know-how' expenditure against your profits in the final trading period.

2.36   Mines, oil wells and dredging

Expenditure after 31 March 1986 on dredging generally qualifies for a 4% writing down allowance on a straight line basis. Prior to that date, expenditure attracted an initial allowance of 15% as well as the 4% writing down allowance.

Expenditure before 1 April 1986 on mines and oil wells attracted initial and writing down allowances related to output, etc. Expenditure after that attracts a writing down allowance of 25% or 10%, depending on the type of expenditure involved. In general, pre-1 April 1986 balances qualify for the new reliefs.

2.37   Class IV National Insurance contributions

For 1985–86 and subsequent years, relief may be claimed for half of your Class IV contributions. Your total income is accordingly reduced. Further details of the contributions, which are payable if you are self-employed, are contained later in this chapter (2.47).

2.38 Earnings basis and cash basis

Where you carry on a trade, you will normally be taxed on an 'earnings basis'. Your sales for each accounts period will be included as they arise and not when you receive the money. Generally, sales arise when they are invoiced. However, in a retail shop, sales normally arise as customers pay at the till. Similarly, your expenses are deductible on an arising basis and the date of payment is irrelevant.

However, should you carry on a trade or vocation, the Revenue may tax you on a 'cash basis', by reference to the actual cash received, ignoring uncollected fees at the end of each accounts period. This basis is usually used for barristers. Other professions are generally required to prepare their opening accounts on an earnings basis, having the option of switching to a cash basis later. Expenses are generally calculated on an arising basis. However, in some small cases, the actual expense payments are used ignoring accruals.

2.39 Post-cessation receipts

Post-cessation receipts are amounts received relating to your trade, profession or vocation after it has permanently ceased. An example is where you receive a late fee payment that had not been included in your accounts because they were prepared on a cash basis or the fee was not included in your debtors. Post-cessation receipts are generally taxed under Case VI of Schedule D and treated as earned income. You cannot set off unrelieved losses and capital allowances from before your cessation. However, you can elect that any post-cessation receipts for the first six years after cessation should be added to your income from the business, on its last day of trading.

A special relief applies if you were born before 6 April 1917 and were in business on 18 March 1986. Only a fraction of your post-cessation receipts will be taxed, varying between 19/20ths and 5/20ths. The latter fraction applies if you were born before 6 April 1903. If you were born before 6 April 1904 the fraction is 6/20ths and so on.

2.40 Losses

Special rules apply where your adjusted results show a loss. If you have an adjusted deficit of income compared with expenditure for any year, then your assessment under Case I or Case II of Schedule D will be nil for the related tax year. For example, if your annual accounts run to 31 December and you make an adjusted loss of £10,000 for 1987, your 1988–89 assessment will be nil. The 1987 loss of £10,000 must be augmented by your 1988–89 capital allowances (say £2,000) and the resultant loss of £12,000 is available for relief. This is applied:

(a) First against your other income for the tax year in which you suffer the loss. (This income includes your business assessment on the profits for the year prior to the loss.)
(b) Then against your income for the following tax year.

Although the rules require you to apportion your loss to the actual tax years that span your accounts year, the Revenue normally allows you to allocate the loss for a given accounts year to the tax year in which it ends. (This does not apply to the first year of trading.) Thus the £12,000 loss for the year to 31 December 1987 is allocated to 1987–88, your relief being set against other income for 1987–88 and 1988–89.

You must follow a strict order of set-off. The loss is first set against your other earned income for the year and then against your unearned income, followed by your wife's earned income and lastly her unearned income. This loss relief is given under TA 1970, s 168 (now TA 1988, s 380) and must be claimed within two years of the end of the tax year to which it relates, by election to your Inspector of Taxes. Should your loss not be completely relieved in this way, you can claim that the balance is carried forward and set against your future profits from the same trade, profession or vocation (TA 1970, s 171, now TA 1988, s 385).

You are not allowed to carry a loss forward from one trade to another. Remember this, should you change businesses. However, a move to a nearby shop in the same trade may be in order.

Concerning your first year of assessment of a new business, pre-trading expenditure of a revenue nature augments your losses. This applies to individuals and partnerships concerning expenditure within three years before trading commences.

Loss relief is given before personal reliefs, etc which cannot be carried forward. This may result in allowances being lost through your income being absorbed by losses. To avoid this, carry the losses forward where possible, so that your allowances are not wasted.

Losses on certain disposals of unquoted shares in trading companies by the original subscribers (6.13) may qualify for income tax relief. Such losses take precedence over claims under s 168.

2.41   Example: Relief for losses

Jack Box made a loss of £20,000 in his business for the year to 31 December 1986 having made a profit of (£6,000 for 1985. In 1987, his profit is £20,000. His only other income is taxed dividends (including tax credits) amounting to £5,000 for 1986–87, £5,500 for 1987–88 and £6,000 for 1988–89. Loss relief can be obtained by Jack as follows:

Jack's loss of £20,000 for the year to 31 December 1986 will be allocated to the year 1986–87 (2.40).

	£
1986–87 loss relief (s 168)	
(1) Against 1986–87 Schedule D Case I assessment	6,000
(2) Against 1986–87 dividends	5,000
	£11,000

1987–88 loss relief (s 168)	
Against 1987–88 dividends	£ 5,500

1988–89 loss relief (s 171)	
Against 1988–89 Schedule D Case I assessment	£ 3,500

(Case I assessment for 1988–89 becomes £20,000 — £3,500 = £16,500).

2.42   Loss in new business

A special relief is available where you carry on a business or profession personally or in partnership. The relief applies to any loss in your first year of assessment or any of the next three years. A written claim is needed within two years of the end of the year of assessment. The losses include capital allowances and certain pre-trading expenditure. They are set against your income for the three years of assessment prior to that in which the losses are made, taking the earliest first.

2.43   Terminal losses

You are able to obtain relief for a 'terminal loss'. This is an adjusted loss made in your last complete year of trading, where you have ceased to carry on a trade, profession or vocation. The relievable loss is augmented by your capital allowances apportioned to your last 12 months of trading. Your terminal losses are allowed against your business assessments for the three years prior to that in which you ceased to trade.

2.44   Farming

Carrying on farming or market gardening business in the UK is treated as carrying on a trade, assessable under Schedule D Case I (2.9). As well as the normal Schedule D Case I rules, some special ones apply, including the following:

(1) Should you have more than one farm, they will all be assessed as one business.

(2) Grants received under various Ministry of Agriculture, Fisheries and Food grant schemes are treated as either capital receipts or revenue receipts for tax purposes according to their nature. For example, field husbandry grants are revenue and grants concerning the reclamation of waste land are capital.

(3) Where deficiency payments are received from the Government in respect of certain crops, etc, by concession these are included in your taxable profits for the year when they are received, rather than when the crop is sold.

(4) A special *agricultural buildings allowance* is available (2.32).

(5) Livestock is normally treated for tax purposes as stock in trade. However, if you have any 'production herds', you can elect for the 'herd basis' to apply. 'Production herds' are those kept for the purpose of obtaining products from the living animal, such as milk, wool etc. A 'herd basis' election must be made within two years from the end of your first year of assessment. Where an election has been made, the initial cost of the herd is not charged against your profits, but capitalised with the cost of any additional animals. You also capitalise the cost of rearing the animals to maturity. Sale proceeds are taxable and the cost of replacement animals is deducted from your taxable profits. Where you sell your entire herd, you are not taxed on the proceeds.

(6) Loss relief is restricted if you carry out 'hobby farming' without any reasonable expectation of profit. Generally, subject to certain relaxations, a restriction applies when you made your sixth consecutive annual loss, so that you are no longer allowed relief against your other income. However, you are still able to carry your unrelieved farming losses forward to set against future farm profits.

(7) Where your farming profits fluctuate, relief is available. This applies to partnerships as well as individuals. You average the profits of any pair of consecutive years of assessment, provided you make a claim to this effect within two years of the end of the second year. If the taxable profits for either year are later adjusted, the original claim is set aside but a new one can be made by the end of the tax year following that in which the adjustment is made. Averaging is only allowed where the profits for the lower year are no more than 70% of the profits for the better year. (Limited spreading is allowed if the lower profits are between 70% and 75% of the higher ones.) If a loss

is made, for the purposes of the spreading rules, the profits are treated as nil and the loss relieved as usual.

2.45 Sub-contractors

Should you be an independent or self-employed contractor (not engaged under a contract of employment), you will be taxed under Schedule D Case I and not Schedule E. Generally, this should prove advantageous since you will be able to deduct various expenses such as travelling from your home or other base of operations to the site, etc where you are working. Special rules apply to payments made by a building contractor, etc to a sub-contractor concerning building and construction work. These extend to non-building firms whose average annual construction expenditure on a three-year basis exceeds £250,000.

The contractor must deduct tax at 27% from each payment made to the sub-contractors who work for him, unless they have exemption certificates. This tax must be paid over to the Revenue. When the sub-contractors prepare their own accounts under Schedule D Case I, they are credited with the tax already paid.

As a sub-contractor in the building trade, you are able to apply for an exemption certificate from your Inspector of Taxes. Requirements include having a regular place of business in this country and having been employed (or undergoing full time education or training) or being in business in the UK, making full tax returns for the three years up to the application.

2.46 Authors' copyright sales and royalties

Where patent royalties are paid to individuals, basic rate income tax (27%) is generally deducted. However, copyright royalty payments to authors, etc are made gross without the deduction of income tax. If you receive such amounts as an author or composer, then your royalties will normally be taxed under Schedule D Case II as part of your professional earnings (2.9). Otherwise, the royalties may be assessed under Schedule D Case VI.

Any sum that you receive for assigning the copyright in the whole or part of a work is taxable by reference to the tax year or accounting period when received. However, a spreading election can normally be made to the Revenue, as follows:

(1) Spreading depends on the time that you took to prepare the work of art. If this was more than 12 but less than 24 months, half of your

proceeds is taxed as if received when paid to you and the other half one year earlier. If the preparation time was more than 24 months, you are taxed on 1/3rd of the proceeds as if received when paid to you, 1/3rd as if received one year earlier and the remainder one year earlier still.

(2) Where you assign the copyright of an established work not less than ten years after its first publication, you can spread any lump sum received. This relief also applies where you grant an interest in the work for a period of at least two years, and the sum which you receive may be spread over the lesser of six years or the duration of the grant or licence.

2.47   The assessment and payment mechanism

Detailed coverage of how your income tax is assessed is included in the *Allied Dunbar Tax Guide*. In general, assessment will follow the submission of your income tax return, business accounts and tax computations. You have the right to appeal against an assessment within 30 days of its issue, or longer in special circumstances.

The due date for paying income tax is normally 1 January in the year of assessment (ie tax for 1988–89 is payable on 1 January 1989). However, income tax assessments under Schedule D Case I and II on your business and professional income are payable in equal instalments on 1 January and 1 July in the year of assessment, as is Class 4 National Insurance (2.48). Higher rate income tax on your 'taxed investment income' is payable on 1 December following the year of assessment. (If an assessment is issued later than 30 days before the above dates, the tax payment date is normally 30 days after the assessment is issued.)

Interest is payable on overdue tax at $8\frac{1}{4}$% from 6 December 1987 (for earlier interest rates see 4.6). However, the Inland Revenue normally excuse you interest if it is less than £30 in total for one assessment. If you obtain an income tax overpayment, you may qualify for a repayment supplement (4.6).

2.48   Class 4 National Insurance

As a person who is self-employed or otherwise liable to Schedule D income tax under Cases I and II you may be charged an earnings related amount under Class 4. This is in addition to your normal flat-rate Class 2 (self-employed) contributions (£3.85 per week for 1987–88 — see 9.29). The following should be noted:

(1) The contribution rate for 1987–88 is 6.3% which applies to your

Cases I and II income between £4,590 and £15,340. The maximum is thus 6.3% × £10,750 = £677.25.

(2) The rate for 1986–87 was 6.3 per cent, which applied to the income between £4,450 and £14,820.

(3) Class 4 is payable on your Schedule D assessments under Cases I and II for the tax year, after capital allowances, but with no deduction for personal allowances, pension contributions etc. Your share of partnership income is thus included.

(4) If your wife has self-employed earnings, these are also charged to Class 4 as if her earnings were separate from yours.

(5) Class 4 does not apply to men over 65 at the end of the previous year of assessment and women then over 60.

(6) Your contributions for each year of assessment are normally collected through your Case I or II Schedule D income tax assessment. Thus it is payable in two instalments.

(7) It is possible to defer your Class 4 payments in certain cases, such as where you also pay Class 1 contributions.

(8) Class 4 only applies if you are UK resident.

3 Partnership taxation

3.1 Introduction

The simplest form in which you can carry on a trade or profession is as a sole trader. However, your business may grow and you may wish to take in others as partners. A particular example would be your husband or wife, when tax advantages are likely (3.10). It is also possible that several individuals commence trading in partnership at the outset. Regardless of the circumstances, special tax rules apply to partnerships and these are considered below.

3.2 Partnership defined

Partnership is the relationship which exists between two persons carrying on business together with the object of making profits (5.77). It is not necessary to have a written partnership agreement. However, the partnership must exist in fact and if none actually operates, a written agreement would not make the partnership exist.

The Revenue will seek to establish whether a partnership actually exists. Particular points to consider include:

(1) The existence of a written partnership agreement.
(2) Whether the partners' names appear on business stationery.
(3) The arrangements existing for dividing the profits; also the assets on dissolution.
(4) Whether the partners can close down the business.
(5) Whether or not the partners are personally liable for the debts.

3.3 The taxation of partnership income

The partnership profits are adjusted in accordance with the rules which apply to businesses (2.9). A joint assessment to income tax is then made under Case I or Case II of Schedule D on the partners in respect of the adjusted partnership profits. The assessment covers both basic rate

(2⅚%) and higher rate (if any). The rules as for individuals are generally followed in respect of the opening years (2.13), closing years (2.15) and capital allowances (2.19). Special rules apply concerning partnership changes (3.6). Each year, a joint return must be made for the partnership, normally by the senior partner.

If any investment income has been included in the partnership accounts, this must be split between the partners in their profit-sharing ratios but it does not form part of the trading profits. The partners personally pay any income tax arising.

When the partnership trading or professional income has been determined, it must be split between the partners according to the way in which they share profits during the tax year. This provides the split of the Schedule D Case I or Case II assessments.

It should be noted that the proportions in which the assessments are split between the partners are not always the same as the profit sharing ratios for the year when the profits were made.

For example, if Jack and Jill are in partnership and make £20,000 in the year to 30 April 1987, when they split profits three to two, their partnership assessment for 1988/89, which is on the preceding year basis, is £20,000. This is split in the ratio in which they divide profits for the year to 5 April 1989. If the ratio is altered so that they divide profits equally from 1 May 1987, they will each be assessed on £10,000 for 1988/89.

Where a partner is remunerated partly by salary and partly by a profit share, the salary is not normally assessed under Schedule E. It is included in the profit share assessable under Schedule D Case I or Case II. Similarly, interest paid to partners on their capital is also treated as part of the profit shares and assessed under Schedule D, Case I or II. This interest is not an annual payment and it is not taxed as investment income.

3.4　Example: Partnership assessments

Jack, Jill and George trade in partnership sharing profits equally after the interest and salary allocations shown below. They prepare accounts to 5 April showing the following:

			Interest		Salary	
	Profits	Jack	Jill	Jill	George
5 April 1988	£16,000	£500	£500	£1,000	£2,000
1989	£20,000	£400	£600	£2,000	£2,000

The 1988–89 assessment under Schedule D Case I is as follows:

			TOTAL £	Jack £	Jill £	George £
Net profit (preceding year) —						
year ended 5 April 1988			16,000			
Add:	Interest	Jack	500			
		Jill	500			
	Salary	Jill	1,000			
		George	2,000			
			£20,000			

			£				
Less:	Interest	Jack	400		400		
		Jill	600			600	
	Salary	Jill	2,000			2,000	
		George	2,000				2,000
				5,000			
Balance split equally			15,000	5,000	5,000	5,000
Total assessment			£20,000	£5,400	£7,600	£7,000

Notes:

(1) In addition to the above, the normal Schedule D Case I adjustments must be made.
(2) The interest and salaries for the year to 5 April 1988 are added back to the profits.
(3) The 1988–89 assessments split includes the interest and salaries for the year to 5 April 1989

3.5 Losses

Where in any accounting period a partnership has an adjusted loss, this is split between the partners in the same proportions as a profit would have been. This means that the loss is split in the profit sharing ratios applicable to the year of assessment corresponding to the tax year when the loss is made. Thus, a loss made in the year to 5 April 1988 is split between the partners in their profit sharing ratios for 1988–89 (assuming that the preceding year basis of assessment is applicable).

Each partner is free to use his losses as he chooses, according to the rules. He can thus claim for his partnership loss to be relieved against his other income tax assessments for the year of assessment in which the loss is actually made or the following year. As a result, relief can be obtained against the previous year's partnership profits. (This applies even if the partnership had been treated as discontinued, because of a partnership change.)

You may be a limited partner, in which case your risk is generally limited to the capital which you have invested. Losses arising to limited partners after 19 March 1985 are broadly restricted to the capital which they have invested.

3.6   Changes of partners

Subject to a continuation election, which is described below (3.7), if there is any change in the make-up of a partnership, it is treated as ceasing for taxation purposes. Such changes include where a partner leaves or dies or a fresh partner joins.

A cessation caused by a change of partners has similar effects to any other Schedule D Case I or Case II cessation (2.15). The assessment for the final year is based on the actual profits. Furthermore, the Revenue have the option to increase the assessments for the two previous years to the actual profits for those years.

For changes after 19 March 1985, the first four years are assessed on an actual basis. The previous year basis then applies unless you elect for years five and six to be on an actual basis. This is subject to a continuation election (3.7).

3.7   Continuation election

Where there is a change in the members of a partnership, the old partnership is normally treated as having ceased to trade and the new one as having just started. However, within two years of the change, an election can be made to the Inland Revenue (under TA 1970, s 154, now TA 1988, s 113) that the partnership should be taxed on a continuation basis. This election, which is often made, needs to be signed by all of the partners in both the old and new partnerships. Another requirement is that at least one of the partners in the old partnership remains as a partner in the new one.

As a result of the election, the partnership is not treated as ceasing for tax purposes at the date of the change. What happens is that the Schedule D Case I or Case II assessment for the tax year when the change takes place is apportioned up to the change. Thus, the old partners are assessed on their share of the assessment apportioned up to the change. Similarly, the new partners are assessed on the proportion after the change.

3.8   Overseas partnerships

Special rules apply concerning partnerships which are treated for tax purposes as being non-resident. This happens if you are in partnership carrying on a trade or business and the control and management is outside the UK. The partnership is then regarded as being non-resident, even if you or some of your other partners are resident here and some of the business is carried on in this country.

Where a partnership is non-UK resident, any profits arising from its trade or business in this country are assessed here under Schedule D Case I, in the name of any partner resident in the UK. Partnership profits earned abroad are assessable on the partners resident in the UK, in respect of their profit shares, according to the special rules concerning Schedule D Case V. In general, this applies even where, under a double tax agreement, the profits arising abroad are exempt from UK tax.

3.9 Partnership capital gains

The assets of a partnership are regarded as being owned by the partners. Thus, when an asset is sold in circumstances that would have given rise to capital gains tax, had it been owned by an individual, this tax is assessed on the partners according to their shares in the assets. For example, if a capital gain of £15,000 is made from the sale of a partnership property on 1 January 1989 and Tom, Dick and Harry share equally in all the partnership assets, a capital gain of £5,000 must be included in the capital gains tax assessments for 1988–89 for each of them.

If a partnership share changes hands, a share in all of the assets is treated for capital gains tax purposes as also changing ownership. This might give rise to capital gains or losses for any partner disposing of his share. For example, if Tom, Dick and Harry are equal partners and Tom sells his partnership share to Jim, Tom is regarded for capital gains tax purposes as disposing of a one-third share in each partnership asset to Jim. However, in certain circumstances, concessional Inland Revenue treatment introduced in 1975 (SP/D12) may apply. (Various concessions were introduced at that time, concerning partnership capital gains tax, which are considered beyond the scope of this book.)

3.10 Husband and wife partnerships

For the sake of convenience, this section reflects a husband taking in his wife as a partner. However, the reverse may well take place.

If you are in business, it is beneficial from a tax point of view to employ your wife. However, it is necessary that she performs sufficient work to justify the salary which she is paid. Otherwise, the Revenue may seek to disallow part or all of her salary as a deduction from your taxable business profits.

It is particularly beneficial for your wife to receive earned income, so that she obtains the benefit of the wife's earned income allowance (maximum £2,425). Of course, if she already has another job, this allowance would normally be absorbed in any event.

If her work for you justifies a larger salary and particularly if she also has other sources of earned income, an election for the separate taxation of her earnings will be worthwhile. This will involve your losing your married man's allowance. You will each obtain the single allowance, however, and the election is normally worthwhile for 1987–88 if your combined incomes total £26,870 of which your wife's earned income is £6,545. The higher the incomes, the greater the savings, which are brought about because your wife's earned income is subjected to a separate set of tax rates, so that she has £17,900 at the 27% basic rate and so on. (From 6 April 1990, the income of husband and wife will be taxed separately in any event — see the 1988 Budget Notes.)

In order to make the most of the wife's earnings election, the wife should have as large an earned income as possible. However, as mentioned above, it may be difficult to demonstrate that she does sufficient work to support this. In these circumstances, it is most helpful if she is a partner. Provided that she can be shown to take part in the management of the partnership, it will not be necessary that she works full-time. There should be a properly drawn partnership deed, stipulating her share in the capital and revenue profits and losses.

In general, the level of the wife's National Insurance contributions will be diminished if she is a partner. As an employee, she will be liable to pay her own contributions and the employers will do likewise. However, as a partner, she will be responsible for paying her own Class 2 and Class 4 contributions, whilst half of the latter will be deductible for Schedule D income tax purposes.

3.11 Example: Husband and wife partnership

Jack and Jill are husband and wife. Jack is in business as a sole trader and his assessable profit for 1987–88 is £38,000 after paying a salary of £2,000 to Jill for limited assistance. The following illustrates (a) the income tax and (b) the National Insurance contribution effects if instead Jill is an equal partner and an election for the separate taxation of her earnings is made.

(a) *Income Tax 1987–88*

	Jack – Sole Trader		Jack and Jill Partnership	
	Jack	Jill	Jack	Jill
	£	£	£	£
Earnings	38,000	2,000	20,000	20,000

Less:
50%

	£	£	£	£
Class IV Contributions (below)	339		339	339
	37,661	2,000	19,661	19,661
Personal allowances:				
Married	3,795			
Wife's earnings		2,000		
Single			2,425	2,425
	£33,866	Nil	£17,236	£17,236

Income Tax	£		£	£
17,900 at 27%	4,833.00		4,653.72	4,653.72
2,500 at 40%	1,000.00			
5,000 at 45%	2,250.00			
7,900 at 50%	3,950.00			
566 at 55%	311.30			
£33,866	£12,344.30		£4,653.72	£4,653.72
				£9,307.44
INCOME TAX SAVING				£3,036.86

Note: When Jack employs Jill at a salary of only £2,000, an election for the separate taxation of her earnings is not beneficial. However, that level is below the National Insurance contributions threshold of £2,028.

(b) *National Insurance contributions 1987–88*

	Jack – Sole Trader		Jack and Jill Partnership	
	Jack	Jill	Jack	Jill
	£	£	£	£
Class 1		Nil		
Class 2	200.20		200.20	200.20
Class 4 (maximum)	677.25		677.25	677.24
	£877.45		£877.45	£877.45

Additional contributions payable by Jill as a partner	£ 877.45
Saving in income tax as in (a) above	£3,036.86
Net saving	£2,159.41

Note: If instead of being a partner, Jill is employed by Jack at £20,000 per annum, an election for the separate taxation of her earnings will produce commensurate income tax savings. However, she will need to work full-time and demonstrate that her services are of special value. Otherwise, the Revenue may seek to restrict the deduction from Jack's taxable profits.

The National Insurance contributions for Jill will be far higher. Assuming she has not 'contracted out', she will pay 9% on £295 per week as an employee under Class 1 making *£1,380.60*. At the same time, Jack as employer will pay 10.45% on £20,000, making *£2,090*. However, £2,090 will be deductible from his taxable profits and so his income tax bill in this example will be reduced by £2,090 at 27% = *£564.30*. Thus the partnership route is significantly better regarding National Insurance contribution levels.

4 The taxation of companies

4.1 Introduction

Unlike individuals and partnerships, companies are taxed separately from their owners. In other words, whilst partners pay income tax on the profits made by their partnership, in the case of a company the shareholders or directors generally only pay tax on their dividends or remuneration. The company itself pays corporation tax on its profits.

4.2 Corporation tax

All the income assessable on a company for a year is subject to corporation tax, at the present rate of 35%. This rate is reduced if the taxable profits are less than £500,000 (less if there are associated companies — see 4.4). Profits for corporation tax purposes include capital gains. (Before 17 March 1987, only a fixed fraction of a company's capital gain was liable to corporation tax.)

Corporation tax is charged on a company according to the actual income assessable for each accounting period (4.5), according to the rules of the various cases of Schedule D (2.2) and other applicable Schedules. The corporation tax rate is fixed by Parliament in the Finance Act each year, for the preceding 'financial year'. Such a year commences on 1 April so that the financial year 1988 is the year to 31 March 1989. The 35% rate has applied since 1 April 1986, prior to which it was 40% for one year, 45% for one year, 50% for one year and 52% back to 1973.

4.3 Small companies rate

A special reduced corporation tax rate called 'small companies rate' is charged on company profits not exceeding certain limits. For the purposes of these limits, both profits on which corporation tax is to be paid, and 'franked investment income' (4.9) must be taken. The rate has recently moved in line with the basic rate of income tax and is 27% from 1 April 1987, having been 29% for the previous year.

Small companies rate of 27% is charged on the profits of a company, provided these do not exceed £100,000 and there are no 'associated companies' (4.4). Where profits are between £100,000 and £500,000, marginal relief is available. The tax is then broadly the full 35% corporation tax rate on the profits, less a fixed fraction of the amount by which they fall short of £500,000. The fraction was 3/200 for financial year 1986 and is now 1/50 for financial year 1987. This means that for 1987, there is a marginal rate of 37% which applies within the £100,000–£500,000 profit range, assuming that there are no 'associated companies' (see below).

The figures of £100,000 and £500,000 mentioned above must be divided by one plus the number of 'associated companies' connected with the company in question. For example, if four associated companies comprise a group, they will each pay 27% corporation tax on their profits for the year to 31 March 1988, if these are no more than £25,000 (£100,000/4) each. Where any of those companies have profits between £25,000 and £125,000 (£500,000/4), marginal relief is obtained.

From 1 April 1988, small companies rate is 25% (see the 1988 Budget Notes).

4.4 Associated companies

Associated companies are those which are under common control or where one controls the other. Control broadly means voting power or being entitled to the greater part of the profits or of the assets on liquidation.

For the purposes of common control, the shares held by husband, wife and minor children are considered as one. However, if you control one company and a more distant relative, such as your brother, controls another, the two companies are not generally regarded as being 'associated' unless there is a large amount of inter-company trading.

4.5 Accounting periods and payment dates

Profits for corporation tax purposes are computed for 'accounting periods'. Such periods normally coincide with those for which a company draws up its annual accounts. However, 'an accounting period' must not be longer than 12 months in length. Where accounts are prepared for a longer period, of say 18 months, the first 12 months constitute one accounting period. The other six months are regarded as a second accounting period.

The normal payment date for corporation tax is nine months from the end of an accounting period or, if later, 30 days from when the assessment is issued. However, where a company traded before April 1965, there may have been a longer interval between the tax due date and the company's accounting date. This had been retained.

The rules for companies formed before April 1965 were changed for accounting periods starting after 16 March 1987. After a three year transitional period, corporation tax will be payable nine months after the end of each accounting period. The payment interval during the transitional period will be reduced to nine months in three equal stages. Thus, a company with a payment interval of 21 months and an accounting period ending 31 March has successive payment dates as follows:

Accounting period	Payment interval	Payment date
1.4.86–31.3.87	21 months	1.1.89
1.4.87–31.3.88	17 months	1.9.89
1.4.88–31.3.89	13 months	1.5.90
1.4.89–31.3.90	9 months	1.1.91

4.6 Interest and repayment supplement

If corporation tax is not paid when it is due, interest may be charged at $8\frac{1}{4}\%$ (from 6 December 1987). If, however, you appeal and obtain a postponement (ie permission to hold over some of the tax), interest on that part may not be payable until 15 months after the end of the accounts period.

If your company receives a tax repayment more than a year from when corporation tax is due for the accounting period, a repayment supplement generally arises. (Another condition is that the repayment must be at least £100.) The tax-free repayment supplement is calculated from one year after the due date for paying the corporation tax until 'the tax month' in which the repayment is made. 'The tax month' ends on the fifth day of the following month. The interest rates for repayment supplements are the same as those payable on overdue tax and recently have been as follows:

From	Rate %
6 May 1985	11
6 August 1986	$8\frac{1}{2}$
6 November 1986	$9\frac{1}{2}$

6 April 1987	9
6 June 1987	8¼
6 September 1987	9
6 December 1987	8¼

4.7 The imputation system

The present system of corporation tax is known as 'The Imputation System'. This is because shareholders are imputed with tax of currently 27/73rds of their dividends. Thus, as a shareholder, you would obtain a tax credit of this amount and are only liable for tax at the higher rate if applicable. When a company pays dividends, these are paid gross to the shareholders and tax of 27/73rds of the dividend is paid over to the Inland Revenue. This is known as 'Advance Corporation Tax' (ACT). (Before 6 April 1987, the ACT rate was 29/71sts.) The ACT can be deducted from the company's corporation tax bill.

As a UK shareholder, you obtain a tax credit of 27/73rds of your dividends, but pay higher rates on your dividends plus tax credits. For example, if you receive a dividend of £73, you are imputed with a tax credit of 27/73rds × £73 = £27. If your income is sufficiently high, you will pay higher rates of tax on £73 plus £27 = £100. However, the £27 tax credit will be deductible from your total tax bill.

4.8 ACT on dividends etc

Companies pay advance corporation tax (ACT) on their dividend payments and other 'qualifying distributions' (4.9). Prior to 5 April 1986, the rate was 3/7ths. For the year to 5 April 1987 it was 29/71sts and then 27/73rds. For 1988–89 ACT is 25/75ths (see the 1988 Budget Notes).

Companies must account to the Inland Revenue for ACT, normally on a 3-monthly basis to 31 March, 30 June, 30 September and 31 December. However, if the company accounting period does not end on one of those dates, the company must submit an additional return for the period from the end of the last quarter to the end of the accounting period.

ACT returns must include 'franked payments' (4.9), and 'franked investment income' (4.9) received, together with the amount of ACT payable and certain other details. In calculating the ACT due for payment, tax credits on receipts of 'franked investment income' during the period may be deducted.

4.9 Distributions and franked payments

Distributions are classified as being either qualifying or non-qualifying. *Qualifying distributions* are dividends and similar payments. *Non-qualifying distributions* are particular types of shares, carrying potential future claims on the company's profits etc. For example, bonus debentures or bonus redeemable shares would come within this category.

Qualifying distributions are subjected to ACT. However, no ACT is payable by a company in respect of non-qualifying distributions which it makes. As a shareholder, you would obtain no basic rate tax credit and would not be liable to the basic rate on the distribution. However, you would still be liable to the excess of your higher rate tax over the basic rate on the actual value of your non-qualifying distribution.

When a company makes a qualifying distribution this, together with the relevant ACT, is defined as a *'franked payment'*. For example a qualifying distribution of £7,300 carries with it ACT of £2,700 and together, they make up a franked payment of £10,000.

A similar term is *franked investment income*. This consists of income from a UK resident company comprising distributions in respect of which tax credits are obtained. A company's franked investment income is the amount including the tax credits. For example, a company receiving a dividend of £730 has franked investment income of £1,000 (£730 + £730 × 27/73).

4.10 Setting off ACT

ACT is a pre-payment of the 'mainstream' corporation tax bill of a company. The 'mainstream' tax is only ascertained when accounts are submitted to the Inland Revenue for each accounting period. At that stage, the full corporation tax is calculated and any ACT paid is set off. However, there is a limit to the amount of ACT which can be set off in this way. The limit is the ACT which would have been paid on a full distribution of the company's pre-tax profits, taking account of the notional ACT payable.

For example, if a company makes adjusted profits of £1 million before tax for the year to 31 March 1988, the maximum ACT set-off is £270,000. On a distribution of £730,000, ACT would be paid amounting to £730,000 × 27/73 = £270,000. As a result, the entire profits of the company would be absorbed. The mainstream corporation tax assessment would be £1,000,000 × 35% = £350,000, from which £270,000 ACT would be deducted, leaving a net amount payable of £80,000.

An important change concerning capital gains took effect from 17 March 1987. For accounting periods beginning on or after that date, but not earlier, ACT may be set off against corporation tax on capital gains (4.17). For accounting periods straddling 17 March 1987, only tax on gains after that date qualifies for set-off.

4.11 Surplus ACT

ACT which is not relieved against the corporation tax payable for the accounting period when the relevant distribution is made because of the restriction rules (see above) is known as 'surplus ACT'. This can be carried back and set off against corporation tax payable for any accounting period beginning in the six years preceding that in which the distribution is made. To make this set-off, you must make a claim within two years of the end of the period for which the surplus ACT arises. The surplus ACT will then be allocated to one or more earlier periods, resulting in a reduction in corporation tax payable or a repayment. Surplus ACT not carried back may be carried forward indefinitely, for setting off against future corporation tax payable.

4.12 Computing the assessable profits

The income assessable under each schedule, as well as under each case of Schedule D, must be computed and aggregated with any capital gains, in order to find the total amount chargeable to corporation tax. However, all corporation tax assessments are made on an actual basis, instead of the preceding year basis that sometimes applies for income tax. The profits shown by the accounts will need adjusting in accordance with rules which follow, with some modifications, those applicable for income tax assessments (2.9). For example:

(1) Deduct any franked investment income.
(2) Add back payments for non-business purposes.
(3) Add back capital losses and payments. Deduct capital profits and capital receipts. Compute the capital gains less losses for the accounting period according to the capital gains tax rules (4.17).
(4) Add back business entertaining unless in connection with overseas customers or the company's own staff. (Gifts of advertising articles of less than £10 value to each customer are also allowable.)
(5) Add back depreciation and amortisation of fixed assets charged in the accounts.
(6) Adjust interest payable and receivable to the actual gross payments and receipts during the accounting period.
(7) Deduct capital allowances for the accounting period (4.13), adding back balancing charges and deducting balancing allowances.
(8) In some cases, notional income tax at the basic rate must be added

to any building society interest received. This is calculated by multiplying the actual interest received by 27/73. The notional tax is then deducted from the total corporation tax payable.

4.13 Capital allowances

The capital allowances rules for businesses (2.17) apply to companies subject to certain special rules including the following:

(1) Where a company obtains first year allowance (2.20) in respect of capital expenditure, if this results in an adjusted corporation tax loss, the loss may be carried back and set against profits for the three preceding years. (Expenditure after 31 March 1986 generally no longer attracts first year allowance.)

(2) Where one company takes over all of the assets and business of another company, the former continues to receive exactly the same capital allowances on the assets transferred as the old company would have obtained. For this to apply, there must be a 'company reconstruction' without change of ownership. This takes place if at any time during the two years following the reconstruction, no less than 75% of the acquiring company belongs to the same people who owned no less than 75% of the old company.

4.14 Example: Corporation tax computation

Box Ltd has no associated companies and prepares its accounts to 31 March each year. Its pre-tax profits for the year to 31 March 1988 amount to £80,000 which includes a dividend of £800 received in December 1987 which comprises its only franked investment income for the year. Also included is a profit on asset sales of £10,000 in respect of which a chargeable gain (4.17) of £8,800 has been computed. The profit is after charging £6,000 depreciation. Capital allowances of £9,000 are due for the year. A dividend of £2,260 was paid for the year in December 1987.

Assuming no other taxation adjustments are required apart from those noted above, compute:

(a) The corporation tax liability of Box Ltd for the year to 31 March 1988.
(b) Its ACT liability.

Box Ltd

(a) Corporation tax computations—
    Accounting period to 31 March 1988

	£	£
Profit per accounts		80,000
Add: Depreciation		6,000
		£86,000
Less: Franked investment income (excluding tax credit)	800	
Capital allowances	9,000	
Profit on asset sales	10,000	
		19,800
		66,200
Schedule D Case I assessment		
Chargeable gain		8,800
Assessable profits		£75,000
Corporation tax payable at 27%		
(small profits rate)		£20,250

(b)   ACT liability

	£
Dividends paid December 1987	£2,260
Less: Dividends received December 1987	800
	£1,460
Net ACT due £1,460 × 27/73	£ 540

Note: ACT of £540 will normally be payable with the return for the three months to 31 December 1987 by 14 January 1988. The remainder of the corporation tax of £19,710 (£20,250 — £540) will normally be due on 1 January 1989.

4.15 Losses

Where a trading loss results for an accounting period of a company, after the necessary corporation tax adjustments, a repayment of the tax on an equal amount of the profits (of any description) for the previous accounting period is obtainable under TA 1970, s 177(2) (now TA 1988, s 393(2)). Note that a loss for a period can only be set against a profit from a previous period of equal length. Thus, where a loss is made in a nine month period, it can only be set against profits for the previous nine months. The time limit for making claims to the Inland Revenue is within two years of the end of the accounting period of the loss.

As an alternative, tax credits on dividends can be reclaimed by offsetting trading losses.

For the above purposes, trading losses are effectively augmented by capital allowances and annual charges. Any unused balance is available for carrying forward to be set against trading profits for future years.

Where there is a 'company reconstruction without change of ownership' (4.13), so that one company takes over the trade and assets of another, any trading losses are carried over with the trade. This broadly applies where the two companies are under at least 75% common ownership. However, the unused tax losses may not be fully available if the original company is insolvent when the trade is transferred.

4.16 Terminal losses

Relief for terminal losses is available (under TA 1970, s 178) to a company in much the same way as for an individual ceasing to trade (2.43). A company is therefore able to make a claim to set off a loss incurred in its last 12 months of trading against the profits for the three prior years.

4.17 Capital gains and losses

From 17 March 1987 capital gains realised by companies are charged to corporation tax at the normal rates. Thus, if a company has £1 million profits, it will pay 35% corporation tax on its capital gains. However, a gain of £20,000 made by a company with £50,000 other taxable profits carries the small companies corporation tax rate (27%) on the gain. (If the gain arose in the period from 17 March 1987 to 31 March 1987, the rate was 29%).

In any accounting period, capital losses may be offset against gains and only net gains are taxable. An accounting period straddling 17 March was regarded as being two separate accounting periods, one before and one starting on that date for capital gains purposes. Allowable capital losses in the second period could be carried back to set against gains in the first.

Gains realised before 17 March 1987 effectively were taxed at 30%. This was achieved by charging a fraction of the gain to corporation tax at the full rate. Thus, 6/7ths of capital gains were so charged for the period from 1 April 1986 to 16 March 1987.

Capital gains can be relieved by setting off capital losses in the same period or those brought forward from previous periods. Trading losses may be offset against capital profits of the same or the previous period. Capital profits can also be offset by group loss relief claims (4.19). However, note that trading losses brought forward from previous periods can only be set against future trading profits and not against future chargeable gains.

Where a company incurs capital losses, these can only be set against its capital gains for the same accounting period or a future one. However, unused capital losses can be carried forward to future years, even after the company ceases to trade. This contrasts with trading losses which can no longer be carried forward if a company ceases trading.

Normally, overseas companies are not liable to UK corporation tax on their capital gains realised abroad. However, under CGTA, s 15, any shareholders resident and domiciled in the UK can have capital gains apportioned to them if the overseas company would have been close (4.21) if it were resident in the UK. This also applies to UK beneficiaries of an overseas trust owning shares in an overseas company.

4.18   Groups of companies

A variety of special provisions relate to groups of companies, broadly parent and subsidiaries. A subsidiary company is classified according to the percentage of its ordinary capital owned directly or indirectly by its parent company. In particular, a 51% subsidiary is owned as to more than 50% by its parent and a 75% subsidiary is not less than 75% owned by its parent.

4.19   Group loss relief

In a group comprising a parent company and 75% subsidiaries, the trading losses (including capital allowances) of the group members can be offset by way of group relief against the profits of other group members. Points to watch include:

(1)   A claim must be made to the Inland Revenue within two years of the end of the accounting period.
(2)   For full relief, there must be a group relationship throughout the respective accounting periods of the loss-making and profit-making companies. Otherwise, profits and losses are apportioned on a time basis to the period during which the group relationship exists.
(3)   Parent and subsidiaries must all be resident in the UK.
(4)   The parent company must have at least a 75% interest in each of the subsidiaries, and be entitled to at least 75% of the distributable profits of each subsidiary and 75% of the assets available on liquidation.
(5)   Group relief also applies to a consortium of UK companies which, subject to the rules, owns 75% or more of the loss-making company. No member of the consortium may own less than 5% and

thus the maximum number of members is 20. In addition, losses made by consortium companies can be surrendered down to a company which is jointly owned.

(6) If a company joins or leaves a group during its accounting period, a time apportionment basis is normally applied in calculating group relief. However, this can be set aside if it operates unfairly. A 'just and reasonable method' is then used.

(7) No group relief is now available for the losses of dual-resident investment companies.

4.20 Groups — Other reliefs

As well as group loss relief (4.19) various other reliefs are available for groups of companies including the following:

(1) Dividend payments from 51% subsidiaries to their parent may be made without having to account for ACT. A prior election to the Revenue is needed, however. A similar rule relates to inter-group interest payments. (In both cases, the companies must be resident in the UK.) Payments from a consortium-owned company to the consortium members are included, provided the consortium owns at least 75% of the ordinary shares.

(2) Subject to certain rules, a parent company can transfer to its subsidiary relief for ACT. Thus, if the parent pays a dividend of £7,300, it obtains £7,300 × 27/73 = £2,700 ACT relief. However, instead of taking this itself, it can surrender the relief to its subsidiary which then deducts £2,700 from its corporation tax bill. It is necessary for the parent company to hold more than 50% of the ordinary shares of the subsidiary and to be entitled to more than 50% of the distributable profits and more than 50% of the assets on liquidation.

(3) No capital gains tax generally arises where assets are transferred within a group consisting of a parent and its 75% subsidiaries (all UK resident). However, when the asset leaves the group, capital gains tax is paid on the entire chargeable gain whilst it was owned by any group company.

(4) Capital gains tax 'rollover relief' (6.24) applies to a UK group consisting of parent company and 75% subsidiaries. The gain on an asset arising to one trading company may be 'rolled over' against the purchase of an asset by another trading company in the group. For these purposes, property holding companies which hold assets used for trade by trading companies in the group are also included.

4.21 Close companies

Special rules relate to 'close' companies. These are broadly those under the control of five or fewer persons and their 'associates' (or the directors). The term 'associates' includes close family, such as husband, wife, father, mother, brother and sister. A quoted company is not 'close', however, if the general public own at least 35% of its voting shares.

A UK subsidiary of an overseas parent company is 'close' if the overseas parent would have been a close company itself if resident in the UK. Thus, most small or medium companies are likely to be 'close' companies unless they are subsidiaries of non-close companies. In particular, most 'family companies' are 'close'. Although the rules concerning close companies are not nearly as harsh as they were prior to 27 March 1980, it is still important to have regard to these provisions, some of which are noted below.

4.22 Apportionment of income

The Revenue may apportion the excess of the 'relevant income' of a close company over its distributions for an accounting period among its shareholders. However, no apportionment will be made for a trading company or member of a trading group, if the excess is under £1,001. Furthermore, by concession, no apportionment is made for a property investment company whose excess is under £251. Also, an individual is exempt from apportionment if his or her share of the total apportionment amount is less than both 5% and £1,000.

'Relevant income' consists of not more than the company's 'distributable investment income' plus 50% of its estate (property) income (subject to abatement — 4.23) and in certain cases 50% of its trading income. 'Distributable investment income' is calculated after tax interest and dividends (without tax credits). Dividends from companies in the same group, known as group income, must be included. A deduction is made from the investment income of the lower of £3,000 and 10% of the company's trading and property income.

The trading income of a trading company or member of a trading group is excluded from its 'relevant income'. (This applies for periods ending after 26 March 1980). However, 50% of the property income is still included.

If a company can prove that it cannot distribute its 'relevant income' because the money is needed for business purposes, a reduction might be obtained by negotiation with the Revenue. Business purposes include expansion and the acquisition of a business as well as the repayment of loans originally obtained for these purposes. If, however, a property investment company spends its profits purchasing land or buildings (not farm or market garden improvements) this money is regarded as available for dividends and thus apportionable. However, income which cannot be legally distributed is excluded from apportionment.

If a company pays dividends within a reasonable time, these are set against the 'relevant income' in arriving at the amount to be apportioned. For these purposes, 'a reasonable time' is accepted by the Revenue to be not less than 18 months.

4.23 Abatement

In order to understand how abatement works, it is easier first to consider periods ending prior to 27 March 1980, when trading income for trading companies was liable to apportionment. However, if a close company had no 'associated companies' (4.4) the first £25,000 of the company's trading or property income after tax was not regarded as 'relevant income' (4.22). If such after-tax income was between £25,000 and £75,000, you reduced this income by half of the difference between it and £75,000. This is known as abatement.

Where a company had one or more 'associated companies' (4.4), excluding dormant and non-trading companies, the amounts of £25,000 and £75,000 were reduced by dividing them by one plus the number of 'associated companies'.

For periods ending after 26 March 1980, a proportionate amount of abatement can be obtained. The limits of £25,000 and £75,000 mentioned above must be reduced in the ratio of the estate income (ie property income) to estate and trading income. Thus, if a trading company (without associated companies) has trading income of £30,000 and estate income of £20,000 after tax, it obtains abatement of 1/2 (£75,000 × 2/5–£20,000) = £5,000. The rules for reducing abatement by reference to the number of 'associated companies' remain as previously.

4.24 Close companies — Loans and distributions

Where close companies make loans to their 'participators' or associates of 'participators' the companies are charged to tax at 27/73rds of the amounts. For example, if a company makes a loan of £7,300 to a participator, the company will be assessed to tax amounting to 27/73 × £7,300 = £2,700. This rule extends to loans by companies controlled by or subsequently acquired by close companies (FA 1976, s 44).

A 'participator' broadly means a person having a share or interest in the capital or income of a company. This includes, for example, a shareholder or loan creditor.

The tax is repaid when the loan is repaid to the company. However, the Revenue may assess loans even if they have been repaid, in which case a repayment would follow later. Where a close company lends money to a participator or his associate and then releases the debt, higher rate tax is assessed. This is based on the grossed-up equivalent of the loan. Thus in the above example, if the company releases the participator from his debt, he will pay higher rate tax on £10,000 but will deduct the basic rate tax of £2,700 from the amount which he pays.

In the case of close companies, the term 'distribution' is extended to include living expenses and accommodation, etc provided for a 'participator', unless taxed as a benefit (9.14).

Where a payment is treated as a distribution, it is not deductible from the taxable profits of the company. Furthermore, in the case of a 'qualifying distribution' (4.9) ACT is payable to the Revenue, although offsetable against 'mainstream' corporation tax.

4.25   Cessations and liquidations

Prior to 27 March 1980, if a close company ceased to trade, its distribution requirement included all of its trading and property income after abatement for its final chargeable accounting period and any other chargeable accounting periods ending within a year of the date of cessation. For subsequent periods, trading income is excluded from the distribution requirement but the rule still applies to property income.

4.26   Non-resident companies

A company is deemed to be resident where its central control and management are carried out. Normally, the central control and management would be exercised in the country in which the company is registered. However, this is not necessarily so and if a company simply has its registered office in the UK but carries on all its business from offices abroad and holds its board meetings abroad, it is non-resident. The 1988 Budget includes new rules (see the 1988 Budget Notes).

Taxes Act 1970, s 482 contains penal provisions to prevent UK companies from becoming non-resident without Treasury consent. This consent is also required to transfer part or all of a company's business to a non-resident.

Where a non-resident company trades in this country through a branch or agency, corporation tax is charged in respect of the profits of the branch or agency. However, if those profits are also subject to tax in the country of residence of the company, double tax relief might be available.

4.27 UK companies with overseas income

UK resident companies are subject to corporation tax on the gross amount of their overseas income, if any. However, double tax relief is frequently available where overseas income is taxed both in the UK and abroad. Special rules apply where a UK company receives a dividend from an overseas company from which tax at source has been deducted (withholding tax). The gross dividend is included in the taxable profits which are subject to corporation tax and, normally, double tax relief for the withholding tax suffered is given against the corporation tax payable.

If the company owns at least 10% of the voting capital of the overseas company, relief is given for the 'underlying tax' (the proportion of the total tax paid by the foreign company attributable to its dividends). The rate of double tax relief is limited to the UK corporation tax rate (35% etc).

4.28 Controlled foreign companies

Anti-avoidance rules enable the Revenue to impose extra tax on UK companies with interests in controlled foreign companies which are under overall UK control, subject to certain rules including the following:

(1) The overseas company must be subject to tax in its own country of less than half that payable if it were UK resident.
(2) The UK company (together with its associates) must have at least a 10% interest in the overseas company.
(3) The charge is excluded if there are acceptable dividend payments. (Only counted if made by a company which is not resident in the UK at the time of payment.) In broad terms, 50% of the available profits of a trading company are required to be paid as dividends and 90% for investment companies.
(4) The charge is excluded if the controlled foreign company satisfies an 'exempt activities' test. This involves having a business establishment where the company is resident and being managed there; also being broadly a trading company or qualifying holding company.
(5) Exclusion is also obtained through a motive test. Requirements are

that the foreign company's transactions are carried out for commercial reasons and not for the main purpose of saving UK tax or diverting profits from the UK.

(6) Certain foreign companies quoted on foreign Stock Exchanges are excluded.

(7) No charge is made if the foreign company's profit for the year is less than £20,000.

(8) The profits of the overseas company are apportioned to any UK companies having at least a 10% interest and corporation tax is charged at the appropriate rate for each. A deduction from the UK tax is then made for an appropriate proportion of the overseas tax and relief is given where dividends are paid by the overseas company.

(9) The Inland Revenue has published a list of excluded countries which will not be regarded as low tax countries for the purposes of the above rules. In general, the list excludes tax havens.

4.29   Demergers

Where two or more trading businesses are carried on either by a single company or in a group of companies, there are special rules to assist in splitting up those businesses. Subject to the detailed provisions, the demerger rules include the following:

(1) Where a company distributes to its shareholders shares in a 75% subsidiary (4.18) this is not treated as a distribution for tax purposes and so no ACT nor income tax arises for the company or its shareholders.

(2) Where one company transfers a trade to a second company which in turn distributes its shares to the shareholders of the first, relief is also available.

(3) Any distribution which you receive in the above circumstances is relieved from capital gains tax until you sell the actual shares.

(4) Anti-avoidance provisions apply to counter, for example, the extraction of tax-free cash from companies, subject to a procedure for advance clearance.

4.30   Unquoted company purchasing its own shares

Company law enables a company to purchase its own shares and issue redeemable equity shares in certain circumstances. If the proceeds exceed the original cost, the surplus would be a distribution and the company would pay ACT at 27/73rds on the excess. An individual receiving the payment would pay higher rate tax on the grossed-up excess less a tax credit. However, relief is provided in certain circumstances so that the company pays no ACT and the shareholder's liability is restricted to capital gains tax (unless he is a share-dealer, in which case the gain is treated as his income). Application for advance clearance may be made to the Revenue.

There are various conditions for relief. For example, the company cannot be quoted and must be a trading company or the holding company of a trading group. The purchase or redemption of the shares must be mainly to benefit the trade of the company or its 75% subsidiary. The shareholder selling back his shares must be UK resident and ordinarily resident, having normally owned the shares for at least five years, and if he keeps part of his shareholding, it must have been substantially reduced (broadly by at least 25%). Furthermore, after selling back his shares, the shareholder must not be 'connected' with the company, which means holding with 'associates' 30% of the shares, etc.

4.31 Business expansion scheme

The business expansion scheme (BES) provides a useful method for suitable companies to raise capital. At the same time, investments carry income tax relief. Thus, if your income is high, you should consider making appropriate BES investments.

The detailed rules are involved and beyond the scope of this book. However, particular points to note include the following:

(1) Both investment in new unquoted companies and the issue of shares by established unquoted trading companies satisfying certain conditions are included.
(2) The scheme excludes employees, paid directors and any shareholder owning more than 30%.
(3) Your maximum investment in BES schemes is limited to £40,000 in any tax year. The minimum investment in any company is £500 unless made through approved investment funds. You may now elect to carry back to the previous tax year part of your investment if made prior to 6 October. The carry-back is limited to half such investment or £5,000, if less. Your total relief for any tax year, including the amount carried back, may not exceed £40,000.
(4) In general, you must hold the shares on which relief has been claimed for at least five years.
(5) The relief does not normally reduce the cost for capital gains tax purposes and shares issued after 18 March 1986 are exempt from capital gains tax when first disposed of.
(6) Share capital issued in excess of £50,000 in total in any tax year does not qualify for relief if the company broadly has more than half the net value of its assets consisting of land and buildings.
(7) In order to issue shares under the business expansion scheme, the

company must exist to carry on one or more *qualifying trades*. Such trades are, with some exceptions, broadly manufacturing, wholesale and retail business but not leasing and financial activities, etc.

(8)   The 1988 Budget announced additional points (see the 1988 Budget Notes).

4.32   Future changes

The Keith Committee made certain proposals on filing accounts, interest and penalties. These were enacted in 1987 but will not take effect until April 1992 or even later. Particular points to note are:

(1)   Companies are to pay corporation tax nine months after their accounting dates, whether or not assessments have been raised.
(2)   Tax paid late will carry interest from the required payment date. This also applies to repayments by the Revenue.
(3)   It will be necessary to submit accounts to the Revenue within 12 months from the accounting date.
(4)   Penalties will be charged if accounts are filed late without excuse.

4.33   Deciding whether to incorporate

If you are trading successfully as a sole trader, or in partnership, you should consider seriously whether or not to incorporate. Trading as a limited company has various advantages compared with trading as a sole trader or partnership and also certain disadvantages, such as the need to disclose more about your business to the world at large.

The non-tax advantages and disadvantages, such as the protection afforded by limited liability are dealt with elsewhere (1.13). This section considers only the taxation and National Insurance contribution position.

If your business is not incorporated, you will pay income tax on the profits at the basic and higher rates. Thus, income tax will range from 27% to 60%, depending upon your assessable profits. However, if you are incorporated, any profits which you retain in the company will normally bear corporation tax at the small companies rate of 27% or a higher rate, ranging up to the full corporation tax rate of 35%. If you are considering incorporation, it is likely that your profits are below the small companies rate limit (normally £100,000) and thus the company would pay no more than 27% corporation tax (4.3). This indicates a clear advantage for incorporation, if you are a sole trader with profits of say £35,000 and thus a top income tax rate of 50%. In particular, this will help you to accumulate money in the company, for development.

Once you have incorporated, you will probably become a director of the company and draw out money for your living expenses, by way of director's remuneration. To the extent that you do this, the income tax position will be the same as if you were not incorporated. However, a balance of income is likely to be left in the company where it will simply bear corporation tax. Furthermore, you may be able to regulate the salary which you take from the company, so that the income tax borne is at more moderate rates.

So far as the comparison between income tax on an unincorporated business and corporation tax on a company is concerned, the latter is generally more favourable. However, the position is counterbalanced to some extent by the extra burden of National Insurance contributions on the directors' remuneration, compared with the charge on sole traders and partners.

Directors' remuneration is charged to National Insurance contributions under Class 1 (9.30), whereas sole traders and partners pay contributions under Classes 2 and 4 (2.48). The latter cases carry a strictly limited charge but Class 1 involves substantial contributions for the employee and unlimited ones for the employer. The maximum employers' contribution is 10.45%. This is relieved for corporation tax purposes, but the overall effect of National Insurance contributions on directors' remuneration is significant.

Another factor is the additional tax cost when accumulated money is withdrawn from a company. If this is done on liquidation, capital gains tax will be paid by the shareholders at 30%, subject to indexation. Thus, even though such tax may not be payable in the foreseeable future, the contingency should still be kept in mind.

Another way in which profits may be extracted, either in the year when they are earned or at a future time, is by way of dividend. This may increase the tax burden for shareholders liable to higher rate income tax. However, there is the advantage, compared with directors' remuneration, that no National Insurance contributions are payable.

Thus, it is apparent that evaluating whether or not to incorporate is highly complicated. Many facets need to be considered and it is difficult to give an exact level of profits at which incorporation is beneficial from a tax viewpoint. However, a sole trader earning at least £30,000 per annum and a two-man partnership earning over £60,000 may well gain tax advantages from incorporation. The following example illustrates the position.

4.34   Example: Saving tax by incorporating

Jack Box is single and carries on business as a sole trader. His assessable profits are £35,000. Assuming that he has no other income, his income tax liability and National Insurance contributions for 1987–88 would be:

	£	£
Assessable profits		£35,000
Less personal relief	2,425	
50% of Class 4 NHI contributions	339	2,764
		£32,236

Income tax 1987–88		
17,900 at 27%		4,833
2,500 at 40%		1,000
5,000 at 45%		2,250
6,836 at 50%		3,418
£32,236		11,501.00

National Insurance contributions		
Class 2		200.20
Class 4 (maximum)		677.25
Total income tax and National Insurance		**£12,378.45**

If Jack incorporates his business and makes the same profits in his company, his tax and National Insurance contributions are shown below, assuming he draws salaries of (a) £10,000 and (b) £20,000.

	£	£ (a)	£	£ (b)
Profits		35,000		35,000
Salary	10,000		20,000	
Employer's National Insurance	1,045	11,045	2,090	22,090
		£23,955		£12,910
Corporation tax 27%		£6,467.85		£3,485.70

Jack's income tax and National Insurance

	£		£	
Salary	10,000		20,000	
Less personal relief	2,425		2,425	
Income tax at 27%	£7,575	£2,045.25	£17,575	£4,745.25

	£		£
Class 1 National Insurance at 9%	900.00	(maximum)	1,380.60
	£2,945.25		£5,125.85

Thus, a reduction in total tax and National Insurance contributions is obtained by Jack forming his business into a company, depending upon his salary level as follows:

	(a) £10,000	(b) £20,000
Salary		
Income tax on salary	2,045.25	4,745.25
National Insurance — Jack	900.00	1,380.60
— Company	1,045.00	2,090.00
Corporation tax	6,467.85	3,485.70
	10,458.10	11,701.55
Total tax and National Insurance if not incorporated	12,378.45	12,378.45
SAVING	£ 1,920.35	£ 676.90

Notes:

(1) The savings tend to reduce as Jack increases his salary because higher income tax rates and extra National Insurance are encountered.
(2) If Jack takes dividends instead of more salary, the extra National Insurance is saved.
(3) Future capital tax liabilities must be kept in mind. Capital gains tax may arise on retained profits, whilst if dividends are paid, this may well increase the value of the company shares for inheritance tax purposes.

5   Company and partnership law

Part A   Company law

5.1   Introduction

The following discussion is an outline of some of the main features of company law. It has to be selective and non-exhaustive because of the sheer size of the subject (CA 1985 alone (which is not the only relevant statute) runs to 747 sections). Of necessity, then, certain rules and concepts and detail generally are omitted from this chapter. Finally, as with partnership law (5.77) Scottish law has slightly different rules, on occasions, from those set out here.

There can be various types of companies, those limited by shares (both public and private), those limited by guarantee and unlimited companies. In this chapter we discuss *limited* companies as this is usually the type of company adopted by businesses trading with a view of profit.

5.2   Public companies

A public company is defined as one which carries the name 'public limited company' or 'plc' or, if its registered office is in Wales, 'cwmni cyfyngedig cwhoeddus' ('ccc'), which has a minimum issued share capital of £50,000 (a quarter of which must be fully paid up) and which is otherwise subject to more stringent rules in CA 1985 concerning maintenance of capital and other procedures that do not apply to private companies

5.3   Private companies

A private company is one which is not a public company. It may also not offer its shares to the public.

5.4   Company law in general

Much of this chapter is common to both public and private companies, although significant differences are highlighted where thought appropriate. It is beyond the scope of this book to discuss aspects of company law such as mergers, takeovers and reconstructions of both private and public companies, securities regulation, Stock Exchange rules and specialised rules that apply to public companies only. Nor does this book give any detailed treatment of the Financial Services Act 1986 as far as its relevance to company law is concerned.

5.5   Starting up

Starting a company these days can be quite simple. Companies are often formed by purchases 'off the shelf'. This means that instead of preparing all the formalities yourself, you can contact a company registration agent who may have a number of 'ready made' or 'off the shelf' companies available for purchase. The registration agent will already have completed much of the formality necessary in setting up one of these companies. But the following is a brief description of the procedures.

5.6 Name

First, you have to choose a *name*. The rules here are set out in Part C at the end of this chapter.

5.7   Documents to be delivered

On incorporation you have to deliver to the Registrar of Companies a Memorandum and Articles of Association, a statement of first directors and secretary, a return of subscribers' shares, a notice of accounting reference date, a notification of registered office address and a statutory declaration of compliance with incorporation procedures.

In this chapter we refer to the use of certain forms. Mostly certain types of form are prescribed for lodging information with the Registrar of Companies. These are prescribed under the Companies (Forms) Regulations 1985 and the Registrar may reject forms which do not comply with the rules. But you can get the forms from your professional adviser or from a law stationer.

5.8 Memorandum and Articles of Association

The Memorandum and Articles of Association are the constitutional documents of the company.

The Memorandum contains the following:

(a) the company name;
(b) the country in which the registered office is situate;
(c) the objects clause;
(d) a statement that the liability of the company is limited;
(e) a statement of the authorised share capital of the company.

The Memorandum must be signed by each subscriber in the presence of at least one witness, who must attest the signatures.

The Articles of Association are more to do with internal regulation of members' rights and procedures which companies have to follow to make decisions and to manage their day-to-day affairs. They include provisions about meetings, appointment of directors, company secretary and auditors, sale of shares, borrowing powers, appointment of managing director and procedures for the removal of directors. A model form of Articles is contained in Table A of the Companies (Tables A to F) Regulations 1985. If a company does not incorporate its own Articles expressly it will, by default, incorporate those Articles in Table A. These are suitable for most purposes but not all.

Most companies' Articles adopt Table A for the most part but make some modification where some standard provisions of Table A are considered unsuitable for the particular company in question. A company adopts the Table A relevant to the legislation under which it was incorporated. If your company was incorporated under an earlier Companies Act its Articles may be based on an earlier (and different) Table A, eg CA 1948, Sched 1, Table A. In this chapter, when we refer to Table A, the reference is to Table A under the 1985 Regulations. The Memorandum and Articles will be discussed in more detail later in this chapter (5.24, 5.28).

5.9 Statement of first directors and secretary

Every company must have at least one director (and a public company must have at least two). It is common to have more directors than the legal minimum. But, in the case of a private company, if there is a sole director, that sole director cannot also be company secretary. A form (G10) must be signed by the intending directors/secretary showing their consent to act and this must be sent to the Companies Registry.

5.10   Subscribers' shares

The original subscribers to the company must apply for shares and a return of the issue of these shares to the first members must be delivered to the Companies Registry. It is recorded on Form PUC1. Each company must have at least two members at all times and, therefore, the original subscribers must number at least two. It is important to maintain the minimum membership requirement, for if a company carries on business without having at least two members for more than six months, the sole member, if he is aware of the fact there is only one member, will be liable jointly and severally with the company for the company's debts thereafter. Reduction of the members below two will also give the court jurisdiction to wind the company up under the provisions of the Insolvency Act 1986. Capital duty is payable on all shares issued in the amount of £1 per £100 or part thereof (although the Chancellor's budget statement of 15 March 1988 indicated that it is proposed to abolish such duty) (5.22).

5.11   Accounting reference date

The company must send to the Registrar of Companies within six months of the date of incorporation a notice (on Form G224) of its accounting reference date, ie the date up to which its annual accounts are to be prepared.

5.12   Registered office address

The company must send to the Registrar of Companies (on Form G10) a notice of its actual registered office address (not simply the country in which the address is situate).

5.13   Statutory declaration of compliance with procedures

There must be filed with the Registrar of Companies a statutory declaration sworn either by a solicitor engaged in the formation of the company or by a director or by a secretary that the provisions of the Companies Acts in relation to formation have been complied with. Form G12 is used.

5.14   Certificate of incorporation

Once all this has taken place and been approved, the Registrar of Companies will issue a certificate of incorporation. The company, if it is a private company, is then ready to trade. If the company is a public company it must also apply to the Registrar of Companies (using Form G117) for a certificate of compliance with the capital requirements of CA 1985 as applicable to public limited companies. Before then it may have been incorporated but it cannot trade.

5.15 First meeting of directors

The company will now have directors and a company secretary and will have issued two shares, at least, to the original subscribers. These can be transferred to the real members of the company if, in fact, the original subscribers are merely members of the company registration agency and further shares can be issued to the members of the company if desired. If further shares are issued this is done usually at the first meeting of directors of the company which should take place after incorporation. Any further shares issued are recorded on a Form PUC 2 which is then sent to the Registrar of Companies.

If the authorised share capital is too low to permit issue of the number of shares you want at this stage, it should have first been raised by an ordinary resolution at the *general* meeting (ie by the shareholders). Again capital duty is payable on any shares issued at the rate of £1 per £100 worth of shares or part thereof although the Chancellor's budget statement of 15 March 1988 may affect this and the consequent Finance Act may abolish such duty. (5.22). The first meeting of directors should also deal with the appointment of solicitors and accountants, the appointment of additional directors, appointment of managing director, chairman of the company and any other business.

5.16 Capital structure, borrowing, and other questions

The following is a brief synopsis of how companies are structured. Also explained are a few expressions that are peculiar to company law.

5.17 Capital

We have seen that a company must state in its Memorandum that it has an *authorised* share capital of a certain amount. The *authorised* share capital is also often known as the *nominal* capital (the two expressions have the same meaning). The *authorised* or *nominal* capital is simply a figure of capital which the company may achieve by the issue of shares to that value if it wishes. Thus, if a company is registered with a nominal share capital of £5,000, this means that the company can, if it wishes, issue shares (commonly, these will be of £1 each) of a total value of £5,000. It does not mean that it *has* done so, nor is it obliged (if it is a private company) to do so beyond the two initial subscribers' shares (5.10). The authorised share capital can be raised by ordinary resolution.

When a company does issue shares the value thereof is known as the *issued* or *allotted* share capital. As we have seen, a company can have as little as two members and, therefore, a company could have an issued share capital of as little as £2, assuming shares are of a par value of £1 each. If it has shares of a lower denomination than £1, say, 25p, a company could have an issued share capital of as little as 50p!

A further twist is that not all of the issued share capital (at least in a private company (contrast requirements in relation to a public company (5.2)) needs to be paid up. So issued share capital is not necessarily *paid up* share capital. Naturally, the company can make a call upon members to pay up what is outstanding on the share capital issued but, in the case of a private company, it does not have to do so.

5.18   Limited liability

A member's liability is limited to the amount paid up on shares issued to him or if unpaid, to the amount outstanding on those shares. There is no liability beyond this for the company's debts unless specific rules either in legislation (5.75 and 5.90 for example) or, occasionally, under the general law (5.50) are broken. This makes the limited liability company an extremely attractive proposition for the proprietors of a business.

However, with the capital requirement being so low in the case of private companies this can also lead to abuse. There are many instances of overtrading by under-capitalised companies with resulting hardship for creditors who do not get paid when those companies fold.

And, in practice, the concept of limited liability in the case of small businesses can sometimes be illusory. A company without assets and capital may have difficulty in borrowing without personal guarantees being given by its directors. These may even have to be backed up by the security of their own homes to the bank. If such companies fold, the directors may stand to lose their personal assets notwithstanding the use of a limited company as a trading vehicle.

5.19   Raising capital

A company ordinarily raises capital either by issuing shares in return for money paid by subscribers, or by borrowing. Some companies start up and fund themselves entirely by subscription for shares. It is also possible for companies to ask for further money to be injected into the company by shareholders at a later date. This is sometimes done by means of what is known as a *'rights issue'*, that is to say, an offer of shares giving an equal chance for all to participate in the issue of shares of the company pro rata to their existing shareholdings.

Some articles of association have 'pre-emption' rights written into the articles, making every share issue in effect a rights issue. And CA 1985 will imply such pre-emption rights in most circumstances although they can sometimes be disapplied. Pre-emption rights are important in the context of minority rights, in that they can stop discriminatory share issues that might otherwise have the effect of freezing out a minority.

Otherwise, the company looks to lenders of money for capital. That lender may be a bank or some other financial institution. Some companies exist to provide venture capital to other companies. The Business Expansion Scheme can also be a useful method of raising capital (4.31).

Some lenders may take *debentures* in return for the loan. *Debenture holders* are often contrasted with *shareholders*. Shareholders and debenture holders are, however, very different. Thus:

(1) A shareholder is entitled to participate in capital gains of the company and a debenture holder is not.
(2) A shareholder is a member of the company with constitutional rights under the Articles of Association. A debenture holder is not.
(3) A shareholder may be given a dividend annually on his shares which is not fixed and which is at the discretion of the directors (although preference shareholders often have a fixed dividend). If the company cannot afford to pay a dividend, it should not be declared. This may leave a shareholder with no return on capital. A debenture holder, however, usually receives interest on sums lent to the company at a fixed rate.
(4) A shareholder cannot be repaid his money. He must sell his shares to another or, very exceptionally under certain circumstances, ask the company to repurchase the shares under special provisions in the CA 1985 (5.66). However, a debenture evidences a loan and a loan is repayable under its own terms.

Being a debenture holder might be seen in some ways to be a safer investment than being a shareholder since the money is always repayable and the return on capital fixed. Although a shareholder stands to enjoy capital gain and also to enjoy a reasonable dividend if the company is doing well, he nonetheless stands the risk also of capital loss and no dividend at all if the company is doing badly.

However, lending monies to a company can have its own risk. For
a loan will only be repaid as long as the company survives and has
the money to do so. Therefore, debenture holders who lend large
amounts of money to the company should back up their loan with
the security of a charge either *fixed* on the company's real property
(such as its land or factory) whether freehold or leasehold or *floating*
(5.20). This type of security is usually incorporated into a standard
debenture document.

5.20   Floating charges

A *floating charge* can only be given by companies (see chapter 1)
and is a useful additional form of security to offer a lender. A floating
charge is basically a charge on moveables such as stock in trade,
furniture and other assets, but can also include, for example, book
debts. The advantage of a floating charge is that, as its name implies,
it does not actually fix itself to any particular asset or assets. Whilst
the charge is in place the company is free to trade normally and even
turn over its stock and other assets which are the subject of the charge.
Only upon the occurrence of certain events, for example, the
liquidation of the company, does the floating charge *crystallize*, ie
become fixed. It then fixes on all the assets the subject of the charge
existing at that time.

Most lenders, such as banks, play doubly safe by taking a fixed and
floating charge.

5.21   Receivers appointed by debenture holders

A debenture holder (very commonly, your bank) is also usually entitled,
under the terms of his debenture, to appoint a receiver and manager
to look after the security that has been given by the company. A
receiver is usually appointed upon the occurrence of some event
specified in the debenture, generally when there is default or
threatened default in repayment of the loan or breach of some other
provision in the debenture. A receiver's job is to take charge of the
company for the time being and get in debts owed to the company,
and possibly to sell assets (sometimes this may mean selling the whole
undertaking of the company) to raise money to pay off the debenture
holder.

5.22   Capital duty and stamp duty

At the time of writing, and subject to comment on the 1988 Budget
below, as discussed, *capital duty* is payable on increase of capital by
issue of shares at the rate of £1 per £100 or part thereof. An increase
in the *authorised* share capital *of itself* does not attract capital duty.
Thus if there are only a few of you who are members of the company

and you do not feel the need to capitalise the company by share subscription monies, there is little point in issuing too many shares to yourselves; you will only pay duty thereon. There are certain reliefs from capital duty, for example on corporate reconstructions, such as a transfer of an undertaking or part from a company to another set up for that purpose which is going to remain controlled by the first company. But the conditions are quite complicated and professional advice is necessary. An unlimited company will not have to pay capital duty on a share issue.

The Chancellor's budget statement of 15 March 1988 proposed the abolition of capital duty and subject to Parliamentary approval, the consequent Finance Act may give effect to this proposal.

Stamp duty is payable on transfers of shares for value at the rate of ½% rounded up to the nearest 50p. Generally, transfers not by way of sale, such as dispositions in wills and gifts, will be charged at a fixed rate of 50p. There are reliefs on reconstructions and reorganisations as in capital duty (above) and there can be an overlap, ie double relief. But again the conditions are very complicated and stricter than in the case of capital duty.

Stamp duty reserve tax, introduced by FA 1986, catches certain agreements to transfer securities and the rate of duty in such cases is presently ½%.

Stamp duty will also be payable on property transactions by companies and differing rates apply.

5.23   Transfer of shares

Shares are ordinarily freely transmissible although the directors usually have a discretion to decline to register a share transfer. This is a fiduciary power and must be exercised for proper purposes (5.58). However, in smaller private companies, Articles often have pre-emption provisions restricting the transfer of shares to outsiders without first offering the shares to the other members. These provisions will not be in Table A and special Articles will have to be adopted to give effect to this. It is very wise for members in small private companies to provide for this. After all, a small company is like a partnership and you do not really want to be a partner with a stranger without consenting to it.

Shares are ordinarily transferred by using a standard stock transfer form signed by the transferor on which stamp duty may be payable (5.22). Movements of shares must be recorded in the register of members in the statutory books. A member is entitled to a share certificate which is handed over on sale and a new one issued to the transferee.

Different rules apply, of course, in relation to dealings in shares of public companies, a subject outside the scope of this book.

5.24 The Memorandum of Association and the doctrine of *ultra vires*

The Memorandum of Association which is filed with the Registrar of Companies must contain what is known as an *objects clause* (5.9). Being a creature of statute a company can only do those things which it is set up to do as provided in its objects clause. If a company strays outside its objects clause and does something that it is not set up to do then it acts *ultra vires*. An *ultra vires* act can have very serious consequences for the company, for its directors and for third parties dealing with the company.

At common law, an *ultra vires* contract is void and unenforceable. So at common law, a third party who has delivered goods to the company cannot sue for the money due for those goods and *vice versa*. And, in situations where the company has parted with assets or money under an *ultra vires* arrangement, the directors themselves may be guilty of breach of a fiduciary duty (5.52) and may have personally to reimburse the company for any loss. There is some statutory protection for third parties (5.25) in CA 1985, s 35. But the protection in that provision is not perfect (5.25). Therefore, it is of considerable importance that the company stays within its objects clause.

It has been stated that an *ultra vires* contract is void. This will happen where a company makes a contract and there is nothing in the memorandum to authorise it.

Example A

XYZ Co Ltd is formed to run farms. It contracts to purchase some silicon chips for its unauthorised computer business. The contract is *ultra vires* and void.

However, if a company exercises a *power* which is present in the memorandum and *misuses* that power, ie uses it for an unauthorised business and not its main object, the contract will *not* be *ultra vires*. It will be *voidable* as a misuse by directors of the power in the memorandum. (Powers in the memorandum such as borrowing, giving guarantees, writing cheques and buying land must only be used in furtherance of the main object of the company.) That is to say, the company can avoid the contract if the third party knew of the improper purpose of the transaction, eg:

Example B

ABC Co Ltd is formed to run farms. It borrows money from its bank to buy silicon chips for its unauthorised computer business. There is a power to borrow money in the memorandum. The contract is not *ultra vires*. But it may be avoided against the bank if the bank knew of the purpose to which the loan was being put. If the bank was ignorant of the purpose, it can enforce the contract.

These rules are complicated by the doctrine of *constructive notice* at common law. This says a third party dealing with the company is *deemed* to have notice of certain documents registered with the Registrar of Companies such as the Memorandum of Association, Articles of Association and special resolutions. Thus, you are deemed to know the objects of the company with which you deal. Thus, in Example B, if the bank knows of the *purpose* of the loan, ie to buy the chips, it will stand the risk of the contract being avoided. The bank may well not actually appreciate that the company should not be buying chips. But it will be *deemed* to know it is set up to run farms and will be *deemed* to appreciate it should not deal in computers. Therefore the doctrine of constructive notice at common law can catch out unwitting third parties.

5.25 Protection of third parties by statute

There is some limited statutory protection which deals with the *ultra vires* and constructive notice problem. Companies Act 1985, s 35 gives protection to third parties dealing with the company. If it applies, the third party will *not* be deemed to know the objects of the company and thus can enforce any contract with the company even if the company is acting *ultra vires*. It therefore reverses the common law rules set out in 5.22 as far as third parties are concerned. (The provision does not apply in favour of companies.)

However, there are certain conditions to this protection:

(1) A person dealing with a company must deal in 'good faith'. Thus, for example, if the third party actually *knows* that the company with which it is dealing is acting *ultra vires*, it is suggested that good faith might be absent and the third party cannot claim protection under the provisions.

(2) The transaction in question must have been decided upon by the directors. On a literal reading this implies that there must

have been a board meeting approving the particular transaction in question before the section operates. This is, however, often absent in practice. If so, the section will not apply. The interpretation of this limb is however in a state of flux.

5.26   A director's responsibility for *ultra vires* acts

A director of a company who commits the company to an *ultra vires* contract or other act and causes the company loss can be liable for breach of fiduciary duty (5.52) and liable to reimburse the company. A member of the company will have standing to restrain the commission of an *ultra vires* act and to take action against the directors on behalf of the company if the company declines to do so.

In exceptional circumstances, under CA 1985, s 727 a court may grant an officer of the company relief from liability for breach of fiduciary duty if in the opinion of the court he has acted honestly and reasonably and that in the circumstances he ought fairly to be excused. (This provision is also relevant to the discussion at 5.52 onwards.)

5.27   Alteration of the Memorandum

It is not easy to alter the terms of the Memorandum. The following are the rules:

(1) The name of the company may be altered by special resolution. This often occurs after you buy a company off the shelf or when you take over a company. You may want to adopt a name different from that chosen by former shareholders.
(2) The situation of the registered office cannot be altered. This means you cannot change the country in which the office is situated. You can change the address itself within that country by directors' resolution.
(3) The objects clause in the Memorandum can only be altered under certain circumstances, and for limited reasons, by special resolution. The rules are in CA 1985.
(4) Under certain circumstances, liability of directors can be made unlimited.
(5) The capital of the company can be raised by ordinary resolution and reduced by special resolution (in the latter case, with the consent of the court).

If the Memorandum is altered a reprinted copy as altered should be filed at the Companies Registry.

5.28 The Articles of Association

The Articles of Association are mainly concerned with the regulation of members' rights as between themselves and with other internal company procedures.

5.29 The Articles as a contract

The Articles of Association form a contract between the members and the company and between the members. This is the way in which the Articles may be enforced by the company against its members (eg if the company wanted to sue a member for the amount unpaid on his shares), by a member against the company (eg if the company were to refuse to pay a dividend that the directors have already declared is due) or by a member against another member (eg if one member refuses to sell his shares to another member as required by the Articles of Association).

However, this contract differs from ordinary contracts (see chapter 12) in some significant ways:

(1) Not all of the terms of the Articles are enforceable. For example:
  (a) Only membership rights can be enforced ie only shareholder rights and not rights attaching to an individual in his capacity other than by reason of his capacity as shareholder. Thus in the case of *Eley v Positive Government Security Life Assurance Co* (1876) Mr Eley was unable to sue the company to enforce his appointment as the company's solicitor in the company's Articles since this was an attempt to enforce outsider rights and not rights given to him as shareholder (though of course he might have a separate contract with the company and could certainly sue under that).
  (b) The court will also not enforce *all* membership rights. The courts are reluctant to allow an action to complain of a mere procedural irregularity. Normally the courts require you to show that there has been a substantial infringement of your personal proprietary rights.
(2) Damages cannot be obtained against the company by a member.
(3) The remedy of rectification which may be available in some other contractual situations (chapter 12) is not available where the Articles of Association are concerned.

5.30 Alteration of the Articles

The Articles of Association can be altered freely by special resolution subject to special rules which apply on alteration of class rights (5.32). A printed copy of the altered Articles should be filed at the Companies Registry.

5.31   Shareholder protection and the Articles

Articles of Association can be a useful vehicle for safeguarding shareholder rights (5.29 and 5.32). For this reason companies, especially smaller ones, may wish to depart in significant ways from Table A in order to ensure that the Articles are more tailor-made and contain express provisions to prevent disputes arising and to protect minorities. For example you could provide that *all* shareholders are entitled to be offered a chance to buy shares whenever there is a share issue. Similarly, you could stop another shareholder selling his shares to an outsider without first offering them to you. You could make sure that certain types of resolution (5.46) are needed for certain types of business, creating a right of veto for a minority. So there is a strong case for adopting special articles.

It is also possible to provide for this sort of protection in a separate shareholders agreement, and this has the advantage of being private, as it would not have to be registered.

5.32   Class rights

One special feature of Articles is that they sometimes contain what are known as 'class rights'. This occurs where there are more than one class of shares in the company and the rights attaching to the various classes of shares are different. A common example is the division of share capital between ordinary shares and preference shares. (A preference share commonly has different rights from an ordinary share, such as prior right to a dividend at a certain rate.)

If there are shares in different classes the rights attaching to those shares can only be altered by special procedures, usually in the articles or otherwise implied by CA 1985. Usually these will be that a member of a class whose rights are proposed to be varied is entitled to vote at a separate class meeting on whether he approves the variation of his rights. Only members of the class are entitled to participate in that vote and unless there is a three-quarters consent of the members of the class to the proposed alteration the amendment cannot be made *even if* there is the appropriate majority in the general meeting. Sometimes a simple consent by three-quarters of the class shareholders in writing will do.

This is illustrated as follows:

Example

XYZ Co Ltd has two classes of shares, 'A' shares and 'B' shares. The A shares have three votes per share and the B shares have two votes per share. The A shareholders own 85% of the issued share capital of the company. A proposal is made by one of the A shareholders that the B shareholders have their voting power reduced from two votes to one vote per share. A special resolution may be carried by the A shareholders in general meeting as the necessary majority (75% for a special resolution: 5.46) is there (they have 85%). But the members of the B class who constitute only 15% of the company have, nonetheless, the right at their own class meeting to decide whether or not to approve the variation of their rights and, if less than three-quarters of them consent, the special resolution cannot take effect.

Class rights are thus a very valuable method of entrenching shareholder rights. If the class rights are contained in the Memorandum of Association of the company their position is even more secure. As an extreme example, class rights which are contained in the Memorandum (although this is fairly unusual) which contain no provision for variation in the Memorandum or Articles can only be altered by the consent of all the members of the company.

5.33 Company officers, their appointment, tenure and removal

Each company must have at least one director (a public company must have at least two) and a company secretary. A sole director in a private company cannot be company secretary as well. The directors are appointed by the company in general meeting under the terms of the Articles of Association (for example under Articles 73 to 80 and 84 to 86 of Table A). The directors may appoint and (subject to 5.36) remove a managing director. Form G288 should be filed on change of officers.

5.34 The secretary

Article 99 of Table A provides that the directors shall appoint a secretary for such term and on such remuneration and on such conditions as they think fit and any secretary can (subject to 5.36) be removed by them. A secretary in a public company must have certain qualifications. A secretary customarily is responsible for issuing notices, eg of meetings, keeping records and filing material at the Companies Registry. But he can be employed to do other things.

5.35 The director

A director is ordinarily obliged to retire by rotation (Article 74, Table A) and, as a result, offer himself for re-election (this may not apply in the case of a managing director or other executive: Article 84, Table A). This can be inconvenient and the requirement is often (though not always) excluded in private companies.

A director may be removed by the shareholders in general meeting and, if so, this may be effected by ordinary resolution under CA 1985, s 303. Special notice (28 days) to the director is however necessary before he can be removed under that provision and he is entitled to attend the meeting concerned, whether or not he is a member, and to circularise the members of the company with a statement protesting his removal. Although a director is freely removable under CA 1985, s 303 this is, of course, without prejudice to any claims he may have for breach of a separate contract with the company, for example a contract of employment or any statutory employment claims such as unfair dismissal (5.36 and chapter 10).

Article 81 also provides that the office of a director has to be vacated automatically in certain cases, for example, if he becomes bankrupt, becomes mentally ill, resigns, absents himself for more than six months from directors' meetings and the directors resolve that the position is vacated, or if he is prohibited by law from being a director. Directors can be disqualified now for sometimes long periods for various reasons under The Company Directors Disqualification Act 1986, for example for unsatisfactory conduct and involvement in insolvent companies and for persistent failure to file annual returns and other documents at the Companies Registry.

There are provisions in most sets of Articles for fixing expenses (Article 13, Table A), gratuities and pensions (Article 87, Table A), and remuneration (Article 82, Table A) for directors and there are also, usually, provisions dealing with the appointment of alternate directors.

Table A deals with procedures of directors at board meetings. These are generally less formal than company and general meetings (5.47).

5.36 Contractual or other liability to company officers for dismissal

Although directors, managing directors and company secretaries may be removed under the procedures in 5.33 and 5.34 it is not uncommon for these individuals to have separate contracts of employment or service agreements, and summary termination of these agreements without good cause can lead to considerable claims against the company both for damages for wrongful dismissal and for unfair dismissal (chapter 10).

5.37 Third party protection against internal irregularities and the authority of officers of the company to bind the company

A third party dealing with the company may assume all is in order by reason of a number of forms of legal protection, namely:

(a) the indoor management rule and
(b) some statutory provisions and
(c) agency principles relating to companies.

5.38 The indoor management rule

We have described the doctrine of constructive notice (5.24). This deems a third party dealing with the company to have knowledge of matters published at the Companies Registry, namely: the Memorandum of Association, Articles of Association and special resolutions at least. It is very unfair to third parties (although CA 1985, s 35 can protect a third party and negate the doctrine (see also 5.25)).

However, the counterpart to this doctrine is that anything *internal* and *not* required to be published at the Companies Registry is *not* deemed to be published to a third party. And, further, a third party may *assume* that those internal matters are all in order and does not have to enquire. Such internal matters would include discussions or resolutions at board meetings of directors and even ordinary resolutions at company general meetings, because most ordinary resolutions do not have to be lodged at the Companies Registry (but cf for example, the case of an ordinary resolution increasing capital: 5.46). This is the so-called 'indoor management' rule.

This is illustrated by the leading case of *Royal British Bank* v *Turquand* (1856). There a company under its Articles gave power to its directors to borrow only such sums as were authorised by a 'general' resolution of the company (now this would be an ordinary resolution). But the directors borrowed £2,000 from the Royal British Bank without such resolution having been passed. It was held that the bank was entitled to assume that the resolution had been passed. It had no way of knowing whether or not the resolution had been passed since that sort of resolution was not required to be published at the Companies Registry.

However, the rule does not apply in the following situations:

(1) Where a third party has actual or constructive notice of the irregularity, ie where he actually knows the matter is irregular

or where the defect is or would be apparent from the inspection of the company's documents.

(2) Where there are suspicious circumstances, ie where a third party is put on enquiry.

(3) Where there is a forgery.

(4) 'Insiders' cannot rely upon the rule. The term insiders does not have a fixed definition but has been held to include company directors (although exceptionally, a newly appointed officer who has relatively little inside knowledge about the company might not be an insider for these purposes).

5.39   Statutory provisions protecting a third party against internal irregularities

In addition to the common law indoor management rule there are also some specific statutory provisions.

(1) Companies Act 1985, s 285 provides that the acts of a director or manager are to be valid despite any defect that may afterwards be discovered in his appointment or qualification. However, it is thought that this does not apply where there has been no appointment at all.

(2) Companies Act 1985, s 382(4) provides that where minutes at any general meeting of the directors are made in accordance with s 382 (which provides for proper books to be kept and for minutes to be signed by the chairman) then, until the contrary is proved, any meeting is deemed to have been properly and duly held and all business properly transacted thereat, including the appointment of directors, managers or liquidators.

(3) The Law of Property Act 1925, s 71(1) says a purchaser may assume a *deed* has been duly executed by a company if its seal has been attached and affixed to the deed in the presence of and attested by its secretary and a member of the board of directors. (However this only applies in favour of a purchaser for value from the company and only in relation to a deed and not to other situations.)

5.40   Agency principles in relation to companies

A director or other officer of the company may bind the company to a third party when he has authority to do so. The three types of authority that a third party can rely on to enforce a contract with the company are:

(1) *Actual express authority*
An example of this is where John, a managing director of XYZ Co Ltd is told by XYZ Co Ltd, to make a specific contract for the purchase of a computer with ABC Co Ltd on XYZ's behalf.

He now has *actual express* authority to do so. This is a matter of agreement between the company and the managing director.

(2) *Actual implied authority*

An example of this type of authority would be where John is given no specific instructions by XYZ Co Ltd. But since he is managing director he has, from that position, an implied authority to do everything that is usual for that type of officer to do (5.41). As the actual implied authority of a managing director is extensive (5.41), he would have authority to buy the computer from ABC Co Ltd even without being told to do so by the Board. He would be able to bind the company by virtue of his actual implied authority. The actual implied authority of other officers such as individual directors and secretaries and managers is, however, much more limited than that of a managing director (5.41).

(3) *Apparent or ostensible authority*

Suppose John was never appointed managing director at all or, alternatively, was once managing director but no longer occupies that post. If he contracts with ABC Co Ltd without getting an express mandate from the XYZ Co Ltd he may nonetheless still be able to bind the company. You may find this remarkable, but it may happen where he has been 'held out' or represented by the company as being a particular type of officer and the third party relies upon that holding out or representation.

So if, for example, he has been held out as a *de facto* managing director he may have *ostensible* power to bind the company even if the company does not wish to enter into the contract at all. A 'holding out' or a representation could be by inclusion of a person's name on company notepaper or simply by conduct, in allowing that person to act as if he is managing director even if he is not.

The authority of officers and employees can be clearly limited by a company under the terms of an employee's service agreement or other instructions if issued to an employee or officer. If an employee or officer exceeds such authority, then he may be liable to the company. But if a third party is ignorant of such an express limitation of an officer's authority, that third party may be entitled to assume that the person with whom he is dealing has the authority that that type of company officer normally enjoys under the general law (see (2) above).

So the moral of this discussion is that the company must be very careful about its selection of directors, managers and employees because putting them into a certain position may clothe them with some sort of authority to do certain things (depending on their position) on their own initiative.

5.41   The actual implied authority attaching to various posts

It is unwise to generalise about what you would ordinarily expect of a typical company officer. But some examples can be given. The actual implied authority of a *managing director* is very wide and extends to most transactions short of selling the company.

An *individual director* acting as such has very little actual implied authority but persons specifically appointed to posts of an executive nature (eg a 'sales director' or a 'technical director') may have some authority implied from that executive function.

As to a *company secretary*, the traditional view was that he was merely a 'scribe' who served the Board of Directors as such and had no power himself to contract with third parties on his own initiative. This is now probably not the case and it is thought that the actual implied authority of a company secretary extends at least to entering into contracts of an administrative nature on his own initiative.

Finally a *chairman* of a company usually has no greater authority to contract than any other director.

5.42   Protection under section 35 of the Companies Act 1985

Companies Act 1985, s 35, which we mentioned in relation to *ultra vires* (5.24), may also apply to protect a third party where there is some doubt as to whether the director with whom he is dealing has authority. It says that when you deal with a company you are not deemed to know about any restrictions placed on the authority of officers in the Memorandum and Articles.

However the same conditions apply before it protects the third party, that is to say the third party must be in good faith *and* the transaction must be one decided upon by the directors. The provision is rarely helpful in a case where you are basically deciding whether one individual has authority to act on his own initiative. In a case where the board of directors has in fact decided upon the transaction there is usually no want of authority anyway. In that case there is no need for s 35 to apply but, ironically, due simply to bad draftsmanship, the section only applies in such a case!

5.43   Meetings and resolutions

Company law is complex and very procedural. This applies especially in the area of the law of meetings and resolutions. The reason for this is that companies operate on the principle of majority rule. If majority rule is to prevail then matters should be conducted properly so that all members, including a minority, have a perfectly fair opportunity to receive notice of a meeting and participate in the making of any decision.

It has been held that, in some situations, company decisions can be made informally without the need for meetings at all. However, for this principle to apply the incorporators must be unanimous, and it is not entirely clear, anyway, whether *all* types of company decisions may be validly effected by an informal unanimous resolution of this type. And rarely, save in the smallest of companies, will the consent of the members be unanimous.

So, as a general rule, the procedures laid down in CA 1985 and the Articles of Association of the company must be strictly followed.

5.44 The Annual General Meeting

Every company must have an Annual General Meeting, the first to take place not later than eighteen months after the date of incorporation. In any event, annual general meetings should take place each calendar year and not be more than fifteen months apart. An Annual General Meeting should adopt the accounts of the company, reappoint auditors and deal with any other outstanding business.

5.45 Extraordinary General Meetings

Any other meeting of the company is called an Extraordinary General Meeting. An Extraordinary General Meeting is ordinarily convened by the secretary at the instance of the Board of Directors. If the directors do not convene a meeting the holders of not less than one-tenth of the issued share capital of the company have the right to requisition a meeting.

The length of notice of meetings is governed by the length of notice required under CA 1985 and under the Articles of Association of a company, depending mainly on what sort of resolution is proposed to be passed at the meeting.

Meetings at which it is proposed to pass ordinary and extraordinary resolutions require 14 days' notice and, in the case of special resolutions, require 21 days' notice. An annual general meeting requires 21 days' notice. Some resolutions require special notice (ie 28 days' notice) to be given to the subject of the resolution such as in the case of the removal of a director from office under CA 1985, s 303 (5.35).

5.46   Types of resolution

There are three types of resolution, an ordinary resolution, an extraordinary resolution and a special resolution. An *ordinary* resolution will do to effect any decision unless the provisions of the Articles or CA 1985 say otherwise. An ordinary resolution is one which can be carried by a simple majority (ie by 51%).

Both *extraordinary* and *special* resolutions require 75% approval. Companies Act 1985 and/or the Articles of Association will normally stipulate when an extraordinary or special resolution is required. Extraordinary resolutions are less frequently required than special resolutions. Special resolutions are required, for example, to alter the Articles of Association, to decrease capital, to amend the objects of the company, and generally to effect the more important of company decisions.

It is important to note that copies of special and extraordinary resolutions must be filed at the Companies Registry. So must an ordinary resolution increasing capital (with Form 123). You can often dispense with notice of extraordinary general meetings (other than in cases where special notice is required) if 95% of the members entitled to vote and holding at least 95% in nominal value of the shares giving a right to vote consent to short notice. This is often quite helpful.

Finally, members usually have one vote per share held, but the Articles could create shares with more votes per share (such as in the case of class rights (5.32)).

5.47   Procedure at meetings

The chairman of the company acts as chairman of any company general or board meeting and, if there is none, a chairman of the meeting is elected before the meeting commences. Votes at a general meeting are conducted by a show of hands unless a member requires a poll. (A poll means that the actual votes attaching to the shares held by those present are counted.)

For a board meeting, no particular notice is required (although you do have to give notice). At the meeting votes are by a show of hands and a simple majority commonly suffices for a decision. However, the Articles can lay down a different procedure and even provide for blocking powers in favour of some directors.

The Chairman will have a casting vote both in the general meeting and at board meetings if the standard provisions of Table A are adopted. So these provisions are often excluded.

The Articles will stipulate what quorum is necessary for a meeting.

5.48 Relationship between the general meeting and the Board of Directors

Generally, it is not possible for the general meeting to pass resolutions interfering with the day-to-day management of the company by the Board of Directors unless it does so by special resolution. It has always been thought good policy that there be a separation of functions between the Board of Directors and the general meeting so that the Board of Directors is not prone to interference by the general meeting unless there are special circumstances. But the general meeting has, of course, a powerful residual sanction against the board in the sense that it has the power to remove directors by ordinary resolution if it wishes (5.35).

5.49 Books, records and accounts

A company must keep proper books and accounting records. Its statutory books (eg register of members and minute book) must be written up and available for inspection by members at the registered office of the company.

A company must prepare and file annual accounts for members which include a profit and loss account and balance sheet, directors' report and auditors' report. The accounts must be approved by the general meeting. Directors of small or medium-sized private companies (as defined by CA 1985) may deliver accounts to the Companies Registry in a modified form. Where appropriate, group accounts have to be prepared.

An unlimited company may avoid delivery of accounts if, during the financial year in question, it was not a subsidiary of a limited company or a holding company of a limited company; if the majority of its shares were not held nor its board controlled by limited companies; and provided it was not the promoter of a trading stamp scheme.

There are numerous criminal penalties that can attach to directors for failure to observe the law about books, records and accounts, and this is a matter ordinarily best handled by your professional adviser.

5.50   Directors' duties

One of the main differences between a company and a partnership is the sometimes quite daunting duties placed on directors by both the common law and, more recently, by statute. The extent of these duties often goes unappreciated by those who take on a directorship. It must be remembered that breach can lead to *personal* liability.

5.51   Duties of skill and care

There are said to be three main principles:

(1) A director need not exhibit a greater degree of skill and care than may be reasonably expected of a person of his knowledge and experience. A higher duty may therefore apply to a director who is a solicitor or an accountant than a director who has no experience of professional matters.

(2) A director is not bound to give continuous attention to the affairs of his company. However, this is a very old rule and somewhat unrealistic in many modern situations. Many directors are appointed under service contracts or are otherwise executive directors and, if so, would be required to give proper time and attention to their company.

(3) A director is, in the absence of grounds of suspicion, justified in delegating matters to some other official and justified in leaving that official to it. However, this principle does not mean that the directors can abdicate all responsibility. In *Dorchester Finance Co Ltd* v *Stebbing* (1980) it was held that directors who signed blank cheques and did not verify for what these cheques were being used had broken their duties of skill and care. This was especially so as the directors involved had some accountancy experience (see (1) above).

5.52   Fiduciary duties

A director is a fiduciary and, generally, this will mean that he has a duty not to let his own interest and that of his company conflict. The sections below illustrate some specific examples of this.

5.53   Secret profits

A director may not make a secret profit from his position with the company. Thus a director may not take a bribe, secret commission or kick back and if he does so, this will be recoverable from him.

5.54 Corporate opportunities

There is a strict and severe rule that a person in a fiduciary position like a director cannot profit from that position. If he does so, he is liable to account to the company for any profits made thereby. If a 'corporate opportunity' arises, that opportunity belongs to the company and cannot be secretly taken up by the director himself.

A director can be liable even if he acts in good faith, and even if the company suffered no loss. If the director acted in good faith, however, he may escape liability by having the transaction approved by the company in general meeting (and see also the reference to CA 1985, s 727 at 5.26).

5.55 Misapplication of the company's property

Theft from the company would not only be a breach of fiduciary duty but also a criminal offence. But other examples of misapplication of the company's property giving rise to breach of fiduciary duty can occur when some of the intricate provisions of CA 1985 preventing disposition of corporate property, or the making of contracts without certain procedures being followed, are broken by the directors.

For example, any money paid over by way of unlawful financial assistance to someone for the purchase of shares in a company as prohibited by CA 1985 (5.66) would be a misapplication of company funds and would give rise to a breach of fiduciary duty on the part of the directors. Other examples could be:

(1) A payment of compensation for loss of office made to one of the Board without disclosure to the members (5.59).
(2) Where directors have disposed of the company's assets in a manner which is *ultra vires* (5.24).
(3) Where directors make a payment to a third party that is not necessarily *ultra vires*, but is, nonetheless, in breach of fiduciary duty, or not for the benefit of the company.

5.56 Acting *bona fide* and for the benefit of the company as a whole

A director must make decisions *bona fide* and for the benefit of the company as a whole. He must not therefore act *mala fide*, dishonestly, or otherwise for a non-corporate purpose.

5.57 What is 'the company as a whole'?

Generally (and primarily) this means the shareholders as a body but there can, exceptionally, be other considerations to be taken into account. First, especially where the company is near to insolvency there may be, in effect, a duty also to take into account creditors' interests (5.74). Secondly, CA 1985 requires directors also to have regard to the interests of employees.

5.58 The duty to apply powers for their proper purposes

Powers of directors are numerous and these must be exercised *bona fide* and for the benefit of the company as a whole and *not* for an ulterior purpose. This applies, for example, to powers to allot shares, forfeit shares, make gifts or gratuities, or approve transfers of shares.

5.59 Some statutory rules governing directors' duties and fair dealing by directors

There are certain statutory rules concerning the conduct of directors which include:

(1) A director must declare his interest in a contract with a company to the Board of Directors.
(2) A payment to a director or the transfer of property to a director for compensation for loss of office must be approved by the company in general meeting.
(3) A company cannot give a director a service contract for more than five years without its being approved by the general meeting.
(4) Certain approvals must be obtained in relation to substantial property transactions involving directors and a company.
(5) There are certain restrictions on loans to directors and persons connected with them.
(6) A director may not deal in share options in a company in certain circumstances.
(7) A director must disclose shareholdings in his own company.
(8) In the context of public companies, under the Companies Securities (Insider Dealing) Act 1985 a director may not indulge in insider dealing in listed securities.

5.60 Collective abuse of shareholder power against minorities

Shareholders, when voting through resolutions in general meeting can, in general, consider their own interests.

However the passing of resolutions by majorities against minorities can very exceptionally amount to what is known as a 'fraud on the minority' where the outcome is oppressive to the minority. The courts will impugn a resolution where the majority can be said not to have acted *bona fide* and for the benefit of the company.

As, ordinarily, the courts consider it is for the majority themselves to determine *bona fide* what is for the benefit of the company (unless they have formed a view which is so unreasonable that no reasonable majority would have adopted it), few cases are successful.

5.61 Statutory protection for minorities

The discussion at 5.60 paints a gloomy picture of shareholder rights against majority action at common law, but there are also remedies under statute. These are, first, winding up under the just and equitable ground and second, the statutory petition under which you can claim 'unfair prejudice'.

5.62 The statutory petition to wind up under the just and equitable ground under section 122(g) of the Insolvency Act 1986

Under this heading the company may be wound up at the instance of a member: for example, where the main object of the company has failed or where there is no *bona fide* intention on the part of the directors to carry on the business in a proper manner.

Also, and very importantly, it can be wound up where there has been a breach of an understanding between the members as to the equal rights of participation in management and other matters, and confidence between the parties has broken down. In those circumstances it might be 'just and equitable' to wind the company up.

5.63 Example: Winding up under the just and equitable ground

The leading case is *Re Westbourne Galleries Ltd* (1973). In this case A and B were partners with equal shares in a carpet business. They formed a company to adopt the business. A and B were the first directors and each held an equal shareholding. Later, B's son, C, was made a director and A and B each transferred some of their shares to him. The company made profits which were distributed by way of directors' salary and no dividends were paid. Later, A and B fell out, and when the dispute came to a head, C sided with B and, at a general meeting, C and B procured an ordinary resolution (because their shares gave them the necessary majority (5.35)) to remove A from office.

As a result, A ended up in a position whereby, because of pre-emption provisions in the Articles, he could not transfer his shares outside the company without the other directors' consent. Also he was receiving no dividend and he was excluded from management. It was held that it was 'just and equitable' to wind the company up.

Although these facts are not exhaustive of the situations in which a court will wind the company up under the just and equitable ground, the case forms a very useful example of how the winding up petition can be applied in practice to intra-corporate disputes.

On the other hand, using the winding up petition has been described as using a 'sledgehammer to crack a nut'. It is a drastic remedy and sometimes it may not even be the remedy that the partners would themselves choose as a solution to their dispute, if there were alternatives available. It is sometimes more constructive to try and sort out the dispute rather than dissolve the company. The next section provides an alternative solution.

5.64   The unfair prejudice petition

Under CA 1985, s 459 a member of a company may complain of 'unfair prejudice' by a petition presented to the court. This is a far more versatile legal action than winding up. A petitioner must show that there is an act or omission of the company which is unfairly prejudicial to him or that the company's affairs are being or have been conducted in a manner which is unfairly prejudicial to the interests of some part of the members (including himself at least).

If the petition is successful the court may order or grant such relief as it thinks fit. But it can, for example, regulate the conduct of the company's affairs in future, require the company to refrain from doing something complained of in the petition, allow a shareholder to bring a civil action against someone in the company's name, or provide for the compulsory purchase of a member's shares.

There is some doubt as to whether the petition would apply to the facts of *Re Westbourne Galleries Ltd* (5.63) as a petitioner must complain of prejudice to his *members'* rights. It is not certain whether this would cover a complaint of loss of directorship without more. However, case law is still developing on the meaning of the petition.

5.65   Department of Trade investigations

It may sometimes be possible for the Department of Trade to investigate the affairs of a company and take action arising therefrom in cases of suspected fraud, misfeasance or withholding of information from shareholders, to investigate ownership or control of a company, to investigate directors' share dealings, or to investigate insider dealing. An inspector has powers to call on persons to produce books and records and to require attendances before him.

5.66 Some rules about maintenance of capital

Capital rules are complicated and too detailed to describe in full here. The following, however, indicates the strictness with which the subject is treated.

A company may increase its capital by ordinary resolution and reduce it by special resolution if allowed by the Articles. Reduction requires notice to creditors and the approval of the court.

Subject to the below, a company may not purchase shares in itself, or in its holding company, nor (subject to a limited defence) give financial assistance for the purchase of shares in itself or its holding company. A company may not repay share capital to members. There are also strict rules concerning what money is available to pay dividends, which, in any event, cannot be paid out of capital and can normally be paid only out of realised net profits. A company cannot issue shares at a discount. All these rules are to maintain the company's capital. However:

(1) A company may give financial assistance for the purchase of shares under conditions, in relation to an employee share scheme, and a *private* company may give financial assistance if approved by a special resolution and if there is a declaration of solvency.
(2) It is possible to issue redeemable shares.
(3) It is possible for a company to repurchase its shares with the approval of the members of the company (4.30).

Stricter rules about capital apply in the case of public companies, eg a duty to alert members to a serious loss of capital; to ensure that there is a minimum issued share capital of £50,000, a quarter of which is paid up; and to ensure that there are valuation safeguards on payment for shares by transfer of non-cash assets.

5.67 Corporate insolvency

It is ironically appropriate to close this part of the chapter by discussing the subject of termination of businesses. In this section we look at three stages of insolvency, receivership, administration and liquidation, some of these conditions being more terminal in nature than others.

Before doing this, it may be noted that under the Insolvency Act 1986, it is possible for a company in difficulty to propose a voluntary arrangement with its creditors in composition of its debts or a scheme of arrangement of its affairs. A nominee (who must be a licensed insolvency practitioner) must supervise such a proposal. It may be made either by the directors, before administration or winding up (see below) or by an administrator (5.69) or a liquidator (5.70). If a certain proportion in value of creditors vote in favour of such a scheme it will be binding on all creditors and the company may obtain a new lease of life.

5.68   Receivership

A receiver of a company may be appointed at the instance of a debenture holder (5.19) when the terms of the debenture allow this. This will usually arise as a result of breach of the provisions of the debenture. The receiver appointed by the debenture holder may then enter the company and take charge of its affairs. He will normally be a receiver *and manager* and, for the purposes of the Insolvency Act 1986, will usually be an *administrative* receiver.

He takes charge of the company's business and has the authority to dismiss and engage staff. His function is to get in the company's debts and to realise the company's assets in order to raise as much money as possible (or as is necessary) to discharge the company's liability to the debenture holder. This may in practice involve selling a substantial proportion of the company's assets. Sometimes he may have to sell the entire company's undertaking on the basis that an undertaking or part thereof sold as a going concern is more valuable to a purchaser than a bundle of assets alone.

When the exercise is completed, he will pay the debenture holder, observing the order of priorities of payment in insolvency prescribed by the Insolvency Act 1986 and set out at 5.76. Then, in theory, he is free to hand the company back to the members to deal with as they think fit. In practice, though, there is nothing to hand back and the company inevitably proceeds into liquidation. A receiver may also be appointed by the court, but this is comparatively rare.

5.69   Administration order

A new regime was instituted by the Insolvency Act 1986 as a possible means of rescuing an insolvent company otherwise than by receivership or of saving it from liquidation. A court may make an administration order if:

(1)   the company is or is likely to become unable to pay its debts;

(2) the court considers that the making of an order would be likely to achieve one or more of the following purposes, viz, to secure:
  (a) the survival of the company as a whole or any part of its undertaking as a going concern;
  (b) the approval of a voluntary arrangement;
  (c) the sanctioning of a compromise or arrangement between the company and its creditors;
  (d) a more advantageous realisation of the company's assets than would be effected on a winding up.

An application may be made by petition presented by either the company or the directors or by a creditor or creditors including any contingent or prospective creditor or creditors, or by all or any of those parties together or separately. Upon the making of the administration order an administrator has similar powers to an administrative receiver. An administrator may take control of the affairs, business and property of the company, prepare a statement of affairs, make proposals and eventually seek to be discharged as an administrator.

It is hoped that administration, combined with the possibility of a voluntary arrangement with creditors under the Insolvency Act 1986, may lead to an extension of the life of companies that otherwise would have no alternative but to proceed into liquidation.

5.70 Liquidation

A liquidator deals with the dissolution of the company, that is to say, the (terminal) stage beyond either receivership or administration. Liquidation means a winding up and there are two modes, voluntary and compulsory.

5.71 Voluntary winding up

There are two sorts of voluntary winding up, a *members'* voluntary winding up and a *creditors'* voluntary winding up. A *special* resolution of the members is necessary in the former, and an *extraordinary* resolution in the case of the latter. For the former to take place, the directors must file a declaration of solvency. If this is not possible, the voluntary winding up *has* to take the form of a creditors' voluntary winding up and a creditors' meeting must be convened at the same time as the members' meeting to pass the extraordinary resolution to go into liquidation.

5.72 Compulsory winding up

The ways in which the court can compulsorily wind up a company are set out in s 122 of the Insolvency Act 1986 and are as follows:

(1) The company has resolved by special resolution that it be wound up by the court.
(2) The company is a public company which was registered as such on its original incorporation and has not been issued with a certificate of compliance with the capital requirements of CA 1985 (5.14) and more than a year has expired since it was so registered.
(3) The company is an old public company within the meaning of the Companies Consolidation (Consequential Provisions) Act 1985.
(4) The company has not commenced its business within a year from incorporation or it has suspended its business for a whole year.
(5) The number of members has fallen below two.
(6) The company is unable to pay its debts.
(7) It is just and equitable that the company should be wound up.

It is case (6) which is most relevant here. The other cases do not necessarily mean there is an insolvency. Cases (5) and (7) are discussed at 5.10 and 5.62 respectively.

5.73 Choice of liquidator

In the case of a voluntary winding up, the liquidator is elected by the members or creditors as the case may be. In the case of a compulsory winding up the official receiver takes over as liquidator in the first instance. He may or may not be replaced as liquidator by a liquidator voted in by the first creditors' meeting. If the first creditors' meeting does not elect its own choice of liquidator the official receiver will, in practice, continue as liquidator.

5.74 A liquidator's powers

The liquidator can avoid certain transactions if he thinks fit. For example:

(1) He can avoid transactions at an undervalue within 'the relevant time' (see below). Transactions at an undervalue include gifts and transactions where the consideration received by the company is considerably less than the consideration received by the other party to the transaction, and the transaction is not made in good faith and for the purposes of carrying on the business and generally thought capable of benefiting the company.
(2) The liquidator can also avoid *preferences*, again within 'the relevant time'. A preference is any transaction intended to put

a creditor in a better position in the insolvency than he would have been in had the transaction not taken place.
(3) A floating charge may be invalid insofar as any consideration was not paid at the time of creation of the charge. This is so if it is made within two years of the onset of insolvency in the case of a connected person, and 12 months in other cases and, in any event, at a time between the presentation of the petition for making of an administration order in relation to the company and the making of an order.

The '*relevant time*' in relation to the first two cases above is

(a) in the case of a transaction at an undervalue or of a preference which is given to a person who is *connected* with the company (otherwise than by reason only of being its employee): *two years* before onset of insolvency;
(b) otherwise: *six months* before the onset of insolvency;
(c) in any case any time between the presentation of a petition for the making of an administration order in relation to the company and the making of an order.

Where a company enters into a transaction at an undervalue or gives a preference at a time as mentioned in (a) or (b) above the time is not treated as a 'relevant time' unless the company

(a) is at that time unable to pay its debts or
(b) becomes unable to pay its debts in consequence of the transaction or preference.

A person is 'connected' if he or it is a director, an associate (1.8) or an associated company.

5.75 Wrongful and fraudulent trading

Liability can also attach to individuals for wrongful and fraudulent trading if the circumstances appear to support this during the course of a liquidation.

Fraudulent trading occurs when it appears that any business of the company has been carried on with an intent to defraud the creditors of the company or creditors of any other person or for any fraudulent purpose.

Wrongful trading occurs when the company has gone into insolvent liquidation and at some time before the commencement of the winding up of the company that person knew or ought to have concluded that there was no reasonable prospect that the company would avoid going into insolvent liquidation and that person was a director of the company at that time.

In both cases the court can order a contribution to the company's assets as it thinks fit. That is to say, it can make the individual personally liable. This is an important exception to the concept of limited liability of members of a company (5.18).

5.76   Order of distribution of assets

The order of distribution of assets on insolvency is as follows:

(1)   Costs of the winding up.
(2)   Rights of a fixed chargee.
(3)   Rights of preferential creditors, viz:
    (a)   PAYE debts due to the Inland Revenue;
    (b)   debts due to Customs and Excise;
    (c)   debts due to the DHSS by way of Social Security contributions;
    (d)   contributions to occupational pension schemes;
    (e)   remuneration of employees (subject to limits).
(4)   Rights of a floating chargee.
(5)   Rights of ordinary trade creditors.
(6)   Rights of shareholders to return of capital.

It is important to note that certain individuals may take priority over the above order. These include, for example, those entitled to the benefit of *retention of title* (or 'Romalpa') clauses in relation to goods delivered to a company but not yet paid for. Those entitled to the benefit of reservation of title clauses may come above (3) to (6) above because the beneficiary of the clause may have the right to reclaim the goods himself (although an administrator (5.69) has a power of sale under the Insolvency Act 1986). As those under (3) to (6) can only claim proceeds of sale of assets of the company, those entitled to the benefit of reservation of title clauses may transcend this order because the goods which are the subject of the clause have never been the company's assets (see chapter 12).

In an insolvent compulsory liquidation it is of course most unlikely in practice that shareholders will receive any reimbursement of their capital.

Part B   Partnership law

5.77   Introduction

The following is a brief account of partnership law. The discussion is based on English law; in Scotland there are certain differences which should be separately checked if need be.

5.78 Indicators as to whether a partnership exists

A partnership is defined as the relationship which subsists between persons carrying on business in common with a view of profit. A business includes a trade, occupation or profession.

The Partnership Act 1890 lays down some rules to help determine whether or not a partnership exists. Thus:

(1) Common ownership of property of itself does not create a partnership even if there is sharing of profits.
(2) Sharing of gross returns does not of itself create a partnership.
(3) Receipt of a share of the profits of a business can be evidence that a person is a partner in the business but does not *of itself* create a partnership. Thus:

   (a) Receipt of a debt by instalments from profits of a business does not necessarily make the recipient a partner.
   (b) Remuneration by a share of the profits of a servant or agent of a person engaged in a business does not of itself make the recipient a partner.
   (c) If a widow or child of a deceased partner gets an annuity paid from part of the profits that does not of itself make the widow or child a partner.
   (d) If a lender who makes a loan to a person engaged or about to engage in business gets interest on the loan variable with the profits or interest taking the form of a share of profits, this does not necessarily make the lender a partner (provided that the contract is in writing and signed by or on behalf of all the parties).
   (e) Receipt by a person who has sold the goodwill of a business of part of the profits in payment for the sale does not make that person a partner as such.

Commonly, of course, intending partners sign up to an express partnership agreement (5.81), thus avoiding doubt about the matter.

5.79 Size of partnerships

A firm consisting of more partners than the statutory limit is not permissible. The statutory limit in most cases is 20 (but this limit does not apply to partnerships between solicitors, accountants, persons carrying on business as members of the Stock Exchange or other (mainly professional) partnerships specified in orders made under CA 1985).

5.80   Rules implied by the Partnership Act 1890

Some of the rules implied by the Act are as follows:

(1) Every partner is an agent of the firm and has authority to bind the partners unless this is countermanded by the other partners and the person with whom the partner is dealing knows of the lack of authority.

(2) Every partner in a firm is liable jointly with the other partners for its debts (and, in Scotland, also severally) whilst he was a partner and after his death his estate is also liable.

(3) If a partner commits a wrongful act or omission either within his apparent authority or in the ordinary course of the business of the firm any liability attaches to the firm as well as to the partner committing the act (5.82).

(4) Where a partner misappropriates the property of another received in the course of the firm's business the firm is liable to make good the loss (5.82).

(5) All partners are entitled to share equally in the capital and profits of the business.

(6) All partners must contribute equally towards losses of capital or losses otherwise sustained by the firm.

(7) A partner is not ordinarily entitled to interest on capital agreed to be subscribed by him (but see (8)).

(8) A partner making any payment or advance beyond the capital he has agreed to subscribe is entitled to interest at the rate of 5% per annum from the date of payment.

(9) Every partner can take part in the management of the partnership business.

(10) A partner cannot receive remuneration for acting in the partnership business.

(11) No person can be introduced as a partner without the consent of the existing partners.

(12) On ordinary matters relating to partnership business decisions may be made by a majority of partners but no change in the nature of the partnership business can be effected without the consent of all the existing partners.

(13) The majority of partners cannot expel any partner unless a power to do so has been conferred by agreement.

(14) A partnership is determinable at will upon retirement.

The rules which are implied by the Partnership Act 1890 and which affect partners' relations with each other may well be inconvenient to you. But the Partnership Act 1890 provides that rules about partners' relations with each other (but *not* rules about their obligations to *third parties*) may be modified by express agreement. That is when an express partnership agreement is useful. An express agreement allows you to settle the terms between you and your colleagues in some detail in accordance with your real wishes.

5.81 Partnership agreements

No special form is required for a partnership agreement as a partnership can arise from oral agreement, or even by implication (5.78, 5.80). But you would be well advised to put your agreement into writing.

Partnership agreements can, and very often do, include the following. This, however, is merely a list of common terms and is not exhaustive by any means:

(1) The name of the firm and what it does (as to its name, see Part C of this chapter).
(2) The date the partnership started and how long it is to continue.
(3) The proportions in which the partners are to put in capital.
(4) The firm's bankers and which partners may sign cheques.
(5) Whether all or only some of the partners manage the business, and to what extent, and whether any partner is to be a 'sleeping' partner.
(6) Details of the firm's accountants.
(7) Details of holidays and procedures for taking holidays.
(8) How profits are to be shared and what provision there is for drawings.
(9) What provision, if any, there is as to private income.
(10) Provision for keeping regular accounts and books and records.
(11) What happens on the death or retirement of partners.
(12) What cases will justify expulsion of a partner.
(13) A clause providing for the procedure for giving of notice.
(14) An arbitration clause.
(15) A provision requiring partners to sign a continuation election for tax purposes on a change in the composition of the firm (3.7).
(16) Finally, any special provisions or rules relevant to particular partnerships such as doctors, accountants or lawyers' practices.

5.82 A partner and third parties

A partner is an agent of the firm and of the other partners to do any act for carrying on of the firm's business unless he has no authority to do the act concerned and the person with whom he is dealing knows about this. A partner has authority to make the firm liable on a range of matters. This would not include, for example, execution of a deed or submitting a dispute to arbitration or making his partners partners with others. But in a trading partnership his authority is quite wide. It therefore goes without saying that partners should be chosen with care.

A firm can also be liable for a tort (chapter 12) or other wrongful act to a third party committed by a partner. This is provided that it was committed within the apparent authority of the partner or that it was committed in the ordinary course of the firm's business. Partners can also be liable for fraudulent misappropriation of monies received from a third party in the course of the business if the fraudulent partner is acting within the scope of his apparent authority.

Liability of partners is joint in contract, and joint and several in tort and for other wrongful acts and misappropriations, and this is one of the big disadvantages of being a partner in a partnership (chapter 1). Limited liability is possible in a limited partnership formed under the Limited Partnerships Act 1907, but as discussed in chapter 1, the conditions attaching to this type of structure mean that few of this sort of partnership exist.

5.83   Liabilities of new and retiring partners

Under the Partnership Act 1890 a new partner does not take on liability for obligations incurred by the firm before he became a partner. Nor does a retiring partner cease to be liable for obligations incurred whilst he was a partner once he leaves. A retiring partner ceases to be liable for obligations incurred after he has left.

If a third party who has been dealing with the firm before and after its change has no notice of the change, a third party may be entitled to treat all apparent members of the old firm as still being members. So if you retire from a partnership you should ensure that the letterheading is changed to reflect this and that people you deal with (say as a consultant) know about your retirement. A notice in the *London Gazette* will be sufficient notice of the change in the case of persons who have not previously dealt with the firm.

It is possible for a retiring partner to be released from liability to a creditor *entirely* and a new partner liable in his place under a contract of 'novation', ie a three-party agreement between the retiring partner, the firm newly constituted and a creditor. Such an agreement can be express or implied (eg by conduct), although it would not be easy to infer an implied agreement. A new partner would not be advised to enter into such an express agreement.

5.84 Partners' duties of fair dealing to one another

Partners must deal fairly with one another. For example, partners are bound to render true accounts and full information of all matters affecting the partnership. A partner must account to his colleagues for any benefit received by him without their consent from any transaction concerning the partnership or from using the firm's name, property or connection. And if a partner carries on a competing business of the same nature without the consent of his colleagues he must account for the profits he makes.

Finally, the provisions of the Sex Discrimination Act 1975 (chapter 10) apply to partnerships in that it is unlawful to discriminate against a person on ground of sex in relation to partnership offers, access to benefits, etc in partnerships, and adverse treatment or expulsion. Race discrimination in the same context is similarly prohibited under the Race Relations Act 1976, but in that case, at the time of writing, only partnerships of six or more partners are covered.

5.85 Partnership property

Property acquired on account of the firm or for the purposes of the business or with partnership money is likely to be partnership property subject to any agreement to the contrary. But there can be difficult borderline cases. So ownership of partnership property is best dealt with by express agreement and this is another good reason why an express partnership agreement should be drawn up (5.81).

5.86 Dissolution of partnerships

Under the Partnership Act 1890, a partnership is dissolved:

(1) by expiry of a fixed term;
(2) by termination of the object for which the venture was set up;
(3) by death or bankruptcy of a partner;
(4) by one of the partners giving notice to the other or others in a partnership at will.

It is important to note that the above rules can be modified by agreement. In particular, partners often provide that a partnership cannot be determined by a notice given by one of the partners only, or provide that a minimum period of notice is required (contrast (4) above), and it is often provided that partners may expel another under certain circumstances (eg misconduct) (a power of expulsion is not implied by the Partnership Act 1890). An express partnership agreement will usually cover this (5.81).

Dissolution may be ordered by the court under the Partnership Act 1890:

(1) if a partner other than the partner suing becomes in any way permanently incapable;
(2) if a partner other than the partner suing is guilty of conduct calculated to prejudice the business;
(3) if a partner other than the partner suing is guilty of wilful or persistent breaches of the partnership agreement or other conduct which makes it not reasonably practicable for the other partners to carry on in partnership with him;
(4) if the business can only be carried on at a loss;
(5) if it is just and equitable.

5.87   Order of application of assets on dissolution

On dissolution, assets, including contributions to make good losses of capital, are applied:

(1) in paying the firm's creditors;
(2) in repaying advances by partners;
(3) in repaying capital to partners in accordance with their entitlement;
(4) in dividing any balance as profit.

Losses (including losses of capital) must be made good:

(1) out of profits;
(2) out of capital;
(3) by the partners in the proportion in which they share the profits.

If the losses are too great for all the partners to bear, the result will be insolvency. There are specialised rules relating to partnership insolvency. But at the end of the day, because a partner may be personally liable, the final result in cases of serious indebtedness may be personal bankruptcy. The horrors of this are described in our discussion at 1.8.

Part C Company and business names

5.88 Company names

A company, if private, must have the suffix 'Limited' or 'Ltd' or, if public, 'public limited company' or 'plc' or the Welsh equivalent ('cyfyngedig') if appropriate (ie if the company's registered office is in Wales).

Private companies limited by guarantee with restricted objects, for example for the promotion of commerce, science, art, religion, charity or any profession, and whose profits have to be applied therefore, and which prohibit payment of dividends to members and require assets on a winding-up to be transferred to a similar body, can omit the suffix 'Limited' or 'Ltd'.

A company name:

(1) must not be the same as one on the Register already;
(2) must not constitute a criminal offence;
(3) must not be offensive;
(4) must not have a suffix other than 'Limited' 'Unlimited' 'public limited company' or the Welsh equivalent.

A company name must not give the impression that the company is connected with national or local government or include any word of expression specified in the Companies and Business Names Regulations 1981 without the approval of the Secretary of State. The Regulations contain a schedule of such words and the relevant government department to contact for permission in each case. This is too long to set out here in full but, for example, any use of the word 'midwife' would require the consent of the Central Midwives Board; use of the word 'breeding' would require the permission of the Ministry of Agriculture, Fisheries and Food and so forth. The list ought to be consulted if you are in any doubt.

5.89 Change of name

A company can change its name by special resolution (5.27). A company *has* to change its name if it is, in the opinion of the Secretary of State, the same as or 'too like' a name already on the Register. The Secretary of State may direct this within 12 months of incorporation. The Secretary of State may also direct a change of name if it gives so misleading an indication of the company's activities as to be likely to cause harm to the public. A person who is not a public company is guilty of an offence if he carries on any trade, profession or business under a name which includes the suffix 'public limited company' or its Welsh equivalent. A public company may, on the other hand, commit an offence if it gives a material impression to someone that it is a private company.

5.90 Directors' names

It is optional as to whether the names of directors go on a company's notepaper. But if you do put directors' names on the notepaper all of the names must go on, together with the directors' Christian names or initials.

5.91 Use of company name

A company has to paint or affix its name on the outside of every office or place where it carries on its business. A company's name has to appear:

(1) in all business letters;
(2) in all notices and other official publications;
(3) in all bills of exchange, promissory notes, endorsements, cheques and orders for money or goods;
(4) in all bills of parcels, invoices, receipts and letters of credit.

Although contraventions of the company and business name rules carry criminal liability and fines there is an important civil sanction in relation to use of the company's name on paperwork. For if the company omits its name from or misdescribes it on any bill of exchange, promissory note, endorsement, cheque or order, the signatory can be personally liable to the holder if there is default by the company. This is an important exception to limited liability.

Every company must have a company seal with its name legibly engraved.

Finally, a company has to have the following information on any business letters or order forms:

(1) the company's place of registration and its number;
(2) its registered office address;
(3) if it is an investment company under CA 1985, that fact;
(4) if it is a limited company with permission to omit 'limited', the fact that it is nonetheless a limited company.

If you state the company's share capital on such documentation, this has to be a reference to paid-up share capital.

5.92 Business names

There used to be a Register of Business Names under the Registration of Business Names Act 1916. But it was abolished in 1981 and there is now no central register of business names which you can search.

5.93 Companies and business names

There are similar restrictions as at 5.90 about the use of names which give the impression that there is a connection with local or national government or which are specified in the schedule to the Companies and Business Names Regulations 1981. Further, a company using a business name must still carry its corporate name on letters, written orders for goods and services, invoices, receipts and written demands for payment together with an address for service. It must also display its corporate name at premises to which customers and suppliers have access.

5.94 Business names for individuals and partnerships

The Business Names Act 1985 provides that if you carry on business under a name which is different from your own, or in the case of a partnership, does not consist of all surnames of the partners, the provisions of the Act apply. Certain words and expressions are restricted and require the Secretary of State's approval as in the case of companies.

If a partnership, you have to include the name of each partner (and if an individual, the individual's name) on all letters, written orders for goods or services, invoices, receipts and written demands for payment of debts. There must also be address for service. There must also be a note of the place of business of the firm where customers or suppliers have access.

A partnership of 20 or more individuals may exclude the names of partners from its notepaper if no partner's name appears at all other than in the text or as signatory, and if the letter heading states its principal place of business and a list of the partners' names is available for inspection at that address.

Breach of the business name provisions may lead to a novel civil remedy if a person dealing with the firm suffers loss as a result of the breach. This is, that if the firm in breach sues someone, the defendant to the action can plead the breach and ask that the claim be dismissed because of the breach. The court will allow this defence unless it thinks it is 'just and equitable' to permit the claim to be continued.

5.95   Passing off and trade marks

You must also ensure that a trading name does not infringe another's trade mark or amount to the tort of 'passing off' (ie is similar to an existing name and the similarity will be injurious to the first owner because it is likely to cause confusion in the minds of the public). Infringement of trade marks and 'passing off' could lead to expensive court action.

6 Capital gains tax

6.1 Introduction

This chapter provides a brief summary of capital gains tax, particularly dealing with special rules and reliefs relating to businesses. Fuller details concerning other matters are contained in the *Allied Dunbar Capital Taxes and Estate Planning Guide* and the *Allied Dunbar Tax Guide*. Most references throughout this chapter are to CGTA 1979 which consolidated the relevant legislation from FA 1965 onwards.

6.2 Capital gains tax and businesses

Capital gains arise both within businesses and on the sale of businesses. Thus, the sale of a business asset might give rise to a capital gain. If you are trading as a sole trader, the capital gain is assessed on you personally and if you are in partnership, you will be charged to capital gains tax on your proportion of the gain (3.9). In either case, the rate of tax is 30% prior to 6 April 1988. From this date, the new budget proposals apply (see the 1988 Budget Notes).

The position regarding a company is different. Companies are taxed as separate entities and so a company is liable to tax on its capital gains (less losses). The rate of tax is the normal company's corporation tax charge (4.17). However, where you have been trading through a company which is sold, you will personally be liable for capital gains tax on the sale of your company shares.

6.3 Liability to capital gains tax

Any taxpayer is liable to capital gains tax on gains accruing in a year of assessment during any part of which he is resident or ordinarily resident in the UK. Even if he is neither resident nor ordinarily resident here, a taxpayer carrying on a trade in the UK through a branch or agency is generally liable to capital gains tax accruing on the disposal of assets in this country used in his trade; or assets held here and used for the branch or agency. Similar rules apply to companies and partnerships etc.

Should you be resident or ordinarily resident in the UK during a tax year, you are liable to capital gains tax on asset realizations worldwide. However, an exception applies if you are not domiciled here. Your capital gains tax liability then only extends to gains which you remit here. For these purposes, a non-Sterling bank account is treated as located outside the UK unless the account is held at a UK branch and you are UK resident.

6.4   Annual exemptions for individuals

If you are in business as a sole trader or partner, your annual net gains (after losses) are not charged to capital gains tax if they do not exceed the annual exemption. The basic rules are as follows and the rate shown is that for 1987–88:

(1) The first £6,600 of your net gains is exempted from capital gains tax. This applies no matter how high are your total business or other gains for the year. Any gains of your wife are included unless you are separated.
(2) Losses for previous years (6.12) are offset, but so as to leave £6,600 of net gains to be exempt. This results in your exemption being protected and it increases your losses to carry forward. However, all losses for the year must be deducted in arriving at the net gains.
(3) As an example of set offs, suppose you have £8,000 of losses to carry forward from 1986–87 and your gains for 1987–88 are £10,000, with losses of £1,000. You must set off the losses of £1,000 leaving £9,000 of net gains for 1987–88. This is then reduced to £6,600, by setting off £2,400 of losses from the previous year. This leaves £5,600 of losses to carry forward.
(4) The annual exemption is to apply for future years, subject to indexation in line with the increase in the retail price index in the December before the year of assessment compared with the previous December. This applies unless Parliament directs otherwise. For 1988–89 there is, in fact, a reduction to £5,000 (see the 1988 Budget Notes). The annual exemptions in previous years have been:

1984–85	£5,600
1985–86	£5,900
1986–87	£6,300

6.5 Liable and exempt assets

Subject to certain exemptions (6.6) all forms of property are regarded as 'assets' for capital gains tax purposes including:

(1) Investments, land and buildings etc.
(2) Options and debts.
(3) Currency other than Sterling.
(4) Property created by the person disposing of it or otherwise coming to be owned without being acquired. (This would cover articles made or works of art created by you, but not normally in the course of your trade or profession.)

6.6 Table — Assets exempted from capital gains tax

The following are some of the main types of assets exempted from charge to capital gains tax, subject to the rules:

(1) Private motor vehicles.
(2) Your own home.
(3) Certain Government savings arrangements, such as National Savings Certificates, Defence Bonds, Development Bonds, Save-as-you-Earn etc.
(4) Foreign currency obtained for personal expenditure abroad.
(5) Decorations for gallantry unless purchased.
(6) Wins on pools, lotteries and premium bonds etc.
(7) Compensation for any wrong or injury which you suffer to your person or in connection with your profession or vocation.
(8) British Government Securities and qualifying corporate bonds, as well as futures and options concerning them.
(9) Life assurance policies and deferred annuities provided you are the original owner or they were given to you. Certain policies assigned after 25 June 1982 may give rise to income tax instead of capital gains tax.
(10) Chattels sold for £3,000 or less.
(11) Assets gifted to charity.
(12) Certain gifts of historic houses, works or art, etc to the nation.
(13) Tangible movable property which is a wasting asset (ie with a predictable life of 50 years or less). This includes boats, animals, etc but not land and buildings, nor assets qualifying for capital allowances.
(14) Disposals by a close company (4.21) of assets which it holds on trust for the benefit of its employees.
(15) The sale of a debt by the original creditor is not liable to capital gains tax, unless it is a 'debt on security' (a debenture etc).
(16) Business expansion scheme shares issued to you after 18 March 1986 provided you are their first holder (4.31).

6.7   Disposals for capital gains tax purposes

Examples of circumstances in which you will be treated as making a disposal or part disposal of an asset include the outright sale of the whole or part of an asset. The gift of an asset constitutes a disposal although there is generally scope for electing to hold over the gain (6.23).

The destruction of an asset, for example, by fire is treated as a capital gains tax disposal. Another example is if you sell any rights in an asset such as by granting a lease. This is a part disposal, although if you obtain a fair rent, there is normally no capital gains tax liability.

Another example of a disposal is where you receive a capital sum in return for the surrender or forfeiture of any rights. For example, if you receive a sum of money for not renewing a lease, although you had an option to do so.

Gifts or sales of assets to your spouse are not treated as disposals for capital gains tax purposes, provided he or she is living with you during the relevant tax year. Furthermore, the transfer of an asset as security for a debt or to someone else to hold as a nominee does not count as a capital gains tax disposal, provided you retain the beneficial ownership.

6.8   The computation of chargeable gains

(1) In general, you must take the consideration received for each of your disposals during the tax year. (Accounts period for a company 4.5.)

(2) Deduct from the disposal consideration in respect of each asset the original cost, together with any incidental expenses in connection with your original acquisition and with the disposal of the asset. Also deduct any 'enhancement expenditure', ie the cost of any capital improvements to the assets not including any expenses of a revenue nature.

(3) Your incidental costs of acquisition and disposal include surveyors', valuers' and solicitors' fees, stamp duty and commission in connection with the purchase and sale; also the cost of advertising to find a buyer and accountancy charges in connection with the acquisition or disposal. However, no expenses may be deducted if they have already been allowed in computing your taxable revenue profits.

(4) Deduct (if applicable) indexation allowance (6.9) based on the original cost, etc of the asset.

(5) Special rules apply in the case of leases and other wasting assets (6.22).

(6) Special rules also apply regarding assets originally acquired prior to 7 April 1965 (6.15).
(7) In certain circumstances, it is necessary to substitute the open market value of the assets for the proceeds (if any). Such circumstances include gifts of assets, transfers of assets by gift or sale to persons *connected* with you including your business partner and close relatives other than your wife; also, other disposals of assets not at arm's length. A further example is where transactions are such that the sale proceeds cannot be valued.
(8) From 1988–89, rules for rebasing are to apply (see Budget Notes).

6.9 Indexation allowance

Indexation relief is available for disposals after 5 April 1982 (31 March 1982 for companies). The original cost and enhancement expenditure are scaled up in proportion to the increase in the retail price index (6.10) between March 1982 and the month of disposal. If the asset was acquired subsequent to March 1982, indexation runs from the month of acquisition until the month of disposal.

The full benefit of indexation relief is available, even to the extent that it creates or enlarges a loss. (This did not apply prior to 6 April 1985.)

If you acquire an asset from your wife, your deemed acquisition cost is taken to be hers, augmented by any indexation allowance which she had accrued up to the transfer date. When you sell the asset, you calculate indexation allowance on your deemed acquisition cost from the date you took the asset over from your wife. Similar treatment covers transfers between companies in the same group (4.18) and certain reconstructions.

Special indexation rules cover assets which you held on 6 April 1965 (6.15) and 31 March 1982. The latter extends also to assets which you obtained subsequently on a 'no gain–no loss' basis from someone who had held them at that date. Within two years of the end of the tax year in which your disposal is made (accounting period for a company), you have the option of electing for your indexation relief to be based on the *market value at 31 March 1982* of the relevant assets, rather than cost.

6.10   Table: Retail prices index

	1982	1983	1984	1985	1986	1987
January	310.6	325.9	342.6	359.8	379.7	394.5/ 100.0*
February	310.7	327.3	344.0	362.7	381.1	100.4
March	313.4	327.9	345.1	366.1	381.6	100.6
April	319.7	332.5	449.7	373.9	385.3	101.8
May	322.0	333.9	351.0	375.6	386.0	101.9
June	322.9	334.7	351.9	376.4	385.8	101.9
July	323.0	336.5	351.5	375.5	384.7	101.8
August	323.1	338.0	354.8	376.7	385.9	102.1
September	322.9	339.5	355.5	376.5	387.8	102.4
October	324.5	340.7	357.7	377.1	388.4	102.9
November	326.1	341.9	358.8	378.4	391.7	103.4
December	325.5	342.8	358.5	378.9	393.0	103.3
January (1988)						103.3

*Note: At January 1987 the index base was changed to 100.0. Thus assets acquired before January 1987 and sold after that time must be indexed using both scales. For example, the index figure for March 1987 is taken as 394.5 × 100.6 = 396.9.

6.11   Example: Capital gains tax – Indexation relief

John has a retail business and in January 1988 sells a freehold shop which he personally owns for £105,000 (legal and other expenses on sale £5,000). The cost including legal expenses, stamp duty, agents' fees, etc in May 1978 was £50,000 and the value on 31 March 1982 was £75,000. In September 1980 he made capital improvements costing £10,000. Assuming the Retail Price Index is 300 for March 1982 and 400 (adjusted to previous base) for January 1988 and that John has no other gains in 1987–88, his capital gains tax will be as follows:

	£
Proceeds	105,000
Less legal and selling expenses	5,000
	100,000
Less cost	50,000
	50,000
Less indexation * £75,000 × (400–300)/300	25,000
Chargeable gain	25,000
Less annual exemption	6,600
	£18,400
Capital gains tax liability at 30%	£ 5,520

*An election should be made to use the value at 31 March 1982 for indexation purposes.

6.12 Capital losses

Your chargeable gains during a tax year are reduced by any capital losses arising on disposals during that year. The capital losses are computed in the same way as capital gains and are augmented by indexation. Any remaining surplus of losses after setting-off all chargeable gains during the tax year are then carried forward to be set against future capital gains of your spouse and yourself.

The position regarding capital losses made by a company (4.17) is similar to those of an individual. However, the company's accounting period must be considered rather than the tax year. A further point to note is that whilst a company can set a trading loss against capital gains within the same chargeable accounting period or the previous one, an individual is only able to offset capital losses against capital gains.

6.13 Loss on unquoted shares in trading companies

Provided you or your spouse was the original subscriber of shares in a 'qualifying trading company', you can elect to obtain income tax loss relief for any loss on a fully priced arm's length sale. The same applies to a loss on liquidation. It is necessary to elect within two years after the tax year in which the relief is to be used.

Complicated rules define a 'qualifying trading company'. The requirements include trading for at least six years or from within one year of incorporation if less. The company must be unquoted and may not deal in land, shares or commodity futures. The company is permitted to have stopped trading within the previous three years provided it has not, meanwhile, become an investment company.

6.14 Assessment and payment of capital gains tax

Capital gains are treated as arising on the actual date of sale (or gift). Where there is a sales contract involved, such as regarding shares or land, the date of the contract applies rather than the completion date, if different. Your capital gains tax assessments are raised for each tax year, as soon thereafter as the Revenue obtain the necessary information. However, for a company, the gains are included in its corporation tax assessment which is due for payment according to the special company rules (4.5).

For individuals, capital gains tax assessments are due for payment on 1 December following the tax year in which the respective gains are made, or 30 days after the assessment is issued, if later. Thus, capital gains tax on disposals during 1987–88 are due for payment on 1 December 1988, provided they are assessed by 1 November 1988.

Interest at the normal rates (8¼% etc) is payable on overdue capital gains tax, generally from the earlier of 1 June following the year of assessment or when the tax becomes due and payable. However, in no event does interest normally run from a date earlier than 30 days after the issue of the assessment.

In general, even if the sales consideration is paid by instalments, the gain is assessed for the tax year of disposal. However, if you can satisfy the Revenue that undue hardship would otherwise be suffered, payment of the tax can be spread over the period of the instalments with a maximum of eight years.

6.15   Assets owned on 6 April 1965

The current system of capital gains tax only applies concerning sales after 6 April 1965. Rules therefore operate to relieve such part of your capital gains as relate to the period prior to 7 April 1965. The general rule is that you assume that your asset increased in value uniformly and you are relieved from capital gains tax on such proportion of the gain as arose on a time basis, prior to 7 April 1965.

The foregoing is known as the 'time apportionment' method and it operates as follows. If your gain is G on an asset which you have held for A months before 6 April 1965 and B months after that date until sale, your taxable chargeable gain is G × B/(A + B). The gain to which you apply time apportionment is net of any indexation allowance available and A is limited to 20 years.

The market value of an asset disposed of may be substituted for its cost instead of using time apportionment. In order to do this, it is necessary to make an election to the Revenue within two years of the end of the tax year in which the disposal is made. In the case of a company, however, the election must be made within two years of the end of the accounting period of the disposal. The election is not allowed to increase a capital loss. Furthermore, if it converts a gain into a loss, you are regarded as having made no gain and no loss on the transaction.

Note that the 'time apportionment' basis does not apply to quoted shares and securities (6.17), nor to land reflecting development value when sold. Also note that 'time apportionment' applies so as to reduce losses as well as gains.

6.16 Valuations

As has been seen, various circumstances require valuations to be made for capital gains tax purposes. These includes gifts, transactions between connected persons, valuations at 6 April 1965 and 31 March 1982. The general rule is to take the 'market value' of the assets at the relevant time. This means the price which the assets might reasonably be expected to fetch on a sale in the open market.

Only the assets being disposed of need to be valued, even though they form part of a larger whole. This is particularly vital concerning the shares in any non-quoted company. Suppose you hold 90% of the shares in such a company which are together worth £450,000. The gift of 10% of the company's shares to your son would not be worth £50,000 because whereas your 90% carried full control, 10% is a comparatively small minority holding. The true valuation of the gifted shares might be only £5,000, depending on the profits of the company and dividends paid. Note, however, that unquoted share valuations must take account of all information which a prudent arm's length purchaser would obtain.

Regarding the valuation of quoted securities, such as shares and debentures, you must normally take the lower of the two prices shown in the Stock Exchange official daily list plus one quarter of the difference between them; or half way between the highest and lowest prices at which bargains (other than at special prices) were recorded in the shares or securities for the relevant day. (A slightly different basis is used at 6 April 1985.) Apart from quoted shares, valuations normally require to be agreed with the Inland Revenue valuation officers such as the District Valuers, who are concerned with valuing land and buildings, and the Shares Valuation Division.

6.17 Quoted shares and securities

Complicated rules apply concerning identification of the shares which you sell out of a holding which you have built up over a period. Broadly, regarding sales from 6 April 1985 (after 31 March 1985 for companies), these are identified with your acquisitions of the same shares on a 'last in–first in' basis. You must keep separate pools of shares acquired after 5 April 1982 and those obtained from 6 April 1965 to 5 April 1982. Also, acquisitions before 6 April 1965 must be kept separately (unless you have made a pooling election in which case they are included in the 31 March 1982 pool).

Sales after 5 April 1985 are first identified with your post-5 April 1982 pool and then with your pre-6 April 1982 holdings; finally with your unpooled pre-6 April 1965 holdings. (For fuller details, reference should be made to the *Allied Dunbar Tax Guide* or *Capital Taxes Guide*.)

Indexation must be calculated separately on the different parts, additional purchases carrying indexation relief from the date of purchase (or 31 March 1982 if later) until sale.

6.18   Company reorganizations and take-overs

If your company has a capital reorganization, in the course of which you receive shares of a different class, either instead of or in addition to your original shares, you are not normally charged to capital gains tax on any of your existing shares which you exchange for new ones. Capital gains tax is only payable when you sell your new holding. These rules include bonus issues which you may receive.

Where you take up 'rights' to subscribe for additional shares in a company of which you are a shareholder, your new shares are treated as having been acquired at the same time as your original shares and the cost of the rights shares is added to the original cost of your shareholding. Selling your rights on the market without taking up the shares is treated as a 'part disposal' and accordingly charged to capital gains tax (6.20). However, any new consideration is treated effectively as a new acquisition for indexation purposes.

Anti-avoidance rules prevent you from obtaining capital gains tax loss relief artificially. Any increase in the capital gains tax acquisition value of shares obtained through a reorganization is limited to the actual increase in value.

To the extent that you receive shares or loan stock, etc in the acquiring company in a takeover situation, you will not normally be liable to pay capital gains tax until you actually sell your new shares or loan stock. However, there are certain conditions and anti-avoidance rules. One of the conditions is that the acquiring company already held, or obtains as a result of the takeover, at least 25% of the ordinary share capital of the other company. The Revenue are empowered to set aside the relief and thus charge capital gains tax on the value of shares which you receive, if they can show that the transactions had as a main object the saving of tax. However, there are clearance provisions. If the company provides full details to the Revenue, they are required to state within 30 days whether or not clearance is granted.

6.19 Unquoted shares

Many of the special capital gains tax rules apply to quoted and unquoted shares alike. However, some are only of application to unquoted shares and these particularly concern holdings at 6 April 1965, where for example the 'time apportionment' rule applies (6.15). This is not the case for shares in quoted companies.

6.20 Part disposals

Should you dispose of part of an asset, the cost applicable to this part must be computed. (This includes part of a 'pool' holding of shares in a particular company.) You multiply the original cost by the fraction A/(A + B) where A is the consideration for the part disposed of and B is the market value of the remainder at the date of the part disposal. This formula is applied before computing the indexation allowances which is not calculated on the cost attributed to the undisposed of part until that is sold.

A special rule covers part disposals of land where the proceeds do not exceed one-fifth of the total market value. Provided the proceeds during the tax year do not exceed £20,000, you may deduct them from your base cost rather than pay now.

6.21 A series of disposals

If you split up an asset or a collection of assets by having transactions (including gifts) etc with two or more connected persons (6.8) all of the assets are valued together in order to find the relevant proceeds. The transactions must be within a total period of six years and must particularly be watched regarding unquoted company shares. For example, if you have 90% of the shares in the company and gift 20% to each of your three sons, the shares must be valued on a control basis of 60% rather than as minority holdings of 20%. (Normally you would make a gifts election, however — 6.23.)

6.22 Leases and other wasting assets

A 'wasting asset' is defined as an asset with a predictable life not exceeding 50 years. This excludes freehold land and buildings, etc. Leases with no more than 50 years to run are separately treated for capital gains tax. The original cost must be written off according to a special formula under which the rate of wastage accelerates as the end of the lease is reached. Should you sell the property and lease back the premises at a lower rent for less than 15 years, you may be taxed on all or part of the proceeds, either as a trading receipt or under Schedule D, Case VI (Miscellaneous Income).

'Wasting assets' which are also moveable property (chattels) are generally exempted from capital gains tax. Regarding other wasting assets apart from leases, the original costs must be reduced on a straightline time basis over the lives of the assets. For example, if you buy a wasting asset for £20,000 with an unexpired life of 30 years and sell it after 15 years for £30,000, on the assumption that the residual value after 30 years would have been nil, your allowable cost is £20,000 × 15/30 = £10,000. Thus your chargeable gain is £30,000 – £10,000 = £20,000.

6.23 Relief for gifts

Originally, gifts relief only applied to business assets. However, general relief now applies for gifts, subject to an election being made by both donor and donee. The gain is then reduced to nil and the recipient deducts the original capital gain from his acquisition value for the asset. (Gifts to a settlement only require an election by the donor.) If you receive any consideration, the claim only covers the gift element, if this is less than the total gain. Where you are entitled to retirement relief (6.26) this reduces the heldover gain.

The general gifts relief covers gifts between individuals, from individuals to trusts and from trusts to individuals. However, it does not cover gifts to non-residents. The old relief for gifts of business assets still applies for gifts to companies.

6.24 Replacement of business assets — Rollover relief

One of the main capital gains tax reliefs for businesses is the facility of 'rolling-over' gains on business assets by purchasing new ones. This applies to individuals, partnerships and companies. Gains realized on sales of assets used in your business may be rolled-over against further business assets purchased within one year preceding and three years after the sale. The effect is that no tax is paid until the new business assets are sold, unless they, in turn, are replaced.

In order to obtain full roll-over relief, you must reinvest the entire proceeds within the time limit. If only part is reinvested, it is taken to be that part of the proceeds excluding the gain, before the gain is covered. Thus, suppose you sell a factory used in your business for £100,000, making a capital gain of £50,000. If you then buy a warehouse for £50,000, by itself this has no effect on your £50,000 capital gain. However, if you now buy a further warehouse for £30,000, within the time limit, this will reduce the original capital gain to £20,000.

Only 'qualifying' assets attract the relief. This means that the old and new assets must be within the folowing categories:

(a) Land and buildings (apart from trading stock).
(b) Fixed plant and machinery not forming part of a building. This excludes items such as motor vans, fork-lift trucks and moveable machines.
(c) Ships, aircraft and hovercraft.
(d) Goodwill.

Both the old and the new assets must be used in the same business. However, if you carry on several trades, they are treated as one for this purpose. By concession, this still applies if there is a gap of no more than three years between one trade ceasing and another starting. Furthermore, rollover relief applies regarding your purchases and sales of personally owned assets used in your 'family company' (6.26).

You can obtain rollover relief by purchasing wasting assets (6.22). However, unless they are replaced by non-wasting assets within 10 years, the rolled over gains become chargeable. This also applies to assets which will become 'wasting' within 10 years, such as a lease with 59 more years to run.

6.25 Transferring a business to a company

If you transfer your business to a company, as a going concern, wholly or partly in exchange for shares, you obtain a form of rollover relief. All of the assets of your business must be transferred, except that you need not pass its cash over to the company. The relief applies to the transfer of a partnership business to a company but not one already carried on by a company.

If your consideration consists entirely of shares in the company, your total gain is rolled over and you pay no tax until you sell some of the shares. However, if part of your consideration takes another form, such as cash, you will be immediately liable for the capital gains tax attributable to that part of the consideration. Thus, if your total gain is £20,000 and your consideration is shares worth £30,000 and cash of £20,000, you will pay tax now on £20,000 × £20,000/£50,000 = £8,000, the remaining £12,000 being rolled over.

6.26   Business retirement relief

If you have reached age 60 and dispose by gift or sale of the whole or part of a business which you have owned for the past 10 years, you are exempted from capital gains tax on the first £125,000 of any gain arising in respect of the 'chargeable business assets' of the business. If you have several businesses, your total relief is restricted to £125,000. From 6 April 1988, additional relief is to apply (see the 1988 Budget Notes).

'Chargeable business assets' includes those used for the trade, of the business and goodwill. Assets held as investments are not classified as chargeable business assets, however. Also excluded are assets which could not attract any capital gains liability if you sold them, such as trading stock debtors or cash.

You do not actually need to retire to obtain the relief. However, after 5 April 1985 you are able to obtain relief if you retire younger than age 60 for reasons of ill health. You will need to obtain a medical certificate and must show that you are likely to remain incapable of performing your previous work.

Retirement relief also covers any disposal of shares in a trading company which has been your 'family company' for at least the last 10 years, during which time you have been a 'full-time director' of the company. *A family company* is one in which you have 25% of the voting rights or your immediate family has at least 50% including 5% held by yourself. You are a *full-time working director* if you are required to devote substantially the whole of your time to the service of the company (or group) in a technical or managerial capacity.

Only the proportion of the gain on the shares attributable to the 'chargeable business assets' of the company compared with its total chargeable assets qualifies for the relief. Since 6 April 1985 (but not previously), the subsidiary trading companies in a group are regarded as chargeable business assets.

The relief also applies where you dispose of an asset which you personally owned and which has been used rent-free by your 'family company' in its trade. You must have been a full-time working director throughout your period of ownership of the asset. Limited relief is available if you receive less than a market rent. Assets owned by partners and used in the partnership business attract similar relief if sold.

Where you dispose of the whole or part of a business which you have owned for less than ten years, you obtain 10% of the full relief if you owned the assets for at least one year prior to disposal, 20%

relief for at least two years of ownership and so on, adding a further 10% for each year up to 100%.

If your wife complies with the requirements, she is eligible for the relief if she disposes of her business or shares in a 'family company'. The relief also covers disposals by a settlement of assets used by a beneficiary for his own business or that of his 'family company'. This also applies to shares in a family trading or holding company. The beneficiary must retire and have an interest in possession in the settlement (ie be entitled to the income).

Capital gains tax retirement relief is of great value and can be maximised by simple planning. For example, if you are approaching 60 years of age, you should delay disposing of your business until you reach that age. Similarly, you should aim to maximise the proportion of chargeable business assets in your company. If you have reached age 60 but worked in your business for less than 10 years, it might be worthwhile working for a few more years, in order to maximise the relief. A further point is to ensure that your directorship of a family company involves you in working sufficient hours to be treated as a 'whole time working director'.

7 Inheritance tax

7.1 Introduction

This chapter deals with inheritance tax, with particular reference to businesses. It covers some basic rules and then outlines special reliefs relating to businesses, including shares in companies.

The following is only a brief outline of a most complicated subject. Furthermore, only details of the present rules are given. Thus, no mention is made of capital transfer tax, which applied for transfers and deaths before 17 March 1986. However, it should be mentioned that many of the old capital transfer tax rules have been incorporated into the present system and the main legislation is to be found in The Capital Transfer Tax Act 1984, which is now known as the Inheritance Tax Act 1984.

7.2 Property chargeable

Subject to various reliefs (7.10 etc), inheritance tax is charged on transfers which you make during your lifetime unless they are potentially exempt transfers (PETs) (7.3). Also, the value of your estate will be charged to inheritance tax when you die, if it is sufficiently large. Lifetime transfers are evaluated by taking the decrease in value of your assets less liabilities which you suffer as a result of any transfer of your assets and this is known as a 'chargeable transfer'.

Normally, arm's length transactions are ignored if they are not intended to confer any gratuitous benefit. Any capital gains tax which you pay is ignored in calculating the decrease. If you are domiciled in the UK or deemed domiciled here (7.5), inheritance tax applies to all your property wherever situated. Otherwise, it only applies to your property in this country.

7.3 Potentially exempt transfers

If you make gifts after 17 March 1986 to other individuals, or certain trusts, they are classed as 'potentially exempt transfers' (PETs). As a result, inheritance tax is not payable on these gifts unless you die within seven years. However, if this happens, the PETs (less exemptions) become 'chargeable transfers'. Your tax is then recalculated using the rate scale applying at death and subject to possible tapering relief (see below).

Gifts to accumulation and maintenance settlements are classed as PETs, as are those to trusts for disabled persons and interest in possession trusts. The latter are broadly trusts where one or more beneficiaries have the income or use of property as of right. Transfers out of such trusts are also PETs, except on death.

7.4 Tapering relief

Where an individual dies within seven years of making a PET, a proportion of the full tax is payable as follows:

Death in Years	%
1–3	100
4	80
5	60
6	40
7	20

7.5 Deemed domicile

You are deemed to be domiciled in the UK if you were domiciled here on or after 10 December 1974 and within the three years preceding the date of the chargeable transfer. You are also deemed domiciled if you were resident here on or after 10 December 1974 and in not less than 17 of the 20 years of assessment ending with that in which you make the chargeable transfer.

7.6 Rate scale

Inheritance tax is charged according to the following table (7.7). This is applied to 'chargeable transfers' and property passing on death after 16 March 1987. Lifetime gifts which are not PETs (7.3) are charged at 50% of the rates shown in the table. This basically covers transfers into discretionary settlements, charges on such settlements and chargeable transfers arising from close company transactions.

Inheritance tax is payable on chargeable transfers soon after they are made, cumulating them with other such transfers within the previous seven years in order to calculate the amount. However, where death occurs within three years, the tax is adjusted using the full rates. Furthermore, the full rates are applied subject to possible tapering relief (7.4) where death occurs in years 4, 5 and normally 6.

Where death occurs within seven years of a PET (7.3), tax must be calculated by treating the PET as a chargeable transfer and cumulating it with any earlier chargeable transfers within seven years before the PET. Inheritance tax is computed using the value of the gift when made. However, you must use the rate scale current at the date of death. Gifts made more than three years before death would qualify for tapering relief (7.4).

7.7   Table: Inheritance tax rates after 16 March 1987

Slice of cumulative chargeable transfers	Cumulative total	% on slice	Cumulative total tax
The first			
£90,000	£90,000	Nil	Nil
The next			
£50,000	140,000	30	£15,000
80,000	220,000	40	47,000
110,000	330,000	50	102,000
The remainder		60	

Note that from 16 March 1988, there is a single rate of 40% applying from £110,000 cumulative total (see the 1988 Budget Notes).

7.8   Valuation

The general rule is that for inheritance tax purposes, your assets are valued at their open market value at the transfer date. Where the value of an asset which you keep is affected by the transfer, you need to value your estate both before and after the transfer, taking account of your liabilities also, in order to calculate the fall in value.

Regarding quoted securities, any sold for less than their probate value within 12 months of death attract special relief. Those liable to pay the inheritance tax can claim that the total of the sale proceeds should be substituted for the original probate values of the investments. However, if the proceeds are reinvested in the same quoted shares or unit trusts and within two months after the last sale, the relief may be reduced or lost.

Where land is sold for less than probate value, within three years of death, the person paying the inheritance tax can claim that the sale proceeds are substituted in calculating the tax liability. There are various conditions, including the requirement that the shortfall is at least the lower of £1,000 and 5% of the probate value of the land.

7.9   Valuation of related property

Related property is that belonging to your wife or in a settlement in which you or your wife has an interest in possession. Also included is property transferred by either of you after 15 April 1976 to a charity or charitable trust.

Where the value of any of your property is less than it would have been if you had taken into consideration any 'related property', your own property must be valued as the appropriate proportion of the whole, including the related property.

This rule is particularly important regarding unquoted shares. For example, if your spouse and yourself each have 40% of the shares in an unquoted company, the value of 80% of the shares is normally much higher than twice the value of 40% of the shares. This is because the 80% holding carries full control of the company. Thus, the related property rule makes the values of your respective shares much higher for inheritance tax purposes.

7.10   Exempt transfers

Various transfers are exempt both during your lifetime and on death. The following are examples:

(1) Transfers between your spouse and yourself. However, the exemption does not apply if the recipient of the property is not domiciled or deemed domiciled (7.5) in the UK. In that case, only the first £55,000 transferred to the non-domiciled spouse is exempt.

(2) Transfers in the course of trade are exempt, if allowed as deductions in computing the profits for income tax purposes. This applies equally to professions and vocations.

(3) Gifts to charities are exempt, including to settlements for charitable purposes.

(4) Gifts to political parties are wholly exempt if made more than a year before death and otherwise a £100,000 exemption applies.

(5) Gifts for national purposes to certain bodies such as the National Trust, gifts for public benefit and property deemed by the Treasury to be of outstanding scenic, historic, scientific or artistic merit and PETs of property held for national purposes are generally exempt.

(6) Gifts of shares to an employee trust are exempt provided the trust will then hold at least half of the ordinary shares of the company.

7.11 Exempt transfers — Lifetime gifts

The following transfers are only exempt if made by an individual and do not normally apply to transfers made by trustees or assets passing on death. In any fiscal year to 5 April, your spouse and yourself can make all of these exempt transfers cumulatively. Furthermore, the rules apply not only to chargeable transfers but also to PETs (7.3). If you make an exempt transfer, which would otherwise be a PET, it will not attract inheritance tax even if you die within seven years.

(1) Transfers each year up to a value of £3,000 are exempt. If you do not use up the full allowance in one year, you can carry the unused part forward for one year only. Should your transfers taken against this exemption reach £3,000 in one year, you will have nothing to carry forward, even though you may have the £3,000 carried forward from the previous year.
(2) Outright gifts to any one person not exceeding £250 for each year to 5 April are exempt. However, the £250 exemption cannot be used against gifts larger than this amount.
(3) Normal expenditure out of income is exempt. This means that there must be an element of regularity and the transfer must come out of your after-tax income and leave you with enough to maintain your usual standard of living.
(4) Gifts in consideration of marriage made to one of the partners of the marriage or settled on the partners and their children etc are exempt. The limits are £5,000 if the donor is a parent of the bride or bridegroom; £2,500 if a grandparent or great-grandparent or one of the parties themselves, and otherwise £1,000.

7.12 Example: Inheritance tax

Jack Box, having made no gifts relevant for capital transfer tax or inheritance tax, gives £56,000 to his son on 30 June 1986 and £100,000 to his wife on 15 September 1986. He dies on 31 January 1988 leaving an estate valued at £300,000, including £50,000 to his wife, £30,000 to charity and the remainder to his son, including his controlling interest in a family company valued at £120,000.

Inheritance tax is payable as follows:

	£	£
30 June 1986 — gift to son		56,000
Less Annual exemption 1985/86 brought forward	3,000	

	£	£
Annual exemption 1986/87	3,000	6,000
Potentially exempt (7.3)		£50,000

15 September 1986 — gift to wife is exempt
provided she is UK domiciled (7.10)

Estate at death 31 January 1988		300,000

Less Bequests free of inheritance tax:

To wife	50,000	
To charity	30,000	80,000
		220,000
Less business property relief (7.14)		
50% × £120,000		60,000
		160,000
Potentially exempt transfer 30 June 1986		50,000
		£210,000

		£
Inheritance tax on £210,000 : £90,000	Nil	–
£50,000	30%	15,000
£70,000	40%	28,000
		£43,000

7.13 Administration and collection

Chargeable transfers must be reported to the Inland Revenue within twelve months from the end of the month of transfer or death. Tax chargeable on death must be paid on at least an estimated figure before probate is granted. Inheritance tax on death is payable out of the residiary estate unless there is a contrary direction in the Will. However, property situated outside the UK bears its own tax. Recipients of PETs are primarily responsible for the relevant tax.

Interest on unpaid tax runs from when the tax is due. The due date is six months after the end of the month in which death occurs. For lifetime transfers, it is six months after the end of the month in which the transfer is made. However, for transfers between 5 April and 1 October, the due date is 30 April in the following year. The rate of interest on overdue inheritance tax is 6% from 6 June 1987.

Inheritance tax on death on certain assets may be paid by annual instalments over 10 years. This applies to land and buildings, controlling holdings of shares in companies and certain other unquoted shares; also business assets. PETs which become chargeable only qualify for the instalments basis if the recipient keeps the property until the death of the donor.

Provided instalments are paid on time concerning the shares and business assets mentioned above, they are free of interest. Land and buildings only qualify for this relief if they are held as business assets. Otherwise, interest is payable, currently at 6%. Inheritance tax in respect of property qualifying for agricultural relief (7.14) may also be paid in interest-free instalments.

The above provisions extend to lifetime transfers if the donee bears the tax; also to settled property which is retained in a settlement. The interest-free category includes lifetime disposals of timber. In the case of minority holdings of unquoted shares, these must be worth at least £20,000 in order to qualify for the instalments option, also being at least 10% holdings. The instalments basis may also be allowed where paying the tax in one sum would cause undue hardship and the recipient keeps the shares.

7.14 Relief for business property

Business property relief applies to 'relevant business property'. The latter includes:

(1) A business or part of a business.
(2) Shares owned by the controller of a company.
(3) Unquoted minority shareholdings.
(4) Land, buildings, plant and machinery used in your partnership or in a company which you control.
(5) Investment company and land or share-dealing company shareholdings generally do not qualify.
(6) UK stock jobbing and 'market making' qualify.

For the purposes of business property relief, the control of a company includes shareholdings which are 'related property' (7.9) in relation to your shares. Normally you must own the business property (or property which has directly replaced it) for at least two years prior to the transfer, otherwise no relief is due.

The relief is given by reducing the value of the assets concerned as follows:

(1) The whole or part of a business — 50%.
(2) Company shares to be valued on a control basis — 50%.

(3) From 17 March 1987, holdings over 25% in an unquoted trading company — 50%.
(4) Property transferred by you which is used in a trade by a company controlled by you or your partnership — 30%.
(5) Shares in an unquoted trading company to be valued on a minority basis (prior to 17 March 1987) — 30%.
(6) Shareholdings of 25% and under in an unquoted trading company from 17 March 1987 — 30%.
(7) The transfer of land or buildings owned by a trust provided that immediately before the transfer, the assets were used in his own trade by a person beneficially entitled to an interest in possession in the trust — 30%.

Before 17 March 1987, shares dealt in on the USM qualified for business property relief. However, this no longer applies.

An important rule applies regarding PETs. Business property relief is available against any PETs which fall into charge following the donor's death within seven years. However, the relief is lost if the recipient disposes of the property before the donor's death. To avoid losing the relief, it is permissible to replace the original gifted business property with other qualifying assets within one year. Furthermore, the property must remain 'relevant business property' during the seven years. The relief is proportionately reduced if the conditions are only satisfied for part of the property. Where part of an estate is left to the surviving spouse, thus attracting no tax, and part to others, the allocation of business property relief and relief for agricultural property (7.15) is subject to special rules. Specific gifts of such property must be reduced by the business or agricultural property relief. Otherwise, the relief is spread proportionately over the estate.

7.15   Relief for agricultural property

Special relief is granted in respect of the valuation of agricultural property for inheritance tax purposes. In order to qualify, you must have either occupied the property for the purposes of agriculture for at least two years before transferring it, or owned it for seven years up to that time with others farming it. The rules are relaxed where you inherit the property or have replaced one agricultural property by another.

If you enjoy the right to vacant possession of the land or can obtain this within the next 12 months, you obtain relief of 50%. Otherwise, it is normally 30% which applies to tenanted situations, etc.

The grant of a tenancy of agricultural property is not treated as a transfer of value if made for full consideration. Similar rules apply to those relevant for business property relief, regarding lifetime gifts within seven years of death and the allocation of relief to partially exempt estates. Thus, if agricultural property is disposed of within seven years of the gift and before the death of the donor, agricultural property relief could be lost.

7.16 Woodlands

Inheritance tax relief against the charge at death on growing timber is available, provided you either owned the woodlands for at least five years or acquired them by gift or inheritance. Inheritance tax is not charged on the timber on your death, provided the inheritor elects within two years of your death. However, should the timber be sold or given away before the recipient dies, tax is charged on the proceeds or value of the gift. The tax rate is found by adding the proceeds to the estate at your death. The relief only applies to the timber and not the land on which it grows; however, the latter may qualify for business property relief.

7.17 Close companies

Although inheritance tax is predominantly of application to individuals, there are rules under which it is charged where a close company (4.21) makes a transfer of value. What happens is that tax is charged on the company as if each of the participators (4.24) had made a proportionate transfer, according to his or her interest in the company.

The rules extend to close companies owned by trusts or those which are the beneficiaries of trusts. Furthermore, transfers of value arising as above from alterations in the capital and associated rights in a close company may attract inheritance tax at once. Such transfers are not classified as PETs (7.3).

7.18 Anti-avoidance

There are a number of avenues which enable the Revenue to challenge arrangements designed to avoid inheritance tax. Two are mentioned here. The first concerns 'associated operations'. Two or more transactions related to a certain property may be treated by the Revenue as forming one 'chargeable transfer'. Where transactions at different times are treated as 'associated operations', the chargeable transfer is regarded as taking place at the time of the last of the transactions.

Another problem area concerns gifts with reservation. If you make a gift but reserve some benefit, this normally results in the property remaining yours for inheritance tax purposes on your death. However, if you subsequently release the reservation, you will be regarded as making a PET (7.3) or chargeable transfer at that time.

7.19   Deeds of family arrangement

Inheritance tax is not charged on certain variations in the destination of property passing on death. Nor is it charged on the disclaimer of title to property passing on death. However, the disclaimer or variation must be made within two years of the death. Furthermore, an election to the Revenue is required within six months after that.

7.20   Settled property

The rules concerning inheritance tax in relation to settled property are most detailed, and wider coverage is to be found in the *Allied Dunbar Tax Guide* and *Allied Dunbar Capital Taxes and Estate Planning Guide*. The following are a few brief notes:

(1)   Broadly any settlement is subject to the inheritance tax rules on its worldwide assets, if at the time it was made the settlor was domiciled in the UK. Otherwise, only assets situated in this country are caught.

(2)   The settlement of any property is treated as a chargeable transfer by the settlor. However, settlements on accumulation and maintenance trusts, or for the disabled are classified as PETs (7.3).

(3)   Where you have an interest in possession in a trust (eg because you receive the income as of right), the relevant property is treated as yours for inheritance tax purposes. Thus, if your interest ends, you are treated as making a transfer of the value of the property concerned. From 17 March 1987, lifetime transactions involving interests in possession are classed as PETs. This covers gifts, setting them up and transfers out.

(4)   If you obtain interest in property in which you previously had an interest in possession, no inheritance tax is payable. However, this does not normally apply to discretionary settlements.

(5)   Quick succession relief is given if an interest in possession comes to an end within five years of a previously chargeable transfer of the settled property. The relief is allowed against the tax due on the later transfer, etc but is calculated as a percentage of the tax payable on the first transfer. The percentage is 100%, 80%, 60%, 40% or 20% where the interval is not more than 1, 2, 3, 4 or 5 years respectively.

(6)   Superannuation schemes and charitable trusts are normally

exempted from inheritance tax, as are employee and newspaper trusts.

(7) Accumulation and maintenance settlements attract special reliefs and are most useful vehicles for inheritance tax savings. Provided that beneficiaries obtain interests in possession in all of the trust property by the time they attain age 25, no inheritance tax is then payable during the currency of the trust, nor when any beneficiary becomes entitled to the income at 25, nor to the capital at any future time.

(8) Complicated rules relate to discretionary settlements, including provisions for them to be charged to inheritance tax every 10 years, and on removals of capital. However, the rate of charge is 30% of half of the inheritance tax rates taken on the assets held on discretionary trusts. Furthermore, capital distributions from the trust during the 10 year period are charged at a correspondingly lower percentage of the full rates, depending on how early or late in the 10 year period they are made.

8   Value added tax

8.1   Introduction

Value Added Tax (VAT) is imposed in the UK at a rate of 15% on:

(1) The supply (ie sale, hire, etc) of goods and services by a business in the UK;
(2) Imports of goods by any person into the UK; and
(3) The import of services by a business, in certain circumstances.

VAT is thus payable whenever goods or services pass from one business to another or to a private consumer. However, when VAT arises on the sale of goods or services from one business to another, it is frequently refunded. This is because each business is normally allowed a credit for the VAT on its 'inputs'.

The total VAT on the 'inputs' of a business is ascertained from the tax invoices given to it by various other businesses which have supplied it with goods or services. A typical tax invoice would show the VAT registration number (8.2) and, for example:

	£
Goods	100
VAT @ 15%	15
Price payable	£115

For VAT purposes, returns must be made to Customs and Excise of the inputs and outputs (supplies of goods and services) for an accounting period (generally three months). At the end of each accounting period, outputs and inputs must be totalled and included in the VAT return. A typical return for an accounting period might show the following:

Total outputs during the period	£100,000	
VAT thereon		£15,000

Total inputs for the period	£40,000	
VAT thereon		£6,000
Balance payable to Customs and Excise		£9,000

As a result of the credit mechanism, although VAT is charged on each business in the chain of import, production and distribution, each such business obtains a credit for the tax on its inputs. Thus, at the final stage, the whole tax is passed on to the consumer. Often, a business will not normally bear any tax, but merely acts as a collection agency. An effect of the credit mechanism is that it is normally neutral between supplies which go through a number of stages and those where the supplier is vertically integrated. In each case, the tax is borne on the amount of the final price to the consumer. However, businesses which make some 'exempt' supplies (8.10) obtain no credit for the VAT on their inputs relating to such supplies.

8.2   Registration

In general, businesses are normally required to be registered with Customs and Excise and have to make returns every three months (8.3). However, certain businesses which are likely to have repayments of tax are allowed to make returns monthly. Furthermore, certain small businesses can prepare returns annually (8.3). When you register, a Customs and Excise VAT officer will allocate to you a VAT registration number, which must appear on your invoices (8.1).

If your taxable supplies are less than £21,300 per annum, you are not liable to be registered, although you can apply to be registered voluntarily. The £21,300 registration limit applies from 18 March 1987, prior to which the level was £20,500. From 16 March 1988, the limit is £21,100 (see the 1988 Budget Notes). If you are not registered and your supplies exceed £7,250 in the preceding three months, you must notify Customs and Excise. They will register you unless you can show that your total supplies in the year will not exceed £21,300.

The effect of a small trader not registering for VAT is that he is put in the same position as a business making only exempt supplies. No VAT is chargeable to the customers and the small trader has to bear the input tax on his purchases, etc. If your supplies are all zero-rated, you can apply to be exempted from registration. You will not then be able to claim a refund of your input tax, but will be excused the administrative burden of making VAT returns.

You are allowed to *de-register* after any quarter, if registration has lasted at least two years. A further requirement is that the taxable (including zero-rated) supplies in each of the two previous years did not exceed £21,300. This figure applies from 1 June 1987, prior to which it was £20,500. However, where the supplies are likely to exceed £21,300 for the next year, de-registration is not allowed. Nevertheless, if Customs and Excise are satisfied that the taxable supplies for the ensuing year will not exceed £20,300, they will normally allow de-registration.

8.3 Accounts and administration

As mentioned earlier, most accounting periods for VAT purposes are three months in length. However, if your business is likely to have tax repayments, you may be allowed to make monthly returns.

A new scheme starts in the summer of 1988. Businesses with annual turnovers of less than £250,000, which have been registered for at least one year will be able to elect for annual VAT accounting. They will then only be required to submit a VAT return once each year. It is also necessary to make nine equal monthly payments on account by direct debit and a tenth balancing amount with the annual VAT return. Such monthly payments will be computed by the authorities with reference to your VAT for the previous year. Electing to come within the new scheme reduces your administrative burden but may be detrimental insofar as you will pay some of your VAT earlier.

In general, VAT returns should be completed for each quarter and the tax paid by the end of the following month. Thus, your return for the three months to 31 March 1988 should be submitted by 30 April 1988 and the tax paid by that date. Any repayments due to you will be paid but payments to you in error may be recovered by assessment. Where there is any unreasonable delay by Customs and Excise in making any repayment to you, a repayment supplement of 5% of the tax or £30 (if greater) will be due.

Rules govern the period into which supplies and inputs fall. For goods, it is normally the date when they are removed or made available. For services, it is the date of performance. Two exceptions should be noted. If an invoice is issued within 14 days of the time mentioned above, the date of the invoice is taken. In practice, this usually applies, so that the VAT return can be made up from the copy invoices. Another exception is for payments in advance, in which case the date of the invoice or payment counts. This is the only time when payment is relevant; normally it is the invoice date which matters, but note the position for bad debts (8.17). By arrangement with Customs and Excise, the last day of the calendar month or VAT accounting period can be used as the time of supply. Similar rules apply regarding the periods into which inputs fall. As a result, input tax relief is often available before the invoices have been paid. (The invoices should be kept as proof.)

There are special rules concerning *imports*. VAT is payable by the 15th of the month following importation. Payment must be by direct debit covered by bank guarantee. However, no tax is due so long as the goods are in a bonded warehouse. Taxable persons pay no VAT on temporary imports for repair, modification, etc provided ownership does not change. Where there are temporary exports for repair, modification, etc, VAT on the re-import only applies to the repairs, etc plus freight and insurance.

8.4   Penalties

There are severe regulations regarding the imposition of penalties in respect of certain VAT offences. The rules were significantly changed in 1985, although certain new provisions do not come into force until 1988 or later. Also, further changes appear in the 1988 Budget (see the 1988 Budget Notes).

Certain offences involve criminal proceedings which may only be initiated by Customs and Excise or a Crown law officer. Such proceedings must be started within three years of the offence.

On conviction or indictment, penalties of any amount may be charged and/or imprisonment can be demanded for up to seven years. (For offences committed before 26 July 1985, the maximum term is two years.)

On summary conviction, the penalty is limited to three times the tax and/or six months' imprisonment.

The offences for which the above penalties may be incurred include:

(1) Fraudulent evasion of tax.
(2) False documents and statements.
(3) Conduct which must have involved an offence (even though the particulars of the offence are not known).
(4) Knowing that evasion has been intended by someone who has supplied you with goods or services.*
(5) Failure to provide security when required to do so by Customs and Excise.*
(6) Bribery and obstruction of officers.*

*Lighter penalties apply.

In addition to the above, there is a wide range of civil penalties. One of the most important of these is the *default surcharge*, applying to accounting periods ending after 31 August 1986. If Customs and Excise have not received your VAT return and tax by the required date (the end of the month following the period), you will be in default. If you are then in default regarding another accounting period ending no more than one year later than the first, you may be charged a default surcharge. Furthermore, if you are then in default regarding another accounting period, no more than one year from the second, a further default surcharge can arise.

The amount of the default surcharge is the greater of £30 and a specified percentage of the outstanding tax. This percentage is 5% for the first default in the surcharge period, 10% for the second default and so on, up to a maximum of 30% for the sixth and any subsequent period.

You will be treated as not liable to a surcharge if you can show that there is a 'reasonable excuse' for not sending the return or the tax; or that the return and/or tax were sent in such manner and at such time as to expect that they would be received by the Commissioners of Customs and Excise within the time limit. Another vital provision is not expected to take effect until July 1989. This concerns serious misdeclarations or neglect resulting in understatements or overclaims.

The penalty is 30% of the tax which would have been lost if the misdeclaration had not been discovered. However, the penalty only applies if the tax which would have been lost is 30% or more of the true VAT for the period; or more than the greater of £10,000 and 5% of the true VAT for the period. (Where there are two such infringements during any period of four years in the last six, 15% is substituted for the 30% figure.)

8.5 Appeals

Independent VAT tribunals deal with appeals about the matters listed below. There are tribunals in London, Edinburgh, Belfast and Manchester. The tribunals consist of a chairman who can sit alone or with one or two other members. The chairman must be a barrister or solicitor of seven years' standing. The procedure is explained in a leaflet issued by the President of VAT Tribunals which is available from Customs & Excise VAT offices.

In general an appeal must be made within 30 days of the issue of the disputed assessment or other document. Normally, it is necessary to pay any disputed VAT in advance of the hearing. However, if this would entail hardship the requirement is sometimes set aside.

The matters over which the tribunals have jurisdiction include the folowing:

(1)   Registration (including groups of companies).
(2)   VAT assessments.
(3)   The amount of VAT chargeable.
(4)   The amount of input tax deductible.
(5)   The apportionment of input tax by partly exempt persons (8.10).
(6)   Special schemes for retailers (8.18).
(7)   The value of certain supplies.
(8)   Repayment of VAT on certain imports (8.3).
(9)   Refunds to do-it-yourself builders.
(10) Bad debt relief.
(11) Voluntary registration of a person whose turnover is below the limit.
(12) Appeals against certain Commissioners' decisions arising from earlier unappealable decisions which they had made.

There is an appeal from the tribunal on a point of law (not fact) to the High Court and from there to the Court of Appeal. There is a final appeal to the House of Lords if leave to appeal is obtained. In Scotland appeals go to the Court of Session and thence to the House of Lords.

8.6   Groups of companies and divisions

A group registration may be made. This involves a group of companies being registered as a single business. As a result, supplies between members of the group will be ignored. One of the companies in the group is responsible for making returns for the group as a whole. Where a company is organised in divisions, each can be registered separately for VAT purposes.

The Commissioners of Customs and Excise are empowered to direct that separately registered businesses are treated as one for VAT purposes. This applies for companies and other traders. The object is to combat artificially splitting a single business to avoid registration, for example where a business with turnover of £30,000 is split into two businesses each with £15,000 turnover.

8.7   Business

The definition of 'business' is central to the VAT system, because the credit mechanism is applied only to a business. The definition includes any trade, profession or vocation; also clubs and associations such as sports clubs and members' clubs. The charging of admission fees is also taxable as a business, for example in the case of the National Trust. Subscriptions to political parties, trade unions or professional bodies do not normally attract VAT.

8.8 Zero-rated

Not all the inputs and outputs of a business are taxable at a positive rate. Certain classes of supply are treated specially either because they are 'zero-rated' or because they are 'exempt'.

Where a supply is zero-rated, no tax is charged on it, but credit is given to the supplier for all tax on his inputs relating to that supply. Exports of goods, for example, are zero-rated. They leave the country free of VAT in the UK, although they may be liable to VAT in the country of importation if that country has a VAT system. Thus, where a business exports most of its products, its VAT returns for an accounting period will probably show more tax on inputs than on outputs, the majority being zero-rated. (The business can then claim back the difference from Customs and Excise.)

In general, EEC countries operate a VAT system with a similar structure to our own. This is required by the EEC although different rates are allowed. One of the reasons is that the similar treatment of imports and exports promotes equality between home-produced and imported goods. However, the range of zero-rated supplies is not uniform throughout the EEC. For example, food is zero-rated in the UK but positive-rated in certain other EEC countries.

8.9 Table: Zero-rated supplies

The following is a list of the important items. Full details are contained in the General Guide (VAT Notice No. 700) available from Customs and Excise:

Group 1: *Food.* All food except pet foods, alcoholic drinks and certain food products (such as ice cream, chocolate, soft drinks and potato crisps). Meals out are, however, taxable and this includes hot take-away food and drink.

Group 2: *Sewerage services and water.* Water except for distilled water and bottled water; emptying cesspools.

Group 3: *Books etc.* Books, newspapers, magazines, music, maps. But diaries and stationery are taxable.

Group 4:	Talking books and tape recorders for the blind and handicapped and wireless sets for the blind.
Group 5:	*Newspaper advertisements.* Advertising in newspapers, periodicals and journals only, including advertising agency charges. From 1 May 1985, however, all of these items are fully taxable.
Group 6:	*News services.* News services supplied to newspapers.
Group 7:	*Fuel and power.* Coal, gas, domestic heating oil, lubricating oil, electicity.
Group 8:	*Construction of buildings, etc.* Sale of the freehold or grant of a lease for more than 21 years of a building by a builder; construction and demolition of buildings but not repairs. Sales by a builder's merchant, and architects' and surveyors' fees are, however, taxable. A person building his own house (not merely conversions and alterations) can reclaim tax paid on items purchased. Conversions, reconstructions, alterations and enlargements are standard rated and sales of reconstructed buildings are exempt.
Group 8A:	*Protected buildings.* This includes alterations and reconstructions of listed buildings, ancient monuments and listed churches.
Group 9:	*International services.* Exports of services, such as professional advice to non-residents (except individuals in a non-business capacity who are resident in the EEC) and overseas insurance. In some cases, the 'import' of professional services is charged to VAT.
Group 10:	*Transport.* Passenger transport (inland and international) including travel agents (except in relation to hotels in the UK or package tours) and international freight transport. Taxis and hire cars are, however, taxable, as are pleasure boats and aircraft.
Group 11:	*Caravans and houseboats.* Caravans which are too large to be used as trailers on the roads (22.9 feet in length or 7.5 feet in breadth). But smaller caravans are taxable.
Group 12:	*Gold.* Transactions on the London Gold market.
Group 13:	*Bank notes.*
Group 14:	*Drugs, medicines, medical and surgical applicances.* Drugs dispensed by a registered pharmacist on a

doctor's prescription. Other drugs purchased without a prescription are taxable. Medical and surgical appliances for the disabled and certain donated computer and other equipment.

Group 15:   *Imports, exports, etc.* This group has limited application.

Group 16:   *Charities* (8.20) including certain equipment, vehicles and also drugs used in research.

Group 17:   *Clothing and footwear.* Clothing for young children, industrial protective clothing and motor-cyclists' crash helmets.

Export of Goods. This does not include exports to Northern Ireland, which is part of the UK, or to the Isle of Man.

8.10 Exemption

The exemption of a supply of goods or services is not as favourable as zero-rating. As with zero-rating, there is no VAT on the supply but no credit is allowed for the corresponding tax on the inputs of the business. For example, life assurance is one of the exempt items so that there is no VAT on any premium which you pay on a life policy, but the life assurance company gets no credit for the tax on those inputs which it uses for its life assurance business. This introduces a hidden tax cost to its business. Note that zero-rating has priority over exemption if a supply falls into both categories.

Where a business supplies taxable (including zero-rated) and exempt goods and services, it is classified as *partly exempt*. When claiming credit for the tax on its inputs from Customs and Excise, it is entitled to a credit for the tax on those inputs which it uses for its taxable supplies. However, it is not entitled to credit for tax on those inputs used for its exempt supplies. Normally, a proportion of its input tax which corresponds to its taxable supplies is allowed. However, certain exempt items are ignored for this purpose.

Regarding a *partially exempt* business, VAT is only recoverable if attributable to:

(1) Taxable business supplies.
(2) Supplies outside the UK which would have been chargeable or zero-rated if made here.
(3) Business supplies of certain warehouse goods disregarded for VAT.
(4) Overheads supporting the above.

8.11　Table: Exempt supplies

The following is a list of the more important items. Full details are contained in the General Guide (VAT Notice No 700) available from Customs and Excise:

Group 1:　　*Land.* Sales, leases and hiring out of land and buildings (unless within zero-rating Group 8). But hotels (excluding conference facilities), holiday accommodation, camping, parking, timber, mooring, exhibition stands and sporting rights are taxable.

Group 2:　　*Insurance.* All types of insurance and insurance brokers and agents. Both premiums and the payment of claims are exempt.

Group 3:　　*Postal services.* Post, except telegrams. But telephones and telex are taxable.

Group 4:　　*Betting, gaming and lotteries.* Bookmakers, charges for playing bingo. But admission or session charges, club subscriptions and takings from gaming machines are taxable.

Group 5:　　*Finance.* Banking, buying and selling stocks and shares and from 1 May 1985 charges from credit card companies to retailers etc, accepting the cards. But stockbrokers' commissions and unit trust management fees are taxable.

Group 6:　　*Education.* Schools, universities, non-profit-making institutions teaching pupils of any age, or providing job training; private tuition by an independent teacher.

Group 7:　　*Health.* Doctors, dentists, dental workers, nurses, midwives, registered opticians (including spectacles supplied in the course of treatment), chiropodists, dieticians, medical laboratory technicians, occupational therapists, orthoptists, physiotherapists, radiographers and remedial gymnasts, hearing aid dispensers, registered pharmaceutical chemists, medical and surgical treatment (except health farms, etc).

Group 8:　　*Burial and cremation.* Undertakers, crematoria.

Group 9:　　*Trade unions and professional bodies.*

Group 10:　　*Sports competitions.*

Group 11:　　*Certain works of art, etc.*

8.12 Motor cars

Special VAT rules apply to motor cars. In general, no deduction is allowed for input tax on cars required for use in your business. The same is true regarding the acquisition of hire cars and taxis, apart from London-type taxis. However, the tax on the hire charge is available for credit as input tax. The definition of 'motor car' for this purpose excludes commercial vehicles, vans without rear side windows and vehicles accommodating only one person or more than 11.

By contrast, a car dealer can claim a credit for input tax in the normal way on car purchases. However, if he takes a car out of stock and uses it in his own business, tax must be paid which is not available for credit. The 'self-supply' rules (8.15) normally apply.

The input tax on petrol used for business purposes is deductible. However, if it is supplied free of charge or below cost for private journeys, a quarterly scale corresponding to the income tax figures (9.13) is used for each person concerned. The employers are then charged to VAT on the scale figures which counteract the appropriate input tax. The scale figures from 6 April 1987 are as follows:

Cylinder capacity	Scale £
Up to 1400cc	120
1401–2000cc	150
Over 2000cc	225

The scale charge does not apply where a car is wholly used for business purposes, nor where it is used entirely for private purposes, in which case input tax is not deductible. If the business buys any private petrol, it may elect that the scale charges should not apply. However, in that case no deductions of input tax are allowed on petrol and diesel, even for vans and lorries.

8.13 Business entertainment

In general, input tax on business entertainment is not deductible. However, an exception is made concerning reasonable entertainment for overseas customers. Entertainment includes meals, accommodation, sporting facilities and theatre etc. But concerning subsistence expenses refunded to employees, deduction of input tax is normally allowed.

8.14   Second-hand goods

In general, second-hand goods are chargeable to tax in the normal way. However, dealers in certain qualifying items can pay tax under special schemes. These provide that VAT is payable only on the dealer's mark-up.

Second-hand schemes apply to cars, motor cycles, caravans, boats and outboard motors, original works of art, antiques over 100 years old, collectors' pieces, electronic organs, aircraft, fire arms, horses and ponies. With the exception of cars, these provisions only apply when no tax was charged on the dealer's acquisition or when tax was charged on another dealer's mark-up. Full VAT is payable on new goods supplied even though goods are taken in part-exchange.

8.15   Self-supply and personal use

Since a business which makes exempt supplies obtains no input tax relief, it is normally advantageous for it to produce goods for its own use. However, certain rules have been introduced to prevent undue distortion in certain areas.

For example, printed stationery is charged to tax even though supplied to oneself, so that a bank, which is exempt, would be charged tax on the value of any stationery which it prints itself and could not obtain relief for the tax. Similarly, a rule applies to cars which prevents avoidance of the general non-deduction of input tax (8.12).

If you acquire goods in the course of your business and apply them to your own personal use, tax is payable on their market value. This would apply, for example, if you are a shopkeeper and take goods from the shelf.

8.16   Gifts

Gifts of services are not subject to VAT. However, business gifts of goods are taxable on the cost price. (Items costing under £10 in aggregate for each recipient can be ignored.)

8.17   Bad debts

Limited relief for bad debts applies where the debtor goes bankrupt or goes into liquidation. The amount excluding VAT is claimed from the liquidator, etc. The VAT must be reclaimed from Customs and Excise. Retailers operating special schemes (8.18) effectively obtain bad debt relief since they only account for VAT on the amounts received.

8.18 Retailers

Retailers are frequently unable to record each sale separately and so there are special schemes for calculating the amount of VAT which they pay. The schemes also deal with problems arising where retailers sell both zero-rated goods (eg food) and standard-rated goods (eg kitchen equipment). Details of the schemes are to be found in Customs & Excise Notice number 727 and supplements.

At present, there are nine retail schemes in operation. These may be used by anyone dealing mainly with the public and unable to issue tax invoices for all their sales. In all cases, gross daily takings must be recorded and used as the basis for computing VAT.

'Scheme A' is used where all supplies are standard-rated. You simply apply the fraction 3/23 to your gross takings and this gives the output VAT. Input VAT is taken in the normal way from your purchase invoices, etc. The other schemes are more complicated, dealing with situations where there is a mixture of standard-rated and zero-rated supplies.

8.19 Tour operators

Previously, the services of tour operators regarding overseas package holidays were not liable to UK VAT. However, new rules have introduced a special VAT margin scheme. As a result, UK based tour operators buying in services will pay VAT on the margin between their buying and selling prices. This will apply if the services are used in the EEC (including the UK). The tour operators will not be able to recover any VAT charged by suppliers for such services.

8.20 Charities

Widespread income tax, capital gains tax and inheritance tax reliefs apply for charitable gifts and to the charities themselves. However, in the case of VAT, reliefs are limited. Sales in charity shops or at fetes, coffee mornings, etc of donated goods are zero-rated if the charity is established for the relief of distress. Apart from this, the business supplies of a charity are treated in the normal way for VAT purposes.

Any non-business supplies by a charity, such as distributions of free goods are outside the tax (unless exported when they are zero-rated).

If a charity has separate branches, they may each be able to benefit from the £21,300 registration threshold. However, the authorities have powers to stop this being exploited (8.6). Further details regarding charities may be found in the VAT leaflet 701/1/84 and the schedule of zero-rated items (8.10).

8.21 Official literature

The main VAT legislation is contained in VATA 1983 together with subsequent Finance Acts. Also, a large number of statutory instruments have been made under powers contained in the various Acts, all of which are available from HMSO.

An abundance of helpful literature has been published by H M Customs and Excise and a list is given below of a selection of the Notices, which are available free of charge from VAT offices. It should be emphasised that, in general, these Notices are guides and they do not have any legal force. A notable exception is Notice number 727, 'Special schemes for retailers' and those parts of the Notices relating to second-hand goods, which deal with keeping records. Some of the Notices are supported by numerous leaflets on specific topics.

Number

700/1/87	Should I be registered for VAT?
41	Trade classifications
101	Deferring duty, VAT and other charges
200	Temporary importations into the EEC
201	Temporary imports from the EEC
480	Special import entry procedures — period entry
700	The VAT guide (the most helpful booklet of all)
702	Imports
703	Exports
704	Retail exports
705	Personal exports of new motor vehicles
706	Partial exemption
711	Second-hand cars
712	Second-hand works of art and antiques
713	Second-hand motor cycles
714	Young childrens' clothing and footwear
717	Second-hand caravans and motor caravans
719	Refund of VAT to 'do it yourself' builders
720	Second-hand boats and outboard motors
721	Second-hand aircraft

722   Second-hand electronic organs
723   Refunds of VAT to European community traders
724   Second-hand fire arms
726   Second-hand horses and ponies
727   Special schemes for retailers
741   International services
742   Land and property
744   Passenger transport, international freight, ships and aircraft
748   Extra-statutory concessions.

9 Tax and National Insurance for employees

9.1 Introduction

For the purposes of taxation, 'employees' normally includes directors. Thus, if you trade through a company, your own remuneration will be subjected to both income tax and social security contributions, on the basis that you are an employee. However, special rules may apply to you as a director, as described in this chapter.

As previously mentioned, if you are a sole trader or trade in partnership, you are subject to income tax under Case I or Case II of Schedule D. However, it should be noted that as a salaried partner, you may be treated as an employee for tax purposes. Income from employments or any office, such as a directorship, is normally taxed under Schedule E.

The distinction between Schedule D, Case I or II and Schedule E is sometimes very fine. For example, where you have a number of part-time employments and do some of the work at home. If you are able to show that you actually work on your own account and are self-employed, then you will be assessed under Schedule D, which normally results in your being able to deduct more of your expenses from your taxable income than if you were assessed under Schedule E. However, particularly where you do work exclusively for one company, etc, the Revenue may try to assess you under Schedule E.

9.2 The three cases of Schedule E

Schedule E is divided into three cases. Of most frequent application is Case I, which applies if you are both resident and ordinarily resident in the UK. Your assessment is usually on the actual income earned here during the tax year. This case also applies to work which you do wholly abroad (unless you work for a non-resident employer and you are not UK-domiciled).

If you are absent from the UK for a continuous period of 365 days or more, you are not charged to UK tax on your overseas earnings during that period. You are allowed to spend up to 1/6th of your time here without losing this relief.

Schedule E, Case II applies if you are not resident in the UK or where you are resident but not ordinarily resident here. In these circumstances, you will normally be assessed to tax under Case II on your earnings for duties performed here.

Case III applies if you are UK resident, working wholly abroad but remitting salary here during the course of your overseas employment. You are assessed on the actual amounts remitted to the UK in the tax year. However, if one of the other cases applies to the income, then Case III does not operate and it now normally only applies to non-UK domiciled people.

9.3   Schedule E income

For Schedule E purposes, any amount that you derive from your office or employment is normally included in your taxable income. This covers the value of payments in kind, as well as cash. The following list gives some examples:

(1) Your normal salary or wage and overtime pay.
(2) Holiday pay.
(3) Sick pay (including statutory sick pay).
(4) Sickness insurance benefits paid to you (benefits are taxable immediately except to the extent that you have paid for these yourself).
(5) Luncheon vouchers in excess of 15p per day.
(6) Cost of living allowance.
(7) Christmas or other gifts in cash (excluding personal gifts like wedding presents).
(8) Annual or occasional bonus.
(9) Commission.
(10) Director's fees and other remuneration.
(11) Remuneration for part-time employment.
(12) Salary paid in advance.
(13) Tips from your employer or from customers or clients of your employer.
(14) Settlement by employer of debts incurred by employee.
(15) Payment of employees' National Insurance contributions by employer.
(16) Value of goods supplied cost-free by employer to employee.
(17) Share options (9.20).
(18) Job release allowances capable of beginning earlier than a year before pensionable age.

(19) Payment for entering into an employment.
(20) Salary in lieu of notice (often tax-free — see 9.26).
(21) Fringe benefits, such as travelling allowances and cars — according to the rules, amounts are frequently taxable (9.10).

9.4 The PAYE system

The 'pay as you earn' system (PAYE) applies to most Schedule E income tax payable on earnings from employment in this country. The employer is responsible for administering the PAYE on the wages of employees, including directors. From each wages or salaries payment which you receive, whether it be weekly or monthly, the employer deducts income tax at the basic and higher rates (if applicable). National Insurance contributions are also deducted. However, if income tax has previously been over-deducted by the employer (for example, where personal reliefs change following the Budget), you may receive a repayment of income tax through the PAYE system.

The employer pays the total PAYE income tax deductions (less refunds) and National Insurance contributions to the Collector of Taxes in respect of the previous month. If payment is not made by the time limit, which is the 19th day of the following month, the Collector may send an estimated demand which must be paid within seven days, unless (1) the correct PAYE is paid; (2) the Collector is satisfied that no more is owing; or (3) the Collector is invited to inspect the PAYE records.

9.5 Your code number

The PAYE system takes account of your income tax allowances and reliefs by means of 'code numbers'. The Inspector of Taxes allocates a code number to you which takes into account all the reliefs to which you are entitled, adjustment being made for other income being set off and any Schedule E income tax underpaid or overpaid for the previous year.

In general, coding notices are only sent out to cover changes. Otherwise, the code for the previous year is normally used at the beginning of the next tax year. The coding notice itemises your allowances and reliefs. Adjustments are also shown and then the balance of your allowances and the corresponding code number. The Inspector of Taxes normally obtains the details for your coding notice from your last income tax return. However, if your return is overdue, your code number may be understated.

To convert your total allowances and adjustments into your code number, you simply divide by 10 and round down to the nearest whole number. Thus, if your allowances, etc for 1987-88 total £2,745, your code number is 274. Your code number normally ends in L, H, P or V, depending on whether it includes respectively single, wife's earning's allowance, married allowance or single allowance plus additional personal allowance, full single age allowance, or full married age allowance. Whenever increases take place in these reliefs, the Revenue instruct employers to change codes ending in L, H, P or V accordingly. Revised coding notices are not then needed in those cases.

The above normally applies to your code number in respect of your main employment. However, where you have, for example, several directorships or employments, other rules apply to them. If the Revenue consider that your net taxable earnings for 1987-88 will not exceed £17,900, you will be coded 'BR' regarding each of your other employments etc. This means that Table B (9.6) must be applied to your total earnings from each employment, except your main one. If, however, your earnings are likely to be more than £17,900, the Inspector of Taxes is likely to allocate you with 'D' codings (9.6) regarding your supplementary employments etc.

9.6 PAYE records and general operation

The employer is allowed to use computerised records. Otherwise, he may use the official deductions working sheet (form P11). These can be used for weekly or monthly paid employees. One form is used for each individual, and for a weekly paid person the following particulars are entered and calculated:

(1) National Insurance contributions.
(2) Gross pay for the week.
(3) Cumulative pay for the tax year to date.
(4) Total 'free pay' to date (see below).
(5) Total taxable pay to date (3-4).
(6) Total tax due to date (see below).
(7) Tax to be paid or repaid for the week (see below).

For monthly paid employees, similar details are entered for each month. Total 'free pay' to date is obtained from 'Table A' which is provided by the Revenue. This table shows for each week the 'free pay' applicable to each code number (9.5). Where your total pay is less than your 'free pay' to date, you pay no more tax for that week and normally receive a refund. You calculate the tax to be paid or repaid for the week (7 above) by subtracting the total tax due to date for the previous week from that for the current week (6 above). Total tax due to date is found each week from the tax deduction tables provided by the Revenue, which give the tax attributable to the relevant total taxable pay to date.

The PAYE tax deduction tables are designated B, C and D. Table B shows tax due for each week or month at the basic rate. Table C shows the amounts to be taxed at each of the higher rates, successive columns covering all of the higher rates of tax from 40% to 60%. Both weekly and monthly tables are provided. Table C is effectively supplementary to Table B.

Where your earnings are substantial and you have more than one employment, etc, the Revenue normally direct that Tables B and C are used for your main employment. For your other employments, you are likely to be issued with Code D1 or D2, etc and you must refer to Table D. This lists the tax payable at the various higher rates from 40% (Code D0) up to 60% (D4). Thus, if you receive £10,000 from a directorship for which your code is D3, PAYE is deducted at 55% on your entire salary, making £5,500. The 'D' codings provide the Revenue with a very approximate means of collecting tax for your supplementary employments, directorships, etc. Once your income tax return is submitted, at the end of the tax year, your income tax is adjusted to the correct figure.

The Deductions Working Sheet (form P11) also provides columns for your earnings related National Insurance contributions. These are calculated either weekly or monthly and are collected through the PAYE system. The total Class I contributions (9.30) are entered together with the employee's amount. The figures are readily calculated from tables provided by the Department of Health and Social Security.

9.7 Employer's PAYE returns

End of year returns P14 must be completed for each employee. These returns are filled in from the forms P11 or other records and should include the National Insurance number, date of birth, final code, total pay, tax and National Insurance contributions. The forms P14 are then sent to the Inspector of Taxes, together with form P35, which is a summary of the total tax due to be deducted for the tax year for all of the employees. The earnings related National Insurance contributions for each employee are also entered on the form P35. The details are obtained from the weekly or monthly records.

The total income tax due to be paid over by the employer is found by adding all of the tax entries on form P35 and the total of the actual payments made is deducted. A similar procedure is followed regarding the earnings-related National Insurance contributions except that the amount to be paid over also includes the employer's contributions. Any amounts shown owing for income tax and National Insurance earnings-related contributions should be remitted when submitting the form P35. (Conversely, any over-payment will be repaid.) Where forms P11D (9.24) are required for the tax year, they should be sent to the Revenue with form P35.

A further part of the year-end procedure is that the employer should issue to each of the employees a form P60. This is a certificate of gross earnings for the year and income deducted under PAYE and now actually forms part of the P14 pack, so that the bottom copy can be used for this purpose.

9.8   Change of employer

Where an employee leaves, the employer should complete a form P45 in triplicate showing the employee's name, district reference, code number, week or month number of the last entries in the tax deduction records, gross pay to date and total tax due to date. The old employer sends Part I of the form to his Inspector of Taxes and hands Parts II and III to the employee who must give these to the new employer.

On receiving form P45, the new employer enters the address and date of starting on Part III and sends it to his Inspector of Taxes. The new employer then prepares tax deduction records (P11) etc from the details on the form P45 and deducts PAYE from future wages, etc in the normal way.

If an employee is not able to provide the new employer with a form P45, the latter must normally deduct tax under the 'emergency' system. This assumes that the employee is single and has no other allowances. If this happens to you, make an income tax return to the Inspector of Taxes or supply the necessary details to him, so that he can issue you with your correct code number which your employer will then use, making any necessary tax payment to you. If an employee does not have a form P45 when starting a new job, it is possible to complete form P46. This form covers whether the employee is a school leaver, or whether it is his main job or an additional one. The P46 enables the employer to know whether to deduct basic rate tax or use an emergency code.

9.9   Fringe benefits

The term 'fringe benefits' is widely used to describe any benefit which you obtain from your employment which is not actually included in your salary cheque. Fringe benefits are taxable according to the rules outlined below. However, the rules provide scope for the emoluments of directors and other employees to be enhanced in a tax-efficient way.

Employees earning less than £8,500 each year, including the value of any benefits, are taxed on their fringe benefits in a comparatively favourable way. However, those earning over £8,500 or who are directors, are normally taxed more strictly on the actual value of the benefits obtained. If you fall into this latter class, then a form P11D (9.24) must be submitted for you to the Revenue each year, by the employer.

For these purposes, you are not treated as a *director* if you work full time for a company and do not own more than 5% of its shares. This includes shares owned by your relatives and other associates. (If you are a director of a charity, you do not need to work full time.) Where you work for a number of companies which are connected, these must be considered together for the purposes of these rules.

9.10 Table: Fringe benefits — Taxation 1987–88

The taxation of certain fringe benefits is summarised below according to whether or not you are a P11D employee (ie a director or earning over £8,500).

	Details	Non-P11D employee	P11D employee or director
(1)	Travelling and entertainment allowances	Generally tax-free if expenses actually incurred (9.11)	(9.11)
(2)	Free private use of motor vehicle supplied by your employers	Tax free (provided some business use is made)	Taxable (9.12)
(3)	Company house occupied rent free	Taxed on annual value of benefit (ie open market rental and expenses paid) unless you need to occupy house to do job properly	Taxed on annual value unless you live there to perform your duties (9.14)
(4)	Board and lodging	If you receive cash you are taxed on it. Otherwise tax free	Taxed on cost to employer of board and lodging subject to a limit (9.14)
(5)	Assets at employee's disposal	Normally tax free	Taxable (9.15)
(6)	Pension and death in service cover	Normally tax free (9.16)	Normally tax free (9.16)
(7)	Interest free loan	Tax free	Taxable subject to certain exceptions (9.17)

(8)	Loan to participator etc of close company	(not Schedule E benefit)	(4.24)
(9)	Employee shareholdings		(9.18)
(10)	Share options	Sometimes taxable (9.21)	Sometimes taxable (9.20)
(11)	Private sickness insurance cover	Tax free	Taxed on premiums paid by your employer
(12)	Working clothing — eg overalls	Tax free	Tax free
(13)	Suits and coats etc	Taxed on estimated second-hand value	Taxed on full cost to employer
(14)	Luncheon vouchers	Tax free up to 15p per day — excess taxable	Tax free up to 15p per day — excess taxable
(15)	Subsidised staff canteen	Tax free	Tax free provided facilities available to all staff
(16)	Employee's outgoings	Tax free	Normally tax free
(17)	Long service awards of articles of employer company shares; after 20 years' service; maximum £20 for each year	Tax free	Tax free
(18)	Cash vouchers	Taxable	Taxable
(19)	Season tickets and credit cards	Generally taxable	Generally taxable
(20)	Scholarship from employer for children of employee	Normally tax free	Taxable with some exceptions for pre 15 March 1983 arrangements and 'open' schemes

9.11 Travelling and entertainment allowances

Where your employer makes any allowance or advance to cover your travelling costs or entertaining or other services, in the course of the business, this is not taxable, provided you actually spend the money for these purposes. (The employer deducts the payments from his taxable profits. However, entertaining expenses are, in the main, only deductible regarding overseas customers and their agents.) Any excess amount which you are allowed to keep is treated as your taxable income.

As a P11D employee (including director, 9.9) allowances to cover your travelling etc are generally included in your form P11D which your company completes for you (9.35) and it will be treated as part of your income unless you actually make a claim for your business travelling expenses, etc to be set against it. However, in general, you are allowed no deduction for travelling costs between your home and your place of business. Thus, any allowance made by the employers towards this expense is wholly taxable in your hands.

The cost of travelling abroad on company business is allowable. However, if you have a holiday at the same time, an appropriate proportion of the cost of the trip is treated as a personal benefit. If your wife accompanies you and the company pays, her own trip would normally be taxed as your personal benefit (assuming she is not also an employee). However, in certain circumstances, some allowance could be obtained such as where she acts during the trip as your secretary or she needs to accompany you because your health is poor.

If you work abroad for at least sixty continuous days, no benefit is assessed on you if your employer pays for your family to visit you. This covers the actual journeys of your spouse and any children under the age of 18 on the outward journey; also journeys by your family in accompanying you at the beginning of your period overseas. The rule covers two return trips for each person in any tax year. Furthermore, provided you are UK resident and working abroad, any travel expenses paid by your employer covering journeys to and from the UK are tax-free.

9.12 Motor cars

Cars constitute one of the most sought after and important 'fringe benefits'. The following rules should be noted, if yours is a director's or higher paid employment (9.9) and a car is provided for you:

(1) If your employment carries a car, you are normally assessed to tax each year on a 'scale benefit' which is fixed according to the size of your engine and the price of your car when new (9.13). However, if your business use is 'insubstantial', you are assessed on 150% of the scale benefit appropriate to your car. Second cars are also treated in this way. 'Insubstantial' means no more than 2,500 miles each year.

(2)   Where your business use exceeds 2,500 miles each year, you are assessed on the actual scale benefit figure (9.13). Thus, if you have a 1500 cc car costing less than £19,250, your scale benefit for 1987–88 is £700. this covers the provision of the car and any expenses borne by your employer except for petrol (see (4)). If your business mileage during the tax year reaches 18,000, your scale benefit is halved.

(3)   Car pools are afforded favourable treatment. Provided you simply take a car from the pool and do not garage it at home over-night, you will not normally be assessed to any benefit. However, you must not have the use of any one particular car and any private use of the car must be merely incidental to your business use.

(4)   Where petrol is provided by the employer, higher paid employees are taxed by applying an additional scale charge. This is equal to the scale benefit figures for new (less expensive) cars. This only applies if your employer bears any of the cost; thus the petrol charge can be set aside if you repay the cost of any petrol provided. Should your business mileage for the tax year reach 18,000, your scale benefit is halved.

9.13   Table: Car and fuel benefit scales 1987–88 and 1988–89

Cylinder capacity (original market value if no cylinder capacity)	Scale benefits assessed				Fuel Benefit (both years)
	Cars under 4 years old		Cars over 4 years old		
	1987–88	1988–89	1987–88	1988–89	
Less expensive cars – cost up to £19,250					
1400cc or less (under £6,000)	£ 525	£1,050	£ 350	£ 700	£ 480
1401cc–2000cc (£6,000–£8,499)	£ 700	£1,400	£ 470	£ 940	£ 600
Over 2000cc (£8,500–£19,250)	£1,100	£2,200	£ 725	£1,450	£ 900
Cars costing more than £19,250					
£19,250–£29,000)	£1,450	£2,900	£ 970	£1,940	£ 900*
(over £29,000)	£2,300	£4,600	£1,530	£3,060	£ 900*
*provided over 2,000cc					

9.14 Living accommodation

Where living accommodation is provided for you because of your employment, in general, you are taxed on the gross rateable value of the property or the actual rent paid by your employer, if this is more. However, anything which you pay towards the cost is deducted. Exemption applies in the following circumstances:

(1) In order to perform your duties properly, you have to live in the accommodation.
(2) In your type of employment, it is customary to have accommodation provided and it helps you to do your job better.
(3) The accommodation is provided with a view to your safety, because your employment involves you in a security risk.

Exemptions (1) and (2) do not apply to directors unless they own broadly no more than 5% of the company's shares and work full time or work for a charity, etc.

In the above circumstances, rates are also covered by the exemption. However, if you are a P11D employee (9.9), you are still assessed on payments made by your employer for heating, lighting, cleaning, repairs, maintenance and decoration, etc. You are also assessed on the value of domestic furniture and equipment provided (9.15). However, the charge for these items is limited to 10% of your net emoluments from your job, after deducting pension contributions, capital allowances and expense claims.

If you are provided with a house costing your employer more than £75,000, there is an additional benefit charge broadly based on the excess of the cost over that sum. This excess is subjected to the rate of interest in force regarding beneficial loans (now $11\frac{1}{2}$%) at the start of the year of assessment (9.17). After you have occupied the house for six years, its market value is substituted for the cost in calculating the benefit. However, this only applies if you first occupied the property on or after 31 March 1983.

9.15 Assets provided for employee

If you are a P11D director or employee (9.9) and your employer places an asset at your disposal for your personal use, your annual taxable benefit is 20% of its market value when you first begin to use it. This does not apply to cars (9.13) nor land, for which 'annual value' is used. If you subsequently become the owner of the asset, you will have a taxable benefit of the excess over anything you pay for the asset, of the original market value less previous benefit assessments. This is increased to the excess of the market value over the price you pay when you acquire the asset from your employers.

9.16   Pension and life assurance arrangements

As a director or other employee, you will need to make National Insurance contributions (9.28). These are not deductible from your taxable income. However, the employer's contributions are deductible from the taxable profits of the company, etc. On retirement, your state pension is taxed as earned income, according to the actual amount for each tax year. Any widow's pension payable to your wife is also taxable in this way. In addition to the basic contributions, there is an earnings related component in the state scheme. However, you may be 'contracted out' which relieves you and your employer of the obligation to pay higher rate National Insurance contributions.

You are taxed on any pension paid to you out of your employer's own pension scheme. The same applies to any retirement pension paid by your employer outside any scheme. In both cases, the pensions are treated as earned income.

If the employer bears the entire cost of a retirement scheme, it is known as 'non-contributory'. Otherwise, if the employee makes his own regular contributions to the scheme as well as the employer, it is known as 'contributory'. For larger companies, a separate pension trust is sometimes set up and investments made on which generally no UK tax is payable, either on income or capital gains. Any employees' contributions are deductible from their taxable earnings and amounts paid by the company are deductible from its taxable profits. No 'benefit-in-kind' assessments are made on the employees. However, Revenue approval is needed in order to obtain this taxation treatment (11.12).

Many employers arrange for their pension schemes to be operated by insurance companies. In return for annual premiums based on the salaries of the employees covered, the insurance company provides retirement pensions and also sometimes lump sum payments in the event of death in service. Subject to Revenue approval (11.12), the company deducts the contributions that it pays from its taxable profits and the employees deduct their contributions from their taxable earnings. Subject to the rules, part of the retirement benefits may be taken as a tax-free lump sum (11.12).

From 1 July 1988, *personal pension schemes* (11.13) are available for those not covered by staff superannuation schemes. The contributions may be paid by the employer or employee. Fuller particulars of these and other matters concerning pensions are contained in chapter 11.

9.17 Beneficial loan arrangements

If you are a P11D director or employee (9.9) and have a loan by reason of your employment at no interest, or at a lower rate than the 'official' one, you are taxed on the benefit of your interest saving compared with the 'official' rate, subject to the rules.

The above also applies to a 'relative' including parent, grandparent, child, grandchild etc, brother or sister; or your spouse, or the spouse of any of the relatives mentioned.

The 'official rate' varies periodically. Recent rates are:

From 6 April 1987	11½%
From 6 June 1987	10½%
From 6 September 1987	11½%
From 6 December 1987	10½%

No charge to tax is made if the cash value of the benefit does not exceed £200 and no tax charge is made if tax relief would have been available for any interest paid on the loan.

9.18 Employee shareholdings

If you are a director or P11D employee (9.9) and acquire shares at an undervalue by reason of your employment, you are taxed on the shortfall of what you pay for the shares compared with their market value when you bought them, as though it was an interest-free loan (9.18). You are regarded as obtaining shares at an undervalue if you pay less than the market value of fully paid shares of the same class at that time, whether or not you are under any obligation to pay more in the future. This continues until the shortfall is ended, or you sell the shares, even if you cease your employment. Note that the shares need not be in the company which employs you, provided you obtain them at an undervalue by reason of your employment.

Share incentive schemes are arrangements under which you are allowed to purchase shares in the company where you work because of your employment or directorship and not simply because of a general offer to the public. If you obtain shares under such a scheme, you are assessed normally to income tax under Schedule E on the increase in market value of the shares between the time when you acquired them and the earliest of the following:

(1) seven years from your purchase;
(2) when in certain circumstances you cease to be a director or employee;
(3) when you sell the shares; and

(4)   when your shares cease to be subject to any special restrictions.

Regarding relevant share acquisition after 25 October 1987, less stringent rules apply, proposed to be contained in the 1988 Finance Act. In particular, there will only be a charge to the extent that value is actually shifted preferentially into the employee shares by lifting or varying restrictions or attaching some new or enhanced rights to the shares.

Certain *profit-sharing schemes* etc are excluded, provided certain conditions are satisfied, including the following:

(1)   the shares are publicly quoted or not in one company which is controlled by another or are shares in an authorised unit trust satisfying certain conditions;

(2)   the shares are not subject to any special restrictions (apart from Stock Exchange 'insider dealing' rules);

(3)   all employees of the company are allowed to belong to the scheme, provided they are aged 25 and over and have at least five years' continuous service;

(4)   your shares are received as part of your earnings according to a pre-arranged basis, which is geared to the profits of the company;

(5)   shares obtained through an approved share option scheme (9.22) are also excluded; and

(6)   a further exclusion concerns offers to employees at the same time as offers to the public of at least 75% of the shares, provided any discount has been taxed under Schedule E.

9.19   Profit-sharing schemes

Tax relief is available for employees participating in a company share scheme approved by the Revenue. Under such a scheme, trustees are allowed to acquire company shares to the value of up to £1,250 for any employee in each tax year. This is increased to 10% of salary (excluding expenses) if higher. For this purpose, you take your salary for the current or previous year, whichever is the higher, but the maximum value of shares is £5,000 in any event.

You must agree to keep your shares with the trustees for at least two years, unless you die, retire or become redundant. The scheme must be open to all employees who have been with the company or group for five years or more, although the employers can allow those with shorter service to join, at their discretion. Dividends on the shares are paid over to the participants.

If the trustees sell any of your shares, 100% is taxable if they had been held for less than four years, 75% if held for four years and the sale is tax-free if the shares are held for five years or more. The percentages are taken on the original value, or the proceeds of the shares if less. However, any capital receipts already charged to income tax are deducted. (The appropriate percentage of capital receipts is charged to income tax less an allowance of £100 maximum.) The charge is abated by 50% for employees who leave due to injury, disability, redundancy or reaching pensionable age.

9.20 Unapproved share option schemes

If you are granted an option to take up shares in the company for which you work, you are assessed to Schedule E income tax on a notional gain, when you exercise your option. (This does not apply to an approved scheme — 9.22.) You pay income tax on the notional gain as part of your earned income. The 'gain' is computed by taking the market value of the shares on the day when you exercise the option and deducting both the price you paid for the shares and the price (if any) you paid for the option. If you subsequently sell the shares at a profit, you will normally have a capital gain (chapter 6) equivalent to your proceeds less the value of the shares when you exercise the option. (For options granted before 6 April 1984, there are certain opportunities to pay the tax by instalments.)

9.21 Savings-related share option schemes

Notional or real gains which you make from an approved savings-related share option scheme are free of income tax, although some capital gains tax may be payable. Under the scheme, you are given an option to buy shares in the company which employs you or its controlling company. However, you are not eligible if you control more than 25% of the shares and the company is close (4.21). You must save the money to buy the shares through a special SAYE contract geared to produce the required cost of the shares on its maturity.

Normally, the option must not be capable of being exercised within five years. Early exercise of the option is only allowed in special circumstances, such as death, disability, retirement or redundancy. Early exercise is also allowed if the company or part of its business, in which you work, leaves the group operating the scheme.

Monthly contributions are limited to £100 and no minimum monthly contribution can be stipulated above £10. The future purchase price of the shares must not be manifestly less than 90% of the market value of the shares when the option is granted. Because of the limitations, if larger benefits are sought, an approved share option scheme (9.22) is likely to be preferable.

9.22 Approved share option schemes

Where you obtain options under an approved share option scheme, the gain is only taxable when the shares are sold and capital gains tax, rather than income tax, applies. The scheme can extend to groups. Conditions for Inland Revenue approval include the following:

(1) You may hold options over shares worth no more than £100,000 at the time of their grant or four times your current or previous year's emoluments if greater. (This limit is applied on a cumulative basis.)
(2) The share price contained in the option must not be much lower than the market value when the option was granted.
(3) You can only exercise your option between three years and ten years after its grant.
(4) When the option is granted to you, you must be a full time director or employee but you are allowed to leave before you exercise it.
(5) You are only allowed to exercise approved options once in every three years.
(6) The options must be non-transferable and the shares fully paid ordinary shares. Shares subject to special restrictions may not be used, although employees may be required to sell their shares when their employment ceases.
(7) Redeemable shares cannot be used except in the case of registered worker co-operatives.
(8) On a takeover, it is possible for a scheme to be transferred from one company to another, subject to certain conditions.
(9) No one with a 'material interest' (broadly 10% of the shares) in a close company or group (4.21) can participate.

9.23 Director's PAYE

If you are a director and your company accounts for PAYE to the Inland Revenue in excess of the amounts which you suffer by deduction, this excess is treated as your income. However, this would not apply to you if you work full time for the company and hold less than 5% of its shares, nor in the case of a charity.

9.24 Form P11D

Forms P11D must normally be completed for each tax year for directors and higher paid employees, in respect of all benefits in kind and expense payments made to them or on their behalf. However, where any directors and higher paid employees do not receive benefits, it is merely necessary for employers to complete a confirmation that all necessary forms P11D have been prepared and returned to the Revenue.

Form P11D requires details covering a wide range of benefits including the following:

(1) Cars owned or hired by the employer.
(2) Cars owned by the employee — allowances from employer.
(3) Entertainment — allowances and reimbursements.
(4) General round sum expense allowances not exclusively for entertaining.
(5) Travel and subsistence — fares, hotels, meals etc.
(6) Subscriptions, private medical and dental care and insurance.
(7) Educational assistance including scholarships awarded after 14 March 1983 to you or your family.
(8) Goods and services supplied free or below market value.
(9) Work done to your home or other assets by employer.
(10) Domestic staff provided by employer.
(11) Vouchers and credit cards given by employer.
(12) Living accommodation provided by employer.
(13) Assets provided by employer.
(14) Home telephone — cost of rental and calls.
(15) Beneficial loans.

The amounts are entered on form P11D according to the instructions and then the employer deducts the amounts of any of the expenses that have been repaid and the amounts included above, from which tax has been deducted under PAYE.

Other information required includes details of payments of remuneration for previous years included in the current form P35 (9.7) and payments relating to that year, to be made after it. Confirmation must be given that PAYE has been paid to the Collector regarding emoluments, including bonuses and commissions for the year in question; otherwise the amounts not deducted but later paid to the Revenue should be detailed.

9.25   Deductions from income

As an employee or director, you may claim any expenses incurred wholly, exclusively and necessarily in performing the duties of your employment, excluding:

(1) Travelling between home and work.
(2) Business entertainment except where disallowed in computing the employer's tax assessment or reasonable entertainment of overseas trading customers.

Directors or P11D employees (9.9) should make a claim to the Revenue regarding allowable expenses included in the form P11D. The claim should certify that the expenses were incurred 'wholly, exclusively and necessarily' in performing the duties of the employment. Provided the claim is accepted, the payments escape tax, whether made to the employee or third parties.

Any expenses that you personally incur as an employee or director in connection with your employment should be included in your income tax return, including:

(1) Overalls, clothing and tools.
(2) Travelling.
(3) Business use of car including capital allowances (2.27).
(4) Home telephone and other expenses.
(5) Professional fees and subscriptions relating to your work.
(6) Your own contributions to any superannuation scheme operated by the employers.
(7) In certain employments (entertainment industry etc) expenses such as hairdressing, make-up, clothes cleaning, etc.

9.26 Compensation for loss of office

Where a 'golden handshake' payment is made to you on your retirement, resignation, redundancy or removal from a directorship or other employment, £25,000 will normally be tax-free. The excess is taxed as your earned income, subject to certain reliefs (see below). 'Golden handshake' payments are normally deductible so far as the employer is concerned, unless, for instance, they are abnormally high payments to controlling directors. It would also be very difficult to obtain any deduction where the payments are in connection with a sale of the actual business or made just before it ceases to trade.

Payments to you arising out of your contract of employment are taxable. For example, if you have a service contract providing for a lump sum payment when you leave your employer, this is liable to income tax.

As mentioned, subject to the rules, the first £25,000 is exempt, the next £25,000 is taxed at half the marginal income tax rate of the recipient and the next £25,000 at 75% of the marginal rate. In other words, 100% relief is obtained on the first £25,000, 50% relief on the next £25,000 and 25% relief on the next £25,000, the remainder being fully taxed. The 1988 Budget announced new rules (see the 1988 Budget Notes).

Due to faultily drafted legislation, the Inland Revenue concede that up to 3 June 1986, higher relief was due. The first £25,000 was exempt, for the next £50,000 the tax was reduced by half and for the next £25,000, the tax was reduced by 25%. As a result, recipients of 'golden handshake' payments from 6 April 1982 to 3 June 1986 may qualify for tax repayments. New legislation took effect from 4 June 1986 so as to apply the rules as originally intended.

Certain payments are normally tax-free including the following:

(1) Ex gratia payments on the death or permanent disability of an employee.
(2) Terminal grants to members of HM Forces.
(3) Ex gratia payments on the termination of an employment where the employee worked abroad, either:

    (a)   For three-quarters of his entire term of service or
    (b)   For the whole of the last 10 years or
    (c)   If the total service exceeds 20 years, half of the total service period including any 10 of the last 20 years.

9.27 Example: Compensation for loss of office

Tom Brown is made redundant in 1987–88 and receives a compensation payment of £35,000 on 31 October 1987. His other income for the year including earnings is £22,795. His personal relief is £3,795 and he has no other allowances. The taxable part of his compensation is £35,000 — £25,000 = £10,000.

Tom Brown 1987–88	*Income Tax*		
	Before lump sum		*Including lump sum*
	£		£
Other income net of personal relief	19,000		19,000
Lump sum — excess over £25,000	—		10,000
	£19,000		£29,000
Income tax:			
£17,900 at 27%	4,833	£17,900	4,833
£1,100 at 40%	440	£ 2,500	1,000
at 45%		£ 5,000	2,250
at 50%		£ 3,600	1,800
	£ 5,273		£ 9,883

Tax payable on lump sum: $\frac{1}{2}$ (£9,883 — £5,273) =   £2,305

9.28   National Insurance contributions

Contributions are payable under four categories known as 'Class 1' (employees), 'Class 2' (self-employed), 'Class 3' (voluntary) and 'Class 4' (self-employed earnings related). Classes 2 and 3 are flat rate contributions and Class 4 is dealt with earlier (2.47).

9.29   Table: National Insurance contributions for 1987–88

The four classes of contributions are as follows:

	Employee	Employer
'Class 1' — employees aged 16 & over:		
Lower earnings limit (LEL) pw	£39.00	
Upper earnings limit (UEL) pw	£295.00	
(a) earnings less than LEL:	Nil	Nil
(b) earnings LEL or more and contracted out: up to LEL		
on balance up to UEL		See Table 9.32
(c) earnings at least LEL and contracted in: on earnings up to UEL		
'Class 2' — self-employed pw		£3.85 (lower earnings limit £2,125)
'Class 3' — voluntary pw		£3.75
'Class 4' — self-employed earnings related		6.3% on annual earnings between £4,590 & £15,340

9.30   Class 1 National Insurance contributions

(1) Contributions are graduated according to earnings up to a certain level and are collected together with income tax under the PAYE system (9.4). They are not allowable for income tax purposes.
(2) The employer supplements each employee's contributions. Employer's contributions are deductible for tax purposes.
(3) No contributions are payable if the weekly earnings are less than £39 but once this level is reached, your entire wages (up to £295) carry the full percentage contribution (9.31).
(4) There is no upper earnings limit for employers. They pay contributions on the total earnings of employees.
(5) If the employers operate an approved pension scheme, they are allowed to contract out of the state scheme. Similarly employees can be contracted out if they have appropriate Personal Pension Plan arrangements (11.12) which result in lower contributions.
(6) Retired employees who have passed normal retirement age (60 for a woman and 65 for a man) do not have to pay contributions.

Those still working beyond age 65 are not liable for contributions, although their employers remain liable.

9.31 Table: Class I National Insurance contributions for 1987–88

Weekly Earnings Band*	Employee		Employer	
	Not contracted out %	Contracted out %**	Not contracted out %	Contracted out %**
Under £39.00	Nil	Nil	Nil	Nil
£39.00–65.00	5.0	2.85	5.0	0.90
£65.00–100.00	7.0	4.85	7.0	2.90
£100.00–150.00	9.0	6.85	9.0	4.90
£150.00–295.00	9.0	6.85	10.45	6.35
over £295.00	9.0% of £295	9% on first £39. 6.85% on earnings between £39 and £295	10.45% on all earnings	10.45% on first £39 and earnings over £295. 6.35% on earnings between £39 and £295

Notes:	*Contributions at the rates shown for each band are levied on all earnings if they reach the beginning but do not exceed the top of the band. **Applies only to earnings between LEL and UEL. Non-contracted out rates apply to part up to LEL (5%, 7% etc).

9.32 Statutory sick pay

Employers generally pay up to 28 weeks statutory sick pay for each employee in any tax year. (The employee does not need to have paid National Insurance contributions.) Only after that is any sickness benefit paid direct by the State (10.52). Employers can deduct their statutory sick pay payments in any month from the total National Insurance contributions which they pay. A similar scheme operates regarding maternity pay (10.51).

For 1988–89 statutory sick pay is paid at the following weekly rates (daily rates are calculated proportionally):

Normal weekly earnings	Weekly rate
Less than £41.00	Nil
£41.00–£79.49	£34.25
£79.50 or more	£49.20

9.33   Profit-related pay

The profit-related pay (PRP) system provides useful tax relief as follows:

(1) Half of your PRP is free of income tax up to £3,000 each year. However, a further limitation of 20% of your PAYE pay also applies. Thus if your pay is £10,000, your tax-free amount is limited to £1,000.

(2) The employer gives tax relief through the PAYE system.

(3) PRP payments qualify for relief only if made under a scheme registered with the Inland Revenue before the start of the first profit period it is to cover.

(4) PRP schemes can be registered for groups, companies, firms or sub-units of any of these.

(5) Certain employers are excluded — mainly those under the control of central or local government.

(6) The rules must show a clear relationship between PRP and profits. Normally, eligible employees will share in a pool representing a stated percentage of the profits. Alternatively, a fixed sum might be stipulated which varies with future profits.

(7) Controlling directors, with interests amounting to 25% or more of the company, must be excluded. Recruits with less than three years' service and part-timers who work less than 20 hours per week may be excluded. Otherwise, in general at least 80% of the employees in an employment unit at the beginning of each period must be eligible for PRP.

(8) Independent audits are required for both the registration application and the general running of the scheme.

10 Employment law

10.1 Introduction

As a business grows, it will inevitably need a workforce. The legal relationship between an employer and his workforce can be extremely complex and impose on him a broad range of obligations. Although, sometimes, a workforce may comprise self-employed sub-contractors, in practice the workforce is usually composed of employees and this chapter concentrates on the main features of individual employment law.

10.2 Recruiting employees

It is at this stage that an employer has most freedom of choice as to whom he wants to work with. There are, however, some important rules about freedom of recruitment.

10.3 Sex and race discrimination and recruitment

Recruitment must not infringe the law relating to sex and race discrimination under respectively the Sex Discrimination Act 1975 and the Race Relations Act 1976. Under these Acts, it is unlawful *directly* or *indirectly* to discriminate upon these grounds. Direct and indirect discrimination are more fully described at 10.41. Direct discrimination could occur where you deliberately refuse to employ for a discriminatory reason (10.41). Indirect discrimination is more difficult. This is where conditions are imposed applicable to all but which some groups may have difficulty complying with. As an example, the following advertisements for jobs could be *indirectly* discriminatory, and therefore unlawful:

(1) 'Wanted: bricklayers. Must be educated to 'A' level standard.'
(2) 'Shorthand Secretary/Typist required (male or female). Must wear a smart blouse and skirt at all times.'
(3) 'Wanted: Mature canteen assistant (age 40 or above) (male or

female). Must have at least 15 years' uninterrupted experience since leaving school.'

All of these advertisements impose conditions which apply equally to both sexes and all races. But the proportion of members of certain ethnic minorities may be less likely to be able to meet the condition in the first advertisement than white applicants. In the second example the number of men who can comply with the condition imposed by the advertisement will be fewer than women and, in the third example, the number of women who can comply with the condition (because of time out of employment through child rearing) may be fewer than men. These conditions could be unlawful unless they were justifiable in the circumstances. In the extreme examples quoted it would be unlikely that the conditions would be considered to be justifiable. The law of sex and race discrimination in employment is discussed more fully at 10.39.

10.4   Rehabilitation of offenders and 'spent' convictions

The Rehabilitation of Offenders Act 1974 provides that certain 'spent' convictions need not be disclosed. This could apply in favour of a person seeking a job with you. A conviction that is deemed to be 'spent' under the Act tends to be of the more minor variety, and certain offences cannot be spent, for example sentences for life imprisonment, custody for life and terms of imprisonment extending beyond 30 months. The rehabilitation periods required before a conviction is spent are set out in the Act and vary according to the type of offence. Certain persons are excluded from the protection of the Act. These include medical practitioners, barristers, solicitors, accountants, doctors, dentists, nurses, midwives and the like.

10.5   Disabled persons

There is a limited protection for disabled persons in recruitment and whilst they are employed. Under the Disabled Persons (Employment) Acts 1944 and 1958 and regulations thereunder a disabled person can apply to be a registered disabled person. If this happens he can receive what is commonly known as a 'green card'.

The Act controls recruitment in two ways. First, in certain employments it is an offence not to take on a registered disabled person unless a permit is obtained from the Department of Employment. So far this only applies to lift operators and car park attendants.

Second, the 1944 Act introduced what is known as the 'quota' system. This applies to all employers employing 20 or more employees. An employer has to seek to ensure that not less than 3% of his workforce comprise registered disabled persons. For the purposes of calculating the number of employees in employment, employees working less than 10 hours a week are ignored, those working between 10 and 30 hours per week count as half an employee and any other employee counts as one. It is a criminal offence to fill a vacancy that arises with an able-bodied person unless the quota is already filled. This can, however, be avoided if permission to employ nonetheless is obtained from the Department of Employment. It is also an offence to dismiss a registered disabled person without reasonable cause, if that dismissal causes the quota to drop below 3%. An employer can obtain a (renewable) permit to ignore the quota from the Department of Employment.

Finally, under CA 1985, companies employing on average 250 employees per week are required to give details in the directors' report in their annual accounts of such policy as the company has applied in relation to disabled employees in the preceding year. Employers even of this size are not actually required to *have* a policy about disabled employees and their recruitment, but it can be argued that the provision indirectly creates an incentive to have one.

10.6 The status of your workforce: Employees or self-employed persons?

Your labour force may well comprise either employees or self-employed contractors, or both. Although most businesses employ employees (and this is the norm), it is possible, to a certain extent, to make a choice in employing these two different kinds of worker. Does the difference matter? The answer is that employing employees generally involves an employer in far greater responsibilities and overhead costs than engaging self-employed sub-contractors. Against this, however, you must compare the advantages of the integration of workers into your business and the relationship of command and subordination which is inherent in an employer/employee relationship as opposed to an employer/self-employed sub-contractor relationship.

There are a number of important points to note if you are employing employees:

(1) The duties on the part of both parties under a contract of employment are more extensive than under a contract for self-employment (10.10, 10.11).

(2)   Employment status gives employees important statutory rights under the Employment Protection (Consolidation) Act 1978 (EP(C)A) and other employment legislation, such as unfair dismissal and redundancy (10.17 onwards).

However *both* employees *and* self-employed persons working for an employer enjoy protection under the 'employment' provisions of the Race Relations Act 1976 and the Sex Discrimination Act 1975 (10.40), and under the Wages Act 1976 (protection against wrongful deduction from 'wages') (10.38). This is because the definitions of the persons covered are wider than under the EP(C)A and include not only persons who work under contracts of employment but also under contracts personally to execute work labour or services.

(3)   Your responsibility as an employer for the deeds of an employee (called, in law, vicarious liability) is considerably wider in the case of employees than independent sub-contractors. Employees can therefore expose you to more liability to third parties for their wrongful acts than can independent sub-contractors.

(4)   Your liability for accidents at work to the individual who works for you is greater in the case of an employee than in the case of an independent sub-contractor. Related thereto, an employer of employees must take out employer's compulsory liability insurance under the Employers' Liability (Compulsory Insurance) Act 1969.

(5)   If you employ employees you will have to deduct tax at source and administer the PAYE system (chapter 9). And you will also have to administer certain other employment payments, responsibility for which has recently been put on the shoulders of the employer, such as statutory maternity pay (Social Security Act 1986) (10.51) and statutory sick pay (Social Security and Housing Benefits Act 1982) (10.52). If you employ employees you will also have to pay employer's National Insurance contributions (chapter 9).

(6)   Sooner or later, you may well come under pressure to provide contractual benefits to an employee that may commonly be enjoyed by other employees in firms like your own, such as a pension scheme, a car, and so forth and you will also have, in any event, to provide employees with working tools, equipment and materials that a self-employed person might supply himself.

(7)   If you engage an independent sub-contractor it is possible to require him to be responsible for his own tax and National Insurance and he will not qualify for statutory maternity pay, statutory sick pay or any other payments arising out of an employment relationship.

(8)   The self-employed person should himself bear in mind that he will not qualify for state unemployment benefit during workless periods or industrial injuries benefit if injured at work.

10.7 How does the law distinguish between employment and self-employment?

Historically there have been a number of tests.

(1) First the courts decided that the issue was best looked at by considering whether the employer *controlled* the worker. Employees could be controlled; the self-employed could not. This, on its own, soon became unsatisfactory as workers' skills became more sophisticated. It is, for example, difficult for an employer to control how a highly skilled employee such as a pilot or a surgeon actually does his job; but this may not mean they are not employees of an airline or hospital respectively.

(2) The courts then developed the so-called 'business integration' test. Under this theory if a worker is thoroughly integrated into the business, rather than appearing to be an outside contractor, he will be more likely to be an employee. But this test, again, does not, of itself, provide the answer in every case.

(3) Another question the courts have asked is whether the worker is in business on his own account. If he is, or he is 'his own boss', to use an expression from at least one of the cases, then it could be that he is self-employed rather than an employee.

(4) At the end of the day, it can appear that no single test is satisfactory because all businesses and all jobs are not exactly the same and may not respond well to a single test.

So the courts developed what was known as the 'multiple' test, ie you have to look at multiple factors to arrive at the answer. And this is, more or less, with some modifications, the approach adopted by courts and tribunals today. Nowadays it is recognised that, in practice, a large number of factors are relevant in deciding between employment and self-employment. These have to be enumerated and then it must be considered whether they are present or absent in the case in question. A useful checklist of the type of factors involved can be found in the case of *Addison* v *London Philharmonic* (1981). These include:

(1) The degree of control exercised by the employer.

(2) Whether the employee's interest in the undertaking involved any prospect of risk or loss.

(3) Whether the employee was properly regarded as part and parcel of the employer's organisation at the relevant time.

(4) Whether at the relevant time the employee was carrying on a business on his own account or carrying on the business of the employer.

(5) Who provides equipment.

(6) The incidence of tax and National Insurance in respect of any contracts.
(7) The traditional structure of the employee's industry or profession and arrangements within it.
(8) Whether the contractual terms are more consistent with a contract of service rather than a contract for services.
(9) What the parties intended.
(10) Also, more recently, in cases concerning the status of casual workers and home workers, the Court of Appeal has coined yet another relevant factor, namely, whether *mutuality of obligation* is present in the relationship, ie whether the worker and employer are mutually bound to each other.

Some of these factors are more helpful in some cases than others. For example the provision of equipment might be relatively unimportant in a white-collar case. 'Mutuality of obligation' is very important in the case of intermittent work provided by casual workers and home workers.

Three final points need to be emphasised.

(1) The label put on the relationship by the parties is not conclusive. On the one hand, all things being equal, the description of the relationship by the parties may be decisive. But the parties may think there is a self-employed relationship whilst all along being mistaken because there may, in truth, be a contract of employment. It is thus possible to look beyond the apparent agreement of the parties.

Certainly, it seems it is not possible for an unscrupulous employer to attempt to get round employment legislation by imposing a self-employed status on an employee that is contrary to the true situation. This might be considered an attempt to contract out of the provisions of the EP(C)A and would be void. This is because section 140 of the EP(C)A prevents parties trying to exclude or limit the provisions of the EP(C)A or to preclude any person from presenting a complaint to or bringing any proceedings under EP(C)A before a tribunal (10.54).

Also, it is not only in the context of the EP(C)A that an inappropriate label put on the relationship can be removed. Thus, the Department of Health & Social Security and the Inland Revenue will be keen to find an employment relationship if at all possible because collection of National Insurance and tax in relation to labour services is more convenient to the relevant authority than if a worker is self-employed (chapter 9).

If what is thought to be a self-employed relationship turns out to be an employment contract for the purposes of tax and National Insurance, the fiscal consequences of unravelling the past relationships (eg sorting out arrears of tax that should have been paid on a different basis and adjusting allowances that should not have been claimed) can be severe.

Thus, putting the wrong label on the relationship can be very dangerous indeed unless you are absolutely sure that it will stand up under scrutiny from such bodies. If in any doubt, when engaging workers, it is prudent to take advice from a lawyer or an accountant and also, possibly, depending on their advice, to clear the matter with the Inland Revenue (see generally chapter 9).

(2) As the issue of whether there is a contract of employment comes up in all sorts of different contexts such as taxation, National Insurance, a claim by an injured worker for accident compensation, unfair dismissal and other statutory rights, different policy considerations and different approaches can be taken by different bodies depending on the context. Our discussion has centred largely on the approach that an industrial tribunal might take if the issue of employment came up in a dispute between the employer and the worker as this tends to be the context in which the issue most commonly arises. But the Inland Revenue or Department of Health and Social Security, for example, may approach the question slightly differently.

(3) A small business in particular might have to consider whether its proprietors themselves are employees or are self-employed. The principles discussed above will usually decide the issue. It is, however, useful to examine our three forms of trading vehicle which we discussed in chapter 1 to illustrate this.

(a) A *sole trader* will be self-employed and cannot employ himself (although he can, of course, employ others including a spouse or other relation).

(b) *Partners* will be self-employed and cannot be employed by the partnership firm. The firm can, of course, employ others.

(c) The position of *company directors* is less straightforward and depends more on the facts of each case. In principle, even the smallest company can be an employer even if, in effect, it is almost wholly owned by one person. This is because of the theory of separate corporate personality discussed in chapter 1. Thus, in *Lee v Lees Air Farming Ltd* (1961) the widow of a pilot who operated his business through his own company was able to claim compensation for his death under a workers' compensation law in New Zealand because Mr Lee was held to be employed by that company. In many, especially larger companies, where directors are executive directors and not solely proprietors, they will commonly be employees (and the Revenue very often will insist upon directors being treated as officers or employees for Schedule E tax purposes (chapter 9)).

However, in smaller companies, the issue may be finely balanced. In *Albert J Parsons and Sons Ltd* v *Parsons* (1976) it was decided that the directors were self-employed and not employed. There the court was influenced by the fact that the directors took their remuneration by way of fees and not salary; they paid their own tax and National Insurance; there was no note of any service agreements at the company's registered office and, indeed, there were no service agreements at all. On balance, these directors were not employees.

10.8 The contents of the contract of employment

A contract of employment may be oral or in writing. Its terms may arise by express agreement of the parties, by implication or by incorporation from other sources such as collective agreements. Incorporation from collective agreements can arise by express reference in the contract of employment itself, by custom and practice and, very occasionally, (though not usually) by agency. Generally, terms in collective agreements must be considered appropriate for incorporation into an individual contract before they can be incorporated. Collective and policy issues, such as long-term planning agreements, are generally regarded as inappropriate. But individual matters such as payment terms and other benefits and conditions to be enjoyed by the employees would be considered appropriate.

10.9 Terms of the contract

Every contract of employment has basic terms which, if not set out by the parties in writing would, in any event, be implied by the courts. These may usefully be separated into employer's obligations and employee's obligations. It is important to note that many of these can be modified by express agreement (10.12).

10.10 The employer's obligations

(1) An employer must pay *wages* or other remuneration. However:

    (a)   This is not always the case when an employee is *sick*. Mostly, these days, sick pay entitlement is covered by express agreement and this is wise (10.13, 10.14). But if not, the position is as follows. For a long time the courts were quite generous and were willing to imply a term that wages should continue during sickness without limit. At one time it was thought that there was a presumption in favour of continuance of wages in the absence of express agreement to the contrary. Nowadays, however, this would be regarded as somewhat out of line with current industrial practice. The more modern view is that there is no such presumption in favour of continuance of wages. The court must have regard to all the circumstances including what the parties thought and what they said and did within the relationship. If there are no factors either way indicating whether such pay is applicable there may still be a residual presumption in favour of payment of wages.

But, in practice, the facts and circumstances of the case will usually provide an indication of whether sick pay is available. It is also thought that if a court *does* imply a right to continuation of wages during sickness, that right will only extend for a reasonable period.

Notwithstanding any right to wages during sickness under the *contract,* a qualifying employee may be entitled to Statutory Sick Pay (10.52). An employer would be advised, however, to provide by contract that contractual sick pay is only available to top up statutory sick pay (or state sickness benefit thereafter) to the level of an employee's normal wages.

Also, an employee may have rights to payment during his period of notice by virtue of the provisions of the EP(C)A, Sched 3 even if he has exhausted or is otherwise not entitled to contractual sick pay.

(b) If an employee absents himself from work on account of a *strike* or other *industrial action* he will not be entitled to wages. The consideration for wages in a contract is the provision of work and if work is not provided no wages are earned.

More complex are cases where the industrial action taken is more sophisticated and does not result in a complete absence from duty, such as in the case of a work to rule or a go slow. This might also affect the right to wages. It is true that deductions of this sort are not covered by the provisions of the Wages Act 1986 which exclude deductions on account of a strike or industrial action from the protection of that Act (see below, (d) and 10.38). But you would be unwise to deduct from pay without taking legal advice as the position is so complex.

(c)   When work is short, an employer may be tempted to lay off without pay. This may be possible within reasonable limits if there is an express power arising from the contract, from a collective agreement or from custom and practice. Nowadays though, it is most unlikely that a court would *imply* a power for the employer to lay off without pay. If he did so without express authority, this would probably be a breach of contract entitling the employee to claim arrears of wages and possibly, in due course, constructive dismissal (10.18). And there may even sometimes be an overlap with the law of redundancy where the right to a redundancy payment can arise after lay off or short-time working (10.25). Under the EP(C)A a qualifying employee may have the right to a modest guarantee payment when laid off (10.32). Collective agreements can also regulate lay off and short time.

(d)   Deductions from wages generally are now covered by the Wages Act 1986 which provides a remedy for improper deductions from wages before the industrial tribunal (10.38).

(e)   Employees on maternity leave may be entitled to Statutory Maternity Pay which is a payment administered by the employer by virtue of the Social Security Act 1986 (10.51).

(2) It is not clear whether an employer has to provide *work* to his employee as long as he pays *wages*. In fact the basic rule (although it is very old) implies that an employer is *not* obliged to provide work as long as wages are paid. This implies that an employer can, in effect, lay off with pay. In more modern cases, courts have doubted whether this is always the case. In 1974 the Court of Appeal expressed the view that there is, by law, a 'right to work' which the employer would breach by laying an employee off even on full pay. But is is doubtful whether there is in fact such a generalised right to work.

Nonetheless, an employee may well have a right to work in certain situations where to carry on working is important to him. For example:

(a)   To ensure his bonus, commission or piece work earnings are maintained by his continuing efforts or

(b)   Where publicity is important to him (such as in the case of an actor) or

(c)   Where reputation in the trade is important to him.

(3) An employer owes a duty of *safety* to his employees by providing competent staff, safe equipment and a safe system of work. This threefold duty was developed at common law but is also enshrined in the Health & Safety at Work Act 1974.

(4) An employee will be entitled to an *indemnity* against expenses

incurred during the course of his employment on behalf of his employer.

(5) Recently, in the context of unfair dismissal cases, courts and tribunals have developed some very up-to-date implied terms. For example, it is now accepted that there is a duty on the employer to maintain 'trust and confidence' in the employment relationship and even, according to one case, to treat an employee as would a 'good and considerate' employer. Breach of these terms often comes up in the context of constructive dismissal (10.18), ie whether an employee is entitled to leave because of an employer's unacceptable conduct.

(6) Any contract, in the absence of an express provision, may be terminated by reasonable notice. So you are bound to give reasonable notice of dismissal to an employee (and *vice versa*) unless you have made an express agreement about length of notice. The length of notice required at common law is a question of fact in each employment case and it is not possible to generalise. In any event, under the EP(C)A an employee is entitled to a *minimum* period of notice of one week for each year of service (subject to a maximum of 12 weeks) (10.36).

10.11   Duties of the employee

(1) An employee is under a duty to *work*. This is the consideration he gives for his wages or salary. Not to work is a breach of contract. There are some problems that arise out of this:

   (a)   It is generally implied that an employee is not in breach of contract by failing to work when he has good excuse, for example, when he is absent through ill-health or sickness. An employer will, however, often provide that it will be a breach of contract not to notify the employer of the sickness and otherwise follow sickness procedures.

   (b)   In a case of a strike or industrial action, not to work may be a breach of contract and there will also be a breach of contract, even when work is done, if it is defectively performed or performed in a way designed to disrupt the employer's business, such as in the case of a go-slow or a work-to-rule.

(2) An employee is under a duty to take reasonable care in and about the performance of his duties.

(3) An employee has to be competent in his job. However, only *gross* negligence will generally allow an employer to dismiss without due notice for incompetence at common law. This applies even more so under the law of unfair dismissal (10.17) and very rarely would a single act of incompetence allow an employer to dismiss fairly. One example however, is the case of *Alidair Ltd* v *Taylor*

(1978) where a single act of negligence by a pilot of a passenger aircraft in landing badly and causing damage to the aircraft was held to justify dismissal.

(4) An employee is under a duty to *obey reasonable commands* of the employer. But

    (a)   an employee is not obliged to follow an *unlawful* order of the employer.

    (b)   An employer cannot dismiss summarily for a single act of disobedience where the act is not serious and the intention of the employee is still, on the whole, to be bound by the contract.

(5) An employee is under a duty of *fidelity* (faithfulness), sometimes called *loyalty*. This means that an employee must be honest and must not steal from his employer. Nor must he take any secret profits or commissions arising out of his duties. He must also respect the confidentiality of the employer's trade secrets. What is confidential and how breach of confidentiality may be restrained is a difficult question and legal advice is usually necessary.

Within employment the employee must not work for others during the time he must work for the employer. This would anyway be a breach of his duty to do work for the employer under the contract. There is, however, nothing, in principle, to stop him working for another employer in his spare time. However, *very* exceptionally, if the spare time work is for a *competitor* of the employer and involves a serious risk to the undertaking of the first employer, even taking on spare-time work could amount to a breach of the duty of fidelity.

Once the employment ends, an employee must not take with him trade secrets and confidential information and give them to another, nor may he take with him customer lists and the like. There is nothing, however, to stop him, in principle, taking with him his skill and know-how if this does not amount to use of his former employer's trade secrets or confidential information.

Further, in the absence of a specific restraint on future employment in the contract of employment, he may, after the ending of the employment, go and work for a competitor (subject again to the rules about use of trade secrets and confidential information). Sometimes this can be quite dangerous for an employer and very often there is written into contracts of employment a restrictive covenant that an employee may not go and work for a competitor for a certain period after the ending of the employment. If this is cast in reasonable terms and is put in for the legitimate protection of the employer's interests, it will be enforceable, but not otherwise (10.14).

(6) There are special rules applicable to *employee inventions* after 1 June 1978. This is provided for by the Patents Act 1978.

Under this Act, an invention belongs to an employer if

(a) it is made in the course of the employee's duties or
(b) it arises as a result of a specific assignment outside the employee's normal duties in circumstances such that an invention might reasonably be expected to arise or
(c) it is made in the course of the duties of the employee the nature and responsibilities of which impose a special obligation to further the employer's interest.

Otherwise, inventions belong to an employee. The terms of a contract between an employer and employee which purport to diminish an employee's rights are unenforceable.

Where a patent is granted in relation to an invention made by an employee but belonging to an employer under the above rules and the patent is of outstanding benefit to the employer (having regard amongst other things to the size and nature of the employer) compensation may be payable where the compensation already paid to the employee (if any) is inadequate. An employee may make such an application for compensation at any time during the life of the patent and during one year thereafter. The court seeks to award a fair share of the rewards or benefits derived from the patent or which are reasonably expected to derive from the patent to the employer.

Copyright in a work arising from employment should also belong to an employer.

10.12 Should a contract of employment be in writing?

As has been seen, a contract of employment may exist orally or in writing, express or implied. If no terms are struck between the parties, the courts may imply some basic terms into the agreement for the parties (10.10, 10.11). However, the EP(C)A requires a *written statement* of main terms and conditions to be issued to an employee after 13 weeks of employment (10.13). And there is every merit in issuing a written document to an employee that goes further than the basic requirements of a statutory written statement. You may find it helpful and prudent expressly to provide for certain matters which the common law will not imply for you (for example a restraint on future employment with a competitor), or to modify common law rules, or to provide more fully about discipline, performance and about your firm's rules generally.

10.13 The written statement under the EP(C)A

Under the EP(C)A, an employer must give a written statement to an employee giving particulars of the major terms of his employment within 13 weeks of the commencement of employment. The items to be included are as follows:

(1) The name of the employer.
(2) The name of the employee.
(3) The date when the employment began.
(4) The rate of pay or method of calculating pay.
(5) The frequency of payment.
(6) Hours of work (including normal working hours).
(7) Holiday entitlement (also enabling the employee to calculate any accrued holiday pay on termination).
(8) Any term relating to sickness and injury and sick pay.
(9) Pension terms.
(10) Length of notice.
(11) Title of employee's job.
(12) Any disciplinary rules applying to the employee or identification of a document where he can find them.
(13) Details of the person to whom the employee may appeal if dissatisfied with any disciplinary decision or if he has any other grievance.
(14) A statement of whether there is a contracting out certificate in force in respect of the Social Security Pensions Act 1975.

Any change in the particulars must be notified in writing to the employee within one month of the change. If the employee does not receive a statement or if he does receive a statement which he alleges is inaccurate or incomplete he may complain to an industrial tribunal and the industrial tribunal may declare what the terms of the employment are or may correct the inaccurate terms (although the employee cannot get compensation from the tribunal for the employer's default).

The written statement is not a contract and is not necessarily conclusive of the main terms of the contract (hence the employee's right to go to the industrial tribunal to complain of any inaccuracy). It is therefore possible (albeit rare) that the written statement can conflict with other terms, eg in a collective agreement, letter of appointment and so forth. This conflict is less likely to arise where a written contract is used (10.14).

10.14 A written contract of employment

Although the written statement is often used in industry quite satisfactorily and is, very often, regarded as accurately reflecting the main terms of the contract (but see 10.13), it is possible to issue a written contract which both covers the requirements of the EP(C)A s 1 and which also covers much more additional ground. Alternatively, if the written statement format is preferred, there is nothing to stop you putting in certain additional clauses or paragraphs. A written contract, or an *expanded* written statement, could make express provision, for example, about:

(1) The way the job is to be performed.
(2) Secrecy and confidential information.
(3) Whether an employee may work for a competitor after the termination of employment.
(4) Sickness and reporting procedures.
(5) Holiday rules.
(6) Bonus calculations.
(7) Special rules in the business that you require to be observed.

Thus the merit of having a more comprehensive document than the minimum required by law can easily be seen. By including additional provisions you can make it much clearer to your employees what their obligations are to you (and, indeed, *vice versa*). To take one example, if you have no express agreement about notice, you will be thrown back on the common law which will imply a 'reasonable' period. This is vague in the extreme. You can instead (subject to the statutory minima specified in the EP(C)A (10.36) declare what the notice on either side shall be and this will override the common law. A clear and express agreement may also be helpful in avoiding disputes and may even help you in unfair dismissal cases (10.23) because you have at least provided some employment rules to be followed.

A contract may not contain anything which is illegal or in restraint of trade. So, for example, a provision in an agreement whereby the parties agree to evade tax will not be enforceable. Further, if an employer tries to restrain an employee for too long and over too wide a radius from working for a competitor after the termination of employment, this may be beyond what is necessary for the protection of the business and what is reasonable and, therefore, may be unenforceable as an unlawful restraint of trade (10.11).

Under the Wages Act 1986 certain deductions from pay are required to have the authority of a contractual provision.

Finally, in the case of contracts given to *directors*, a copy of any service contract, or a memorandum of the terms of any oral contract, must be kept at a company's registered office and be available for inspection by members of a company.

10.15   Statutory employment rights

As we have seen (10.6) statutory employment rights depend, in the main, on there being a contract of employment (but rights under the Sex Discrimination Act 1975, Race Relations Act 1976 and Wages Act 1986 are also available to others (10.6)). Many (although not all) such statutory rights depend also on the employee having worked *continuously* under the contract for a minimum period of time. This period is often called 'the qualifying period'. Our next paragraph therefore deals with the important concept of continuous employment.

10.16   Continuity of employment

The following is a (non exhaustive) table of the main statutory employment rights and the qualifying periods relating thereto.

Right	Qualifying period
Redundancy payment	2 years
Unfair dismissal	2 years
Sex discrimination, race discrimination and equal pay	None
Statement of reasons for dismissal	6 months
Right to return to work after maternity	2 years
Guarantee payment	1 month ending with the day before payment is claimed
Written statement of terms and conditions	13 weeks
Time off for union officers, union members or for public duties	None
Claim for remuneration under protective award	None
Time off for safety representatives or ante-natal care	None
itemised pay statements	None

It is important to note that these periods are subject to change from time to time.

Continuity is accrued by counting weeks of employment. A week counts towards a period of continuous employment if the employee works under a contract of employment for 16 hours or more or works under a contract which normally requires 16 hours or more work.

This 16 hour threshold comes down to eight in the case of employees with five or more years of continuous service. If there is a break of as little as one week in employment that does not 'count', continuous employment is broken and the employee must start again. However, this is subject to some important exceptions, for example:

(1) Periods of up to 26 weeks may count notwithstanding a break due to absence from work in consequence of sickness or injury or wholly or partly because of pregnancy or confinement.

(2) In any case where there is absence from work on account of a 'temporary cessation of work' or absence from work in circumstances such that 'by arrangement or custom' an employee is regarded as continuing in the employment of his employer for all or any purposes.

(3) An employee who is dismissed and then reinstated or re-engaged pursuant to an industrial tribunal award or by a settlement through ACAS may have his continuous employment preserved notwithstanding the break between dismissal and reinstatement.

(4) Finally, there are some complicated provisions preserving continuity notwithstanding that there has been a change of employer. This occurs in the transfer of a trade, business or undertaking, on a change in the composition of personal representatives, on a change in the composition of a partnership, on a transfer by Act of Parliament, upon transfers between associated employers, and upon transfers to and from local authority schools (10.60).

Continuity of employment is not broken by an employee's participation in a strike or a lock-out. But any week during which the strike or lock-out occurs will not actually count towards the period of continuous employment.

10.17 Unfair dismissal

One of the most important statutory employment rights, one of the most commonly litigated and, arguably, the best known is the right of an employee not to be unfairly dismissed. The right is contained in the EP(C)A which provides that an employee has the right not to be unfairly dismissed. The right was introduced by the Industrial Relations Act 1971. This controversial Act was itself repealed in 1974 but the unfair dismissal provisions survived subject to some amendments in the succeeding Trade Union and Labour Relations Act 1974 and other legislation.

There are certain qualifying factors which have to be satisfied before a claim can be made. Amongst these are that an applicant must show:

(1) That he was an employee (10.6).

(2) That he worked long enough continuously under a contract of employment, that is to say, two years (10.13). This qualification does not apply in trade union membership and activities dismissals.

(3) That he is not among the excluded categories of workers not protected by the EP(C)A (eg those whose employment is wholly or mainly outside Great Britain; policemen; a fishermen remunerated by a share of profits).

(4) That there has been a dismissal (10.18).

(5) That he has not attained the age of 65 or the normal retiring age in the firm (Note that the upper age limit of 65 applies to both men *and* women since 7 November 1987 — contrast redundancy payments law: 10.25). This qualification does not apply in trade union membership and activities dismissals.

(6) That he has claimed in time. There is a time limit of three months from the effective date of termination of the employment. This is extendable but only where the tribunal in its discretion considers that it was not reasonably practicable to present the claim within three months. The discretion is rarely exercised.

10.18   Dismissal

This may seem obvious at first, but an employee cannot claim unfair dismissal unless he has been dismissed. There are three kinds of dismissal, viz where:

(1) the contract under which the employee is employed by the employer is terminated by the employer, whether it is so terminated by notice or without notice or

(2) where, under that contract, the employee is employed for a fixed term, that term expires without being renewed under the same contract, or

(3) the employee terminates that contract, with or without notice, in circumstances such that he is entitled to terminate it without notice by reason of the employer's conduct.

Case (1) is what most people would understand as 'giving the employee the sack'. It is an express employer-initiated dismissal. Case (2) is unusual in that it *deems* there to be a dismissal when a fixed term contract comes to an end and *is not renewed*. Case (3) is what is known as a 'constructive' dismissal and merits some further explanation.

Constructive dismissal occurs where an employer's conduct is such that it amounts to a serious repudiatory breach of the contract of employment entitling the employee to resign. If he resigns in the face of such a breach he will have been constructively dismissed. A breach of this sort could be of an express term, eg a demotion, a unilateral reduction in pay, withdrawal of a bonus scheme, unilateral change of location of work and so forth. Or it could be a breach of an implied term, for example that the employee be given work to do or to maintain trust and confidence in the employment relationship (10.10). Examples of breach of the latter duty could be sexual harassment, an unjustified accusation of theft and/or continual undermining of the employee's position.

In relation to Case (2), and to fixed term contracts, section 142 of the EP(C)A allows an employer and employee by agreement in writing to exclude the right to claim unfair dismissal arising out of the non renewal of the contract if the employee is employed under a fixed term of one year or more.

Finally, a contract may sometimes end by frustration (chapter 12), ie by operation of law without the need for action by either party. If so, there will be no dismissal. Frustration can occur in cases of imprisonment or long term illness where the employee's absence makes the contract impossible to perform. Because this doctrine, in effect, prevents an unfair dismissal claim, it is not popular with tribunals and it only rarely applies.

10.19 The test of unfair dismissal

Once a claim is submitted it is for the employer first to show an admissible reason for dismissal. Secondly, the industrial tribunal must be satisfied that the employer acted reasonably in relying upon that reason for dismissal.

10.20 Reasons

The permitted (or admissible) reasons are as follows:

(1) Capability or qualifications.
(2) Conduct.
(3) Redundancy (10.25).
(4) That the employee could not continue to work in the position which he held without contravention (either on his part or on that of his employer) of a duty or restriction imposed by or under an enactment.
(5) Some other substantial reason.

10.21 Reasonableness

The statutory test of reasonableness of the decision to dismiss (and to rely upon one of the above reasons) is as follows:

'. . . the determination of the question whether the dismissal was fair having regard to the reason shown by the employer shall depend on whether in the circumstances (including the size and administrative resources of the employer's undertaking) the employer acted reasonably in treating it as a sufficient reason for dismissing the employee; and that question shall be determined in accordance with equity and the substantial merits of the case'.

10.22   Establishing reasonableness

The test of reasonableness (and therefore, fairness) is a question of fact in each case. The industrial tribunal itself is the judge of what is fair and reasonable in all the circumstances and therefore the judge of what is good industrial relations practice.

To assist it in its determination of this question there are: 'A Code of Practice on Disciplinary Practice and Procedures in Employment' (1977) issued by ACAS and guidelines from time to time issued by the Employment Appeal Tribunal and the Court of Appeal.

(1)   *The Code of Practice* was issued under the Employment Protection Act 1975 (EPA) and is admissible in evidence before an industrial tribunal. It has to be taken into account if relevant; but it is only *one* factor that has to be taken into account. It is however quite useful, stressing as it does, the need for fair implementation of disciplinary procedures. ACAS have recently issued an Advisory Handbook called *'Discipline at Work'* (1987) which, although not issued under the EPA, and which does not have the status of a Code of Practice, is intended to bring the Code of Practice up to date, and may well be influential.

(2)   *Guidelines* issued by the Employment Appeal Tribunal and the Court of Appeal are of use but they must not be treated as rigid precedents and an industrial tribunal would go wrong in law if it slavishly followed guidelines in a particular situation without regard to the facts of each case. Recently the Employment Appeal Tribunal and the Court of Appeal have deprecated the use of guidelines even though many industrial relations specialists agree that guidelines are useful both for those implementing dismissals and those advising the parties as to the merits of particular cases. Many industrial relations pamphlets and periodicals report extracts from cases which can help those implementing dismissals.

Generally, factors related to reasonableness include warnings, consultation and fair investigation before dismissal, clear disciplinary procedures and contractual rules (10.14), observation of mitigating circumstances, length of service and consistency. Very recently the House of Lords in *Polkey v A E Dayton Services Ltd* (1987) has reaffirmed the importance of procedures before dismissal in unfair dismissal cases.

Dismissal for trade union membership or activities is automatically unfair. Dismissal for refusing to become a member of a trade union in a closed shop context will often be automatically unfair, including where the closed shop agreement concerned has not satisfied certain ballot requirements and where the employee has a deeply held personal conviction against union membership, and in other cases also. The Employment Bill currently before Parliament at the time of writing would make virtually all dismissals for refusal to become a trade union member in a closed shop situation automatically unfair.

Dismissal for redundancy where the selection for redundancy either

(1) is for trade union reasons or
(2) breaches a customary or agreed procedure without special reasons for departure from it

will also be automatically unfair.

It is important to note that all trade union membership related dismissals carry additional awards of compensation over and above the ordinary levels (10.24). There is also protection in the EP(C)A to prevent action short of dismissal against an employee on trade union related grounds. An employee dismissed on trade union grounds may also be entitled to interim relief (an order continuing the contract) before his case gets to a tribunal and the final remedy (10.24) is awarded.

There are provisions which state that a dismissal during a strike, lock out or other industrial action cannot be heard by a tribunal, unless there is a discriminatory dismissal or discriminatory non-re-engagement of strikers. Dismissal for pregnancy is not a permitted reason and so will be automatically unfair, unless the employee

(1) is at the date of termination incapable because of her pregnancy of adequately doing her work or
(2) is because of her pregnancy, unable to do her work without contravention (either by her or her employer) of a duty or restriction imposed by some enactment

and in either case there is no suitable alternative vacancy to offer her.

An employee is entitled to ask for a written statement of reasons for dismissal as long as he has been employed for six months or more. In the event of an unreasonable refusal by an employer (or if reasons supplied are inadequate or untrue) an industrial tribunal can award up to two weeks' pay by way of compensation.

10.23   Remedies for unfair dismissal

Complaint is to an industrial tribunal and the remedies available are:

(1)   Reinstatement.
(2)   Re-engagement.
(3)   Compensation comprising

   (a)   a basic award
   (b)   a compensatory award

(4)   If reinstatement or re-engagement are awarded but those orders are not complied with then there may be additional awards.
(5)   Special awards may apply in the case of dismissals for trade union membership or activities or for non membership of a trade union in a closed shop context where statute provides for additional compensation (10.24(2)).

Compensation is the remedy commonly granted although the tribunal has a duty first of all to consider reinstatement/re-engagement.

10.24   Compensation levels

(1)   *Ordinary cases*
   The maximum basic award is £4,740 (£4,920 from 1 April 1988). The maximum compensatory award is £8,500. The additional award for failure to reinstate/re-engage will vary from £2,054 to £4,180 (£2,132 to £4,264 from April 1988) (ie 13–26 weeks' pay) or, in discrimination cases, £4,180 to £8,216 (£4,264–£8,528 from 1 April 1988) (ie 26–52 weeks pay).
(2)   *Other cases*
   In the case of union membership and activity (including closed shop) related dismissals the *minimum* basic award is £2,300 (£2,400 from 1 April 1988) and the *maximum* award is £4,740 (£4,920 from 1 April 1988). The *compensatory* award is the same as for ordinary cases, ie maximum £8,500. There is also a special award in these cases and the minimum and maximum for a special award which is available where there is no order for reinstatement or re-engagement are £11,500 and £23,000 (£11,950 and £23,850 from 1 April 1988) respectively.

   The minimum for the special award where there has been an order for reinstatement or re-engagement which has not been complied with is £17,250 (£17,900 from 1 April 1988) but *there is no maximum in this case* as the award is 156 weeks' pay without limit as to the amount of a week's pay (normally £158 (£164 from 1 April 1988)) to be taken into account.

Awards may be reduced on ground of employee conduct or contributory fault, or, in the case of a compensatory award, on account of the principles relating to mitigation of loss (12.26).

10.25 Redundancy

An individual dismissed by reason of redundancy is entitled to a redundancy payment under the EP(C)A. There are qualifying conditions just as in the case of unfair dismissal (10.17), viz:

(1) The employee must have worked for at least two years.
(2) A redundancy payment is not applicable in the case of a man aged over 65 or a woman aged over 60 (and the amount of a redundancy payment diminishes in any event for a man between 64 and 65 and for a woman between 59 and 60 the closer the individual gets to retirement — although this provision, which discriminates against women and which is out of line with retirement ages and unfair dismissal (10.17), may shortly change (Department of Employment Consultative Document, October 1987). Years of work below the age of 18 do not count.
(3) There must have been a dismissal. The cases are the same as with unfair dismissal (10.18).
(4) The dismissal must fall within the definition of redundancy in the EP(C)A which is as follows:

'an employee who is dismissed shall be taken to be dismissed by reason of redundancy if the dismissal is attributable wholly or mainly to

(a) the fact that his employer has ceased, or intends to cease to carry on the business for the purposes of which the employee was employed by him or has ceased or intends to cease to carry on that business in the place where the employee was so employed, or

(b) the fact that the requirements of that business for employees to carry out work of a particular kind or for employees to carry out work of a particular kind in the place where he was so employed, have ceased or diminished or are expected to cease or diminish'.

A redundancy payment is based on variables including length of service, age and the amount of a week's pay (currently fixed at a maximum of £158 (£164 from 1 April 1988)). The employee is given 1½ weeks' pay for each year of employment when he was at the age of 41 and above, one week's pay for every year of employment when the employee was aged between 22 and 40 and ½ a week's pay for every year of employment when the employee was aged less than 22. The current maximum redundancy payment possible under the statutory scheme is £4,740 (£4,920 from 1 April 1988) (20 + $1\frac{1}{2}$ × £158 (£164). A redundancy payment must be claimed within six months of termination and recovery of the payment, if refused, is from the industrial tribunal. There is a limited discretion for an industrial tribunal to hear late claims.

The right to a redundancy payment may be lost if the employer makes an offer of suitable alternative employment whether in writing or not before the ending of the old employment and this is unreasonably refused by the employee. If the offer of alternative employment is accepted the dismissal by reason of redundancy is deemed not to have taken place, and if the offer is taken up within four weeks of the ending of the old employment, employment is deemed to be continuous.

There is a four week trial period for an employee to try out the new terms and conditions if they differ from the old, and unless the decision to reject the new terms is unreasonable the employee may within the trial period reject the new terms and conditions, even after trying them out, if they are unsuitable. (See EP(C)A, s 84). The right to reject (and therefore the right to the redundancy payment) is lost if the employee stays on after the end of the trial period.

An employee laid off or on short time (10.10) may be entitled to a redundancy payment after a number of weeks of lay off or short time have elapsed. But the conditions are complicated.

Finally, under EP(C)A, s 142, where there is a fixed term contract of two years or more duration the parties may agree in writing to waive the right to a redundancy payment that might otherwise be payable on non renewal after expiry of the contract.

An employer is entitled to a redundancy rebate on any proper (ie paid under the statutory rules) statutory redundancy payment (currently 35% of the amount of the statutory redundancy payment). But the rebate is now confined to employers with less than 10 employees.

Redundancy dismissals also give rise to the right to claim unfair dismissal (10.17). Although redundancy is a permitted reason for dismissal, proper procedures must be followed, such as notification, consultation, fair selection and consideration of possible alternative employment. Otherwise a redundancy dismissal might be unfair and attract unfair dismissal compensation (10.20).

Additionally, in multiple redundancies, the provisions of EPA, s 99 must be observed. Under that provision a recognised trade union must be consulted about the redundancies. If 100 or more employees at one establishment within 90 days or less are proposed to be made redundant, the period of consultation is at least 90 days before the first of those dismissals takes effect. If 10 or more employees are proposed to be dismissed within 30 days or less the period of consultation is at least 30 days. In other cases, consultation has to begin at the earliest opportunity.

An employer has to disclose in writing

(1) the reasons for his proposals
(2) the numbers and descriptions whom it is proposed to dismiss as redundant
(3) the total number of employees of any such description employed by the employer at the establishment in question
(4) the proposed method of selecting the employees who may be dismissed and
(5) the proposed method of carrying out the dismissals, with due regard to any agreed procedure, including the period over which the dismissals are to take effect.

The employer has to consider a trade union's representations and reply to them, stating his reasons if he rejects them.

There is a defence to contravention of these obligations where there are special circumstances rendering it not reasonably practicable for the employer to comply; but this is very narrowly construed indeed and is rarely satisfied. Breach of these provisions leads to the possible award by an industrial tribunal of a protective award (a minimum number of days' remuneration) in favour of affected employees on complaint by a trade union.

There is a duty under EPA, s 100 to notify the Department of Employment of multiple redundancies by notice similar to that under s 99.

Failure to comply with the provisions of EPA, s 99 does not of itself make an individual dismissal for redundancy unfair, but failure to consult with an employee's trade union *may* be relevant to that issue in some cases.

An employee under notice of dismissal for redundancy may be entitled to paid time off to look for other work.

10.26 Wrongful dismissal claims at common law

So far, we have discussed possible claims arising out of dismissal within the industrial tribunal system. In practice, this is likely to be the most common claim an employer will meet in the case of a dismissal which is contested by a former employee. But an employee may have a claim at *common law* in addition to unfair dismissal if he has been dismissed wrongfully, that is to say, summarily, ie without notice in circumstances where he would be entitled to notice.

The law thus operates two systems of dismissal compensation, unfair dismissal and wrongful dismissal. Unfair dismissal involves compensation for *unfair* dismissals under statute (10.17) irrespective of whether the employer complied with his notice obligations.

Wrongful dismissal allows compensation to the employee for the fact that his employment has not been ended in accordance with the contract. This, in practice, means that if he is dismissed without notice in circumstances which do not justify this, he will be entitled to compensation for loss of chance to earn wages during the notice period. In most employments, an employee's right to notice is fairly modest. Very often it follows the statutory minimum (10.36). So, in practice, suing an employer for unfair dismissal is the obvious choice for a former employee requiring compensation, as the compensatory award (maximum £8,500 (10.24)) will usually far exceed the value of a payment in lieu of statutory notice.

However, an employee who has a more generous entitlement to notice (such as a managing director with a two year notice entitlement earning £40,000 per annum) may find his *wrongful* dismissal compensation puts the unfair dismissal maximum compensatory award of £8,500 in the shade. And also employees who have not yet reached the qualifying period to present a claim for unfair dismissal may find a wrongful dismissal claim valuable.

Damages for wrongful dismissal can include compensation for loss wages *and* other fringe benefits such as loss of pension contributions, use of car etc that would have been enjoyed throughout the notice period had notice been given. An employee is under a duty to mitigate loss (and this also applies to unfair dismissal) and if he does so this may reduce his compensation claim.

Many contracts contain procedures that have to be followed before certain dismissals. If these are broken an additional claim for damages may apply.

A claim for damages for wrongful dismissal would ordinarily be brought in the county court if less than £5,000 or in the High Court if greater.

In unfair dismissal, reinstatement and re-engagement are possible. In wrongful dismissal cases, the courts generally do not order specific performance (ie an order to the employer to continue employing the employee) of contracts for personal service, such as employment contracts, after dismissal. Nor will they, generally, grant injunctions to restrain breaches of contract which have the same effect as an order for specific performance. However, injunctions to restrain breaches of employment contracts and orders for specific performance are less uncommon than they were, especially where the employment is in a large (often public) undertaking. For an order for specific performance or an injunction having the same effect to be granted, the court must however be satisfied that mutual confidence between employer and employee still subsists. This will be absent in many cases.

10.27 Inter-relationship between wrongful and unfair dismissal summarised

(1) For a wrongful dismissal there has to be a dismissal in breach of contract. But a dismissal can be unfair even if the contract has been terminated with proper notice.
(2) Wrongful dismissal (usually) compensates an employee over the notice period (if notice has not been given) but not beyond. Unfair dismissal can compensate for loss generally (even if beyond the end of the notice period) but only up to a limit (presently) of £8,500.
(3) There is, in unfair dismissal, additionally, a basic award based on past service. This does not apply to a wrongful dismissal alone.
(4) Reinstatement and re-engagement are theoretically available in unfair dismissal cases as an alternative to wrongful dismissal. But specific performance of contracts in a wrongful dismissal case rarely happens.
(5) Unfair dismissal claims go to an industrial tribunal, wrongful dismissal claims to the county court or High Court.

10.28 Settling dismissal claims

A claim for compensation for unfair dismissal or for damages for wrongful dismissal can be settled 'out of court' and this commonly occurs. Sometimes the dispute between an employer and an employee is settled even before a tribunal claim or court action is instituted. Sometimes these settlements are referred to as 'ex gratia' payments, 'golden handshakes' or 'severance' payments. They have the same effect as settlements of actual or prospective court actions. A sum of money is usually paid in full and final settlement of the employee's claims. Both employers and employees often find settlements attractive for the purposes of avoiding costs, publicity, stress, anxiety and delay involved in court or tribunal proceedings.

All claims within the jurisdiction of an industrial tribunal including unfair dismissal cannot be validly settled unless the settlement is effected through the auspices of the Advisory Conciliation and

Arbitration Service (ACAS). Such a settlement is not binding unless the conciliation officer has 'taken action'. The reason for this is to ensure that individual unrepresented employees are made aware of their rights by an independent person when offered a sum of money by an employer and so as to ensure that they are not being given less than, in the circumstances, they deserve. The procedure is quite important as, if an employer pays a sum of money over to an employee in supposed settlement of his claim, if it is not done through ACAS, the employee can accept the money and still proceed to the industrial tribunal. In other words the settlement will not have been final.

There seems no reason why ACAS settlements, say, about unfair dismissal, cannot also deal with settlements of all other claims (not only other statutory claims but also claims for wrongful dismissal), and this commonly takes place.

ACAS are also available to advise and conciliate in employment cases generally.

Finally, a payment of compensation for loss of office as *director* must be approved by the general meeting of the company making the payment, under CA 1985 (chapter 5).

10.29   The taxation of ex gratia payments

These are treated to favourable taxation rules, particularly, at the time of writing, with regard to the first £25,000, which may be tax free and there is also relief thereafter. However, the key to this treatment is that the payment is a genuine termination payment. Making a payment or even making a contract to pay a sum during employment may prejudice this. You must therefore generally ensure the employment has ended before the deal is implemented. The rules are discussed in detail in chapter 9 (9.26).

The Chancellor's budget proposals of 15 March 1988 are (with effect from 6 April 1988) to increase the tax free threshold to £30,000 but to abolish all relief thereafter.

10.30   Other significant statutory rights in employment

In addition to the right to claim unfair dismissal and redundancy an employee is entitled, if he works under a contract of employment, to enjoy certain other significant rights. These are set out below.

10.31 Maternity rights

(1) *Maternity leave*
Under the EP(C)A, provided that an employee has accrued two years' service and provided also that she works up to and including the 11th week before the expected date of confinement she has a right to return to work after confinement.

She must also comply with various notification requirements, viz:

(a) informing her employer in writing at least 21 days before the beginning of her absence of her intention to take leave, to return and her expected week of confinement;
(b) if requested by the employer not earlier than 49 days after the expected date of confinement, notifying her intention to return in writing;
(c) notifying the employer in writing at least 21 days before the proposed date of return.

She has a right to return to her job or, if not reasonably practicable because of redundancy, a right to return to suitable alternative employment. Failure to permit her to return to work is deemed to be dismissal save in employment where there are less than five employees and it is not reasonably practicable to allow the employee to return.

(2) *Maternity pay*
An employee may qualify for statutory maternity pay (see 10.51).

(3) *Ante natal care*
An employee may be entitled to be paid time off for ante natal care.

10.32 Guarantee payments

An employee who is laid off by reason of lack of work may, under the EP(C)A, be entitled to a guaranteed payment for five workless days per quarter currently at the rate of £11.30 per day. Employees working under fixed term contracts of three months or less do not qualify.

10.33 Written statement of main terms and conditions

The employee is entitled to a written statement of main terms of conditions (10.13).

10.34 Itemised pay statements

An employee is, under the EP(C)A, entitled to an itemised pay statement or a standing statement of deductions. Complaint is to an industrial tribunal which may award an employee an amount up to the amount of unnotified deductions over 13 weeks prior to the application.

10.35   Time off for trade union and other reasons

An employee is entitled to time off for trade union activities without pay and time off for public duties without pay and, if an official of a recognised trade union, to time off with pay for trade union duties. The case law on the meaning of 'time off' in trade union cases in particular coupled with the fairly lengthy statutory provisions means that legal advice should be taken when a difficult point arises. There is also an ACAS Code of Practice (No 3) *'Time off for Trade Union Duties and Activities'* (1977) which is of use and which is admissible in tribunal proceedings.

A woman is entitled to time off for ante natal care (10.31) and safety representatives are also entitled to time off to do with their duties. An employee under notice of dismissal for redundancy may be entitled to time off to look for other work (10.25).

Complaint in all these cases is to an industrial tribunal.

10.36   Statutory minimum periods of notice

As discussed (10.10) every employee is entitled to not less than one week's notice for every year worked, subject to a maximum of 12. An employee is obliged to give at least one week's notice. These are minima, and may be improved by contract.

10.37   Payment of wages — Cash or cheque? The Wages Act 1986

Prior to the Wages Act 1986 employers could not pay wages otherwise than in coin of the realm unless the employee consented to it. Now, as from 1 January 1987 employees can be paid by cheque or credit transfer. The only pitfall might be that, whilst an employer might impose cashless pay upon new employees, an imposition of cashless pay on existing employees who already enjoyed payment by cash might be a breach of contract and this might result in a constructive dismissal and, possibly, unfair dismissal. Whether there was an unfair dismissal (10.17) would depend upon considerations such as consultation, facilities for encashment of cheques on site, and general issues of reasonableness (10.21).

10.38   Deductions from wages and the Wages Act 1986

Under the Wages Act 1986, deductions from pay may only be made if the deduction is made either by a statutory provision (for example, income tax or National Insurance), or by a provision of the worker's contract or if the worker has previously indicated his willingness in writing to it. There is no general control over whether those deductions have to be fair and reasonable (other than, perhaps the rule in contract law about penalties or unfair contract terms (chapter 12)). But a specific restriction is imposed in relation to retail workers in respect of whom a deduction from wages on any pay day cannot exceed one-tenth of the gross amount of wages due to the worker on that day. Also, any sum demanded of such worker by the employer on account of cash shortages or stock deficiencies is subject to a similar limit.

Complaints of breach of the Wages Act can be made to an industrial tribunal which can order repayment of deductions. The following points, however, should be noted (and these are not exhaustive):

(1) In relation to retail workers, although they are subject to the one tenth rule, the one tenth rule only applies to a deduction on a single pay day. If there is a deficiency equal to more than one tenth of a worker's weekly gross wages this may be spread over several pay days, subject only to the one tenth rule on each pay day.

(2) The provisions relating to retail workers do not apply to a final payment of wages or a payment in lieu of notice.

(3) The provisions of the Act do not apply in relation to over payment of wages and expenses.

(4) The Wages Act 1986 does not apply to deductions in relation to employee strike action.

(5) Deductions from expenses and certain other payments otherwise due to the employee are not covered.

Finally, an award of compensation under the EP(C)A for non supply of an itemised pay statement (10.34) is set off against any award by an industrial tribunal under the Wages Act 1986.

10.39 Sex and race discrimination in employment

Discrimination has been briefly discussed already in relation to recruitment (10.3). The principles are similar in relation to employment generally and the subject is given a fuller treatment under this section.

10.40 Discrimination in the employment field: Definition

Discrimination in the employment field is defined as discrimination in recruitment.

(1) in the arrangements an employer makes for the purposes of determining who should be offered employment, or

(2) in the terms on which an employer offers that employment, or
(3) by refusing or deliberately omitting to offer employment,

or in the case of persons employed

(4) in the terms of employment which an employer affords to a person, or
(5) in the way an employer affords a person access to opportunities for promotion, transfer or training or to any other benefits, facilities or services or by refusing or deliberately omitting to afford access to them, or
(6) by dismissing a person or subjecting a person to any detriment.

10.41 Direct and indirect discrimination

There are two types of discrimination, direct and indirect.

Direct discrimination means directly treating another person less favourably on grounds of sex, marital status or race.

Indirect discrimination means where you apply a requirement or condition which

(1) even though it applies equally to all persons is such that the proportion of people of one race or sex who can comply with it is considerably smaller than the proportion in another race or sex;
(2) you cannot show to be *justifiable* on non race/sex grounds;
(3) is to the detriment of the individual because he or she cannot comply with it.

10.42 Genuine occupational qualification

There is also a defence in cases of *direct* discrimination where the discrimination is as a result of a *genuine occupational qualification*. The list of what may amount to a genuine occupational qualification is longer in the case of sex discrimination than in the case of race discrimination, as one would expect. Space permits only a couple of examples. Thus, in the context of sex, this may be because of demands of a job in terms of decency or privacy, or, because, in an artistic performance, authenticity may require members of one sex only. In the context of race, again in an artistic or dramatic context or also in a place where food and drink are consumed, authenticity may require members of one race only (eg Chinese waiters in a Chinese restaurant).

10.43 Discrimination by other bodies

Similar obligations apply also to

(1) partnerships
(2) trade unions
(3) qualification bodies, eg professional associations
(4) vocational training bodies, eg an industrial training board and the Manpower Services Commission
(5) employment agencies.

10.44 Victimisation

It is also unlawful to treat someone unfavourably by way of victimisation which means victimisation against someone who brings proceedings, gives evidence or information, or alleges a contravention of, or otherwise acts under the Equal Pay Act 1970 (10.47), the Sex Discrimination Act 1975 and the Race Relations Act 1976 or intends to do any of those things.

10.45 Remedies

A complaint alleging race or sex discrimination in the employment field can be made to an industrial tribunal and the industrial tribunal can, if the complaint is well founded, make a declaration and a recommendation accordingly. It can also award compensation to an individual applicant which can include damages for injury to feelings. Compensation cannot exceed a limit (presently) of £8,500. In cases of indirect discrimination an industrial tribunal cannot award compensation unless the indirect discrimination was *intended*.

10.46 Formal investigations and the role of the CRE and EOC

The Commission for Racial Equality (CRE) and Equal Opportunities Commission (EOC) can also take action in the employment field or otherwise by way of formal investigations. If successful, investigations can result in the service of a non discrimination order on an employer. If this is not obeyed it can be enforced in the county court.

The CRE and EOC also exist to advise individuals about their rights and, in particular cases, both bodies can support individual claims against an employer. There is also a facility for individuals to prepare a race relations/sex discrimination questionnaire which can be served upon the employer in connection with an industrial tribunal complaint and if an employer declines to answer this questionnaire, or provides misleading answers, this can be taken into account in future industrial tribunal proceedings.

10.47   Equal pay

Under the Equal Pay Act 1970 a woman is entitled to be paid equal pay for like work or work of a broadly similar nature or work rated as equivalent and, since the Equal Pay Act 1970 was amended by the Equal Pay (Amendment) Regulations 1983, for work of equal value.

10.48   Equal pay for like work and equivalent work

The main provisions concern equal pay for like work or work rated as equivalent.

Work is 'like work' if it is of the same or a broadly similar nature but ignoring any differences between the things a woman does and the things a man does if they are not of practical importance in relation to terms and conditions of employment. You also have to have regard to the frequency with which any such differences occur *in practice* as well as to the nature and extent of the differences.

Work is rated as 'equivalent' with that of any man if, broadly speaking, the job has been rated as equivalent under a job evaluation scheme.

10.49   Equal value claims

As has been discussed, even if the comparison between a woman's job and a man's job does not fall within the two categories above, a woman may still be entitled to equal pay if her job (even though different) is regarded as of *equal value*.

10.50   Establishing an equal pay claim

The procedure for a woman who alleges she is entitled to equal pay is for her to allege that she is employed on like work or work rated as equivalent. If she succeeds at this stage, it is nonetheless open to an employer to justify the difference between the man's job and the woman's job on the ground that there is a '*genuine material difference*' between the man's job and the woman's job. A genuine material difference means a difference genuinely due to a material factor which is *not* the difference of *sex*.

Alternatively, a woman may succeed in showing that her job is of 'equal value' to the man she is comparing herself with. At this stage, too, it is open for the employer to allege there is a genuine material difference between the woman's case and the man's. This must again not be based on sex. This material difference in equal value cases in particular can, it is thought, more easily take into account outside circumstances such as market forces which may have meant for example that the employer had to pay more to a particular group of employees at a particular time because of difficulties in recruitment etc, irrespective of the merits of their cases when compared with similar employees already recruited.

If the tribunal has not decided there is no reasonable prospect of success in establishing an equal value claim, the equal value claim is then referred to an independent expert appointed by ACAS who then makes a report to the industrial tribunal. This report is admitted in evidence and can influence the industrial tribunal at the end of the day in deciding whether there is an appropriate equal value claim. Equal value claims can be extraordinarily lengthy and expensive.

If an equal pay/value claim is successful a woman is entitled to the insertion in her contract of an equality clause which entitles her thereafter to be paid at the same rate as the comparator she has chosen. She is also entitled to recover arrears of pay for up to two years at the new rate.

10.51 Statutory maternity pay

Statutory maternity pay was introduced by the Social Security Act 1986. An employer is responsible for administering it and may reclaim the sums he has to pay by deduction from sums he would ordinarily pay by way of employer's National Insurance contributions (chapter 9). A woman must be employed for 26 weeks before she can become eligible and is then entitled to payment at the rate of 90% of her earnings for six weeks and a flat rate for 12 weeks thereafter. Statutory maternity pay commences 11 weeks before the expected date of confinement.

10.52 Statutory sick pay

This was first introduced by the Social Security and Housing Benefits Act 1982. Statutory sick pay is a payment similar to statutory maternity pay which is administered by the employer and paid by him and which is recovered by him by deductions from the employer's National Insurance contributions that he would otherwise make (chapter 9). Subject to qualifying conditions, the payment is made for the first 28 weeks of illness after which state benefit is applicable and statutory sick pay ceases. There is no entitlement to statutory sick pay for various reasons: for example, for the first three days of absence and also, for example, certain individuals such as pensioners, employees on short term contracts of less than three months and those not employed by reason of a trade dispute in which they are interested, amongst other cases, do not qualify.

The qualifying days of statutory sick pay are normally fixed by the employer and the employee and normally relate to the paid days of employment (eg Monday to Friday). The rates are currently

Wages per week	SSP per week
0 — £40	nil
£41–£79.49	£34.25
£79.50 +	£49.20

An employer can require rules as to notification procedures. There are controls on what an employer can require in terms of medical evidence as a pre-requisite for claiming statutory sick pay (although he can operate separate conditions for qualification for contractual sick pay (10.10)).

An employee may be entitled by virtue of his contract to full pay under his contract (10.10) not just statutory sick pay (10.10). An employer would be advised to say in his contracts with employees that an employee is only entitled to such contractual sick pay as is necessary to top wages up to the normal level after payment of statutory sick pay or any state sickness benefit received thereafter.

10.53   Data protection

Under the Data Protection Act 1984 individuals who have personal details about them processed by another on computer recording equipment may have rights to request sight of this. And persons who use computer equipment for recording data have to register with the Data Protection Registrar. This will include employers who store details about their employees in this way (although processing of data relating to basic payroll and pension matters is exempted). If data is processed without registration, use by an employer of such data can be a criminal offence. And an employee's right to see such data as he is entitled under the Act is enforced by withdrawal by the Registrar of the employer's registration. This is an important new concept which all using computer equipment for recording personnel data will have to observe.

10.54   Contracting out of statutory rights

It is generally not possible to contract out of statutory rights such as under the EP(C)A, Sex Discrimination Act 1975, Race Relations Act 1976 or the rules about SSP, SMP and Data Protection. It is possible to contract out of the EP(C)A in limited circumstances, but EP(C)A, s 140 otherwise prevents this. Certain fixed term contracts may exclude unfair dismissal and redundancy rights on non renewal (10.18, 10.25). And we have seen that it is possible to settle EP(C)A claims and also race and sex and Wages Act claims by using ACAS (10.28).

10.55 Selling your business: The Transfer of Undertakings (Protection of Employment) Regulations 1981

This section deals with special employment problems that arise when businesses are being sold or purchased. Although legal advice is normally obtained at this juncture it is important that you should bear in mind that, when a business is bought or sold, the purchaser may well acquire existing employees together with all rights and obligations including continuous employment and potential liability for full redundancy payments and unfair dismissal compensation notwithstanding there has been a change of employer.

10.56 Buying and selling limited companies

If you acquire a firm by buying shares in a company the company you have bought continues as before. Although in reality there is a change of proprietor, in law there is no legal change in the employer. Therefore all employment rights are uninterrupted and continuous. So if you buy the shares in a company which has a workforce you automatically inherit all obligations and duties to that workforce including accrued continuous service for the purposes of unfair dismissal and redundancy and other statutory rights.

10.57 Buying and selling a business which is not a limited company

This does involve a legal change of employer. But there are special statutory provisions which protect employees. Either the provisions of the EP(C)A or the Transfer of Undertakings (Protection of Employment) Regulations 1981 may impose on the purchaser of a business certain liabilities in relation to the workforce including possibly all contractual rights and obligations and accrued statutory continuous employment. This is a fact which often goes unappreciated by purchasers of businesses who automatically assume that when they take on the workforce of a business they take that workforce with a clean break with continuity broken and who also assume that they can impose new terms and conditions on the workforce with impunity. But this may not be the case.

10.58 A business as a going concern

A transfer of a business under the Transfer Regulations or under the provisions of the EP(C)A relating to business transfers (though not all of the provisions of the EP(C)A on change of employer are confined to business transfers (10.60)) means a transfer of a business as a 'going concern'. This means that a transfer of assets only is not a transfer of a business. There needs to be more, such as goodwill, customers, trading name, work in progress, etc.

10.59 The Transfer of Undertakings (Protection of Employment) Regulations 1981

At common law a change of employer is a dismissal and contractual rights are interrupted. Under the Transfer Regulations contracts of employment are automatically transferred on business transfers. All rights and obligations therewith are transferred to the transferee including:

(1)   continuous employment
(2)   redundancy payments and unfair dismissal liability
(3)   liability for accrued wages and other benefits
(4)   contractual seniority rights;

but excluding

(a)   pension rights
(b)   liability for a criminal offence.

Further, a dismissal of an employee in connection with a business transfer (whether by a transferor or transferee) can be automatically unfair (10.17) unless the dismissal is by reason of an economic, technical or organisational reason entailing changes in the workforce. Thus a vendor of a business who dismisses at the request of the purchaser or a purchaser who dismisses after he has acquired the workforce thinking that he no longer needs them may be exposed to automatic unfair dismissal liability. It is true that in many cases such a dismissal will be for an economic, technical or organisational reason (eg redundancy) and the dismissal will not thereby be automatically unfair. But two pitfalls, at least, can arise

(1)   If a vendor is required by a purchaser to dismiss all of the workforce before the transfer the dismissal may be unfair on general principles because there may be insufficient consideration by the parties of whether it is really necessary to dismiss all those individuals (10.21).
(2)   If a purchaser unilaterally changes terms and conditions after the transfer has taken place, and thereby does not expressly, but instead, constructively, dismisses them (10.18) this may be an *automatic* unfair dismissal even if for an economic or technical or organisational reason because the dismissal will not entail a *change* in the *workforce*, but simply a change in the *terms and conditions* that the workforce are obliged to observe. There *could*

therefore under those circumstances be automatic unfair dismissal liability.

Recognition of trade unions and collective agreements are also transferred and there are information and consultation provisions in favour of trade unions that have to be observed long enough before a transfer for consultation to take place. Failure to comply with the information and consultation provisions with trade unions can lead to liability for a protective award of up to two weeks' pay. These are similar to, but less extensive than, the consultation and information obligations that employers have to observe on multiple redundancies (10.25).

10.60 Statutory continuity and transfers

Continuity of employment is preserved on a business transfer both by the Transfer Regulations and by the EP(C)A, and also, even where there is no transfer of a 'business' under the EP(C)A, for example where there is a transfer of individuals within a local authority to and from local authority schools, where there is a change of employer by Act of Parliament, where there is a change in the composition of personal representatives or of partners, and where there is a transfer between associated companies.

10.61 Getting advice on business transfers

The Transfer Regulations and the provisions about continuity are highly complex and legal advice should be sought the moment you are considering buying or selling a business with a workforce. Lawyers will usually be able to draft indemnity clauses that might be appropriate for the parties themselves to apportion liability in these cases by agreement.

11   Life assurance, pensions, and permanent health insurance

by Vince Jerrard, Allied Dunbar Assurance plc

11.1   Introduction

Although the fine print can appear daunting, life assurance, pension and permanent health insurance policies are really just evidence of a contract between the policyholder and the company issuing the policy. In exchange for payment of a contribution or premium, the company promises to make one or more specified payments in certain defined circumstances.

Depending on the type of contract entered into, the payment from the company may be, for example, a lump sum on the death of an individual, an income in retirement for a pensioner or a replacement income for a person prevented from earning by reason of disability

Despite the technical appearance of many of these policies (which is often due to complex tax rules offering relief on payment of premiums or benefits), it is useful to bear in mind the essential simplicity of the idea: payment of premiums (usually regular payments) to the company in exchange for the guarantee or expectation of payments back on the happening of some event in the future.

With life assurance contracts, there is one particular requirement which must be met before a policy can be effected. This is the need for an 'insurable interest'. Broadly, before a person can effect a life policy he must be able to demonstrate that the death of the person whose life is being insured will cause him financial loss. In addition the amount of the assurance must not exceed the amount of that loss.

Individuals have an automatic and unlimited insurable interest in their own life and the life of their spouse. In other cases an insurable interest must be demonstrated before a person can effect a policy on someone else's life (a 'life of another' policy).

This chapter, in Part One, looks at the contracts themselves and gives an outline of the rules which apply to them. Part Two then goes on to consider some basic uses of the contracts with reference to sole traders, partners and small companies.

Part one — The basics

Life Assurance:

11.2   Types of policy

There are three basic types of life assurance policy:

(1)   whole of life policies;
(2)   endowment policies;
(3)   term policies.

Whole of life policies are protection-orientated policies which will pay the guaranteed sum assured on the death of the life assured, whenever death occurs.

As such, they are most appropriate where long term protection is needed, for example to meet the inheritance tax liability on an individual's death or to protect the family from the consequences of the death of the 'breadwinner'. Whole of life policies may, over the years, also acquire significant cash values, although they are not primarily investment vehicles.

Endowment policies pay a guaranteed sum on the death of the life assured during the policy term, or on survival to the end of the term.

Such policies provide a valuable mixture of protection and investment and are often used in conjunction with a mortgage to provide for a lump sum which will pay off the loan at the end of the mortgage term, or on the borrower's prior death.

Term assurance policies pay a guaranteed sum assured only if death occurs before the end of the term. They are for protection purposes only and usually provide no return to the policyholder if the life assured survives the policy term. Term assurance policies are usually the cheapest form of life assurance protection.

The cover provided by term assurances can be widened by use of renewal or conversion options. A renewal option will allow the policyholder to renew the policy at the end of the original term, without further evidence of health being required. A conversion option will allow a policyholder to turn his protection into a whole of life assurance or an endowment policy, should his needs change. A convertible term assurance is particularly useful if the need is for life assurance protection for the whole of the individual's life but it is not possible to afford a whole of life policy at the time.

Term assurance policies can also be effected under some pensions legislation (see 11.11). These policies have the advantage of tax relief on the premiums paid.

11.3   Traditional and unit linked policies

There are two bases on which policies are offered.

Under a traditional policy the life assurance company will estimate future mortality experience, investment return and company expenses. Using these factors the actuary will determine the premium rate for a given sum assured, both of which will then be guaranteed by the company. As the assumptions made by the company would, of necessity, be conservative, the premiums may often be higher than necessary. To counter this, traditional companies developed 'with profits' policies so that those contracts could share in the extra profits being made by the life company.

Extra profits are allocated to the policy by means of bonuses, either during the term of the policy (reversionary bonuses) or on the maturity of the policy (terminal bonuses). Once a bonus has been allocated it cannot be taken away, although the level of future bonuses is not guaranteed.

Unit linked policies are a more recent innovation introduced to the UK in the 1960s. They offer fewer guarantees to the policyholder. Premiums are invested in pooled investment funds maintained by the life company and the performance of the policy is linked directly to the actual performance of the fund. Freed from having to set up the policy with long term investment guarantees, the company can adopt an investment policy which is not unduly conservative and so can provide a fairer level of cover from the outset.

The direct linking of the policy and the investment performance of the underlying fund also mean that the policyholder is not subject to the discretion of the company in deciding the level of bonuses it should declare.

As unit linked policies do not carry the same guarantees as traditional contracts they will usually incorporate the system of reviews by which the company can ensure that the policy stays 'on track'. A review will compare the original assumptions about mortality, expenses and investment return with the actual performance achieved. Unfavourable performance will usually lead to an increase in premium and favourable performance to an increase in benefits.

11.4 Qualifying and non-qualifying policies

The other main method of categorising life assurance contracts is according to whether they are 'qualifying' or 'non-qualifying'.

This categorisation arises solely for the purpose of the taxation of the policy proceeds.

The qualifying rules are detailed and complex but, very broadly speaking, a qualifying policy will be a regular premium policy where the premiums remain fairly level and the sum assured satisfies certain minimum requirements to ensure that it provides a realistic level of life cover protection.

11.5 The advantages of qualifying policies

Premiums paid under qualifying policies issued before 14 March 1984 attracted Life Assurance Premium Relief (LAPR). Qualifying policies issued before that date continue to benefit from LAPR provided that neither the benefits secured are increased nor the term extended after that date.

Subject to meeting the conditions for LAPR, relief was given at approximately half of the basic rate of income tax in force at the time, on up to the greater of $\frac{1}{6}$th of the policyholder's income or £1,500 pa. Where LAPR is still available, it applies at the rate of 15% for the tax year 1988/89 but will reduce to 12½% for the year 1989/90.

The other key advantage of qualifying policies concerns the taxation of policy proceeds. In general, the proceeds from a qualifying policy will be entirely free of tax, provided premiums are kept up for at least 10 years (or three-quarters of the term of an endowment policy, if less).

11.6 Tax treatment of policies

While a policy is in force all the tax on income and gains attributable to the policy is the responsibility of the life company which pays tax on them according to its own corporate taxation position.

The Budget on 15 March 1988 contained proposals for a radical restructuring of capital gains tax (CGT) for individuals. The 'rebasing' of the tax to 31 March 1982 also applies to companies, whose gains continue to be taxed at the appropriate corporation tax rate. However, the special corporation tax rate of 30% which applies to life assurance companies' gains on policyholders' funds remains pending the expected review of life assurance company taxation.

As far as the policyholder is concerned, in most cases life assurance policies, qualifying or not, will be free of any personal liability to CGT. Only if the policy is in the hands of someone other than the original owner who gave consideration for it (ie who bought it or gave something of value for it) will proceeds be liable to CGT.

The taxation of the individual in connection with income tax and life assurance policies revolves around the concept of the 'chargeable event'.

For non-qualifying policies the five chargeable events are:

(1) death of the life assured;
(2) the maturity of the policy;
(3) the total surrender of the policy;
(4) the assignment of the policy for money or money's worth (eg if the policy is sold or exchanged for something of value);
(5) excesses. (The system of 'excesses' allows partial surrenders each year of up to 5% of the premiums paid, on a cumulative basis, up to a total of 100% of the premiums paid. Only if the cumulative 5% 'allowances' are exceeded does a chargeable event occur.)

Chargeable events in the case of qualifying policies are the same as those listed above but with the following amendments:

(1) death or maturity will be a chargeable event only if the policy has previously been paid-up within the first 10 years (or three-quarters of the term of an endowment policy, if less);
(2) a surrender an assignment for money or money's worth or an excess will be a chargeable event only if it occurs before the expiry of 10 years (or three-quarters of the term of an endowment policy, if less) or if the policy was made paid-up within that period.

Assignments between spouses or as security for debts are not chargeable events.

11.7 Gain on the happening of a chargeable event

Where a chargeable event occurs the gain arising on the event must be computed. The calculation depends on the nature of the event but, broadly speaking, it is the investment profit made under the policy, taking into account previous capital benefits enjoyed and the total premiums paid.

Any extra amount received by way of death benefit is mortality profit and would not be included in the gain for tax purposes.

The rules for calculating the gain as a result of an excess following a withdrawal or partial surrender are somewhat different and take into account the 5% allowable withdrawals.

11.8   Taxing gains and chargeable events

The circumstances under which tax is liable on a gain are as follows:

(1)   Gains made on life policies do not give rise to a tax liability at the basic rate of income tax. Accordingly, if the taxpayer's income, including the gain, does not fall into the higher rate tax band there will be no income tax charge on the gain.

(2)   The gain made on the life policy is liable to the higher rate of income tax, where applicable.

(3)   As the gain will have accrued over the life of the policy, it would be rather harsh to treat the total gain as the taxpayer's income in the year of receipt. This could push him into the higher rate tax band in that year despite a relatively low income level. Therefore, a measure of relief is afforded by a process known as 'top-slicing'. This involves calculating the rate of tax appropriate to a part of the total gain (a 'slice') and then applying that rate of tax to the whole of the gain.

(4)   The taxpayer is usually the policyholder. Exceptions to this are that if the policy is held on trust the charge falls upon the settlor (ie the person who established the trust); if the policy is owned by a close company, the amount of the gain is treated as part of the company's distributable income (and top-slicing relief does not apply).

Further details of the qualifying rules and taxation of life policies can be found in the *Allied Dunbar Tax Guide*.

Pensions

11.9   Introduction

Pensions are usually regarded as one of the most attractive investments available. Within limits, contributions are deductible at the highest rate of tax paid by the contributor; the underlying pension funds grow free of UK taxes on income and gains; and in most the pension plan can provide a tax-free cash lump sum to the planholder together with a retirement income in 'old age'.

At the time of writing, the pensions legislation in the UK is undergoing substantial reform and development. The Social Security Act 1986 created the framework for the new 'Personal Pensions' and 'Free-Standing Additional Voluntary Contribution Schemes'; reduced the benefits provided by the State Earnings Related Pensions Scheme (SERPS); increased the scope for individuals to contract out of SERPS; and removed the ability of Occupational Pension Schemes to require compulsory membership for employees.

The legislation also allows, for the first time, banks, building societies and unit trust groups to offer pension plans.

The Finance (No 2) Act 1987 provided much of the necessary tax legislation to support these developments.

The changes come into force over the period between October 1987 and July 1988.

11.10   The State pension scheme

The benefit the State provides to those in retirement falls into two main parts: the basic retirement pension and the supplementary earnings related pension.

Everyone is entitled to the basic retirement pension (payable at state retirement age; 65 for males, 60 for females), subject to payment of the necessary National Insurance contributions. For a married man whose earnings have been at the national average level throughout his working life, the State will provide a basic pension of approximately one-third of his final earnings level.

Note that recent European case law, in requiring the UK to extend unfair dismissal and sex discrimination rights to women up to the age of 65, has not affected state retirement ages or pension entitlement.

SERPS was introduced in April 1978 to provide an additional state pension which is based on earnings (within certain limits) rather than the flat benefit provided by the retirement pension. SERPS also provides a widow's benefit if a husband dies after retirement and also, in certain circumstances, if he dies before retirement.

SERPS is funded by the higher rate National Insurance contributions payable by both employers and employees. The self-employed do not contribute towards, or benefit from, SERPS.

In recent years the State pension scheme has come under pressure from increases in life expectancy and large numbers of retired people in the population. These concerns have led the Government to reduce the benefits under SERPS so that only those reaching state pension age (65 for males, 60 for females) in the years 1998 and 1999 will receive the original maximum benefits.

Those reaching state retirement age in or after the year 2010 will receive a pension of only 20% of their relevant earnings, instead of the 25% originally intended, and the relevant earnings to be taken into account will be the average of lifetime earnings and not the best 20 years of earnings, as was the original rule for SERPS.

A sliding scale will operate for those retiring between the years 2000 and 2010.

11.11   Contracting-in and contracting-out

Those who are participating in SERPS (ie employees earning more than the lower threshold for standard rate National Insurance contributions) are said to be 'contracted in' to SERPS. Since SERPS was introduced it has been possible to opt out of the scheme (referred to as 'contracting-out') in which case National Insurance contributions are reduced for both the employer and employee but with the loss of SERPS benefits.

The original rules only permitted contracting-out through an Occupational Pension Scheme established by an employer, and only where that scheme provided certain guaranteed pension benefits which were broadly equivalent to the SERPS entitlement the employee was giving up.

The new legislation makes significant changes to these rules to encourage contracting-out. In particular:

(1)   contracting-out can be achieved on a 'money purchase' basis so that contributions can be accumulated in a fund and used to buy pension benefits at retirement, without guaranteeing a minimum level for those benefits;
(2)   individuals will be able to take their own decision on whether or not to contract out of SERPS, quite independently of the status of their employer's scheme, or in the total absence of such a scheme;
(3)   an additional 2% (of earnings between the lower and upper National Insurance contribution limits) incentive payment is made by the DHSS where an individual contracts out for the first time (or where he has been in a contracted out scheme for less than two years). The incentive may be paid for up to six years, commencing in tax year 1987/88.

Contracting-out will be possible, once all the legislation and rules are in place, through an Occupational Scheme (as before) or through a Free-Standing Additional Voluntary Contribution Scheme (FSAVC) used by an employee in conjunction with an Occupational Scheme, or a

Personal Pension Plan (PPP) used by an employee not in an Occupational Scheme.

With FSAVC Schemes and PPPs the individual and the employer will continue to make full National Insurance (NI) contributions, the NI reduction being paid by the DHSS direct to the relevant pension plan. Contracting-out through an Occupational Scheme will mean lower National Insurance contributions for employer and employee but the employer is required to make payment of the NI reduction to the Occupational Scheme.

If the individual is contracting-out on a money-purchase basis these NI reductions, plus the 2% incentive where appropriate, are known as 'protected rights contributions' and the fund built up from them must be used to purchase protected rights benefits. It is these benefits which, in effect, replace the SERPS being lost through contracting-out and they are treated more restrictively than benefits built up through the employer's or employee's additional contributions. For example, a protected rights pension cannot commence before state retirement age and cannot be commuted for cash.

Whether contracting-out of SERPS is advisable is a decision to be taken by each employee according to his or her personal circumstances. In general those with more than 15 years to state retirement age (65 for males, 60 for females) should consider contracting-out.

11.12   Occupational pension schemes

These are schemes sponsored by an employer and to which the employer must make a contribution.

Schemes are established on one of two bases: either money-purchase or final salary (often called Defined Benefit Schemes).

With Defined Benefit Schemes the employee is guaranteed a level of pension benefit based on a fraction (typically 1/60th or 1/80th) of his final salary, multiplied by the number of years' pensionable service. A money-purchase scheme will not carry a guarantee of a specific level of pension but will invest the contributions and use the accumulated fund to provide whatever pension can be purchased with the fund, at retirement.

To be tax efficient an Occupational Pension Scheme should be approved by the Superannuation Funds Office (SFO) which is a branch of the Inland Revenue.

'Approval' will prevent contributions paid by the employer being taxed in the employee's hands but the preferable status of 'exempt approval' offers significant further benefits. An exempt approved scheme will be able to invest in a fund free of all UK income and capital taxes; the employee will be able to claim tax relief on contributions he makes to the scheme; and employers' contributions will be deductible business expenses.

To be exempt approved, the scheme must be set up under irrevocable trust for the sole purpose of providing 'relevant benefits'. These are benefits such as an income in retirement, the option to commute part of that income for a lump sum, an income for the employee's widow etc. As a result of the generous tax benefits available to such schemes, there are strict limits on the benefits which may be provided. The limits were further tightened by the Finance (No 2) Act 1987. The application of the new limits is complex, but, in general, they apply to post 17 March 1987 scheme members. For example, the maximum pension which can be provided to the scheme member is usually two-thirds of final remuneration and the minimum period of service required to achieve this level of benefits is now 20 years (previously the maximum benefits could be given after only 10 years' service).

An employee's pension can be commuted for a lump sum, also based on final salary and years of service. The maximum lump sum is one and a half times final salary but is limited to £150,000. The maximum final salary that can be taken into account in the calculation is £100,000. Prior to the Finance (No 2) Act 1987, the only limit was that of one and a half times' final salary.

There are no specific limits on the amount of contributions which can be paid into an Occupational Scheme but monitoring is necessary to ensure that the scheme does not become 'over-funded', ie contributions may have to be limited if projected funds in the scheme are likely to exceed the amount necessary to meet its obligations.

Employees may make personal contributions (of up to 15% of remuneration) to the scheme. This may be done on a voluntary basis (by way of Additional Voluntary Contributions) but the scheme may require some personal contribution from the employee as a condition of membership.

The scheme may also provide a lump sum of up to four times final remuneration on the death, in service, of the employee. This can be paid together with a refund of any personal contributions paid by the employer. It is usually possible to pay the death benefits free of inheritance tax.

It is possible to contract out of SERPS through an Occupational Scheme but the availability of contracting-out is largely in the hands of the employer.

The new FSAVC Schemes (see 11.13 below) can be used by an Occupational Scheme member to contract out on an individual basis, from 1 July 1988. The Finance Bill 1988 also contains a provision to allow a contracted in occupational scheme member to contract out through a Personal Pension Plan, providing no contributions other than the NI rebates, appropriate tax relief and incentive payments are paid to the Plan. This is a change to the original proposals which would not have permitted an occupational scheme member to effect a PPP at all.

11.13 Personal pensions

The period between October 1987 and July 1988 has been one of considerable growth in the number of pension plans available to individuals. Prior to October 1987 the main personal plan was the Retirement Annuity Contract (also called Section 226 Plans, a reference to the legislation giving them tax effect). By July 1988 they will be replaced by Personal Pension Plans and will have been joined by FSAVC Schemes.

The wider scope of the PPPs and the ability of individual employees to contract out of SERPS (back dated, in many cases, to 6 April 1987) means that the individual has never before had such a wide choice of pension planning opportunities.

(1) *Retirement annuity contracts*

It will not be possible to effect a Retirement Annuity Contract after 30 June 1988 but plans in force by that date will be allowed to continue.

An individual is eligible for one of these plans if he has Relevant Earnings. These are earnings which do not carry pension rights, eg the earnings of sole traders, the self-employed, partners and employees in non-pensionable employment. Controlling directors of investment companies are excluded from eligibility.

Unlike Occupational Schemes, these 'Section 226' contracts are not controlled by reference to the maximum benefits which can be provided; rather, restrictions are applied to the amount of contributions which can be made. The contribution limit is $17\frac{1}{2}\%$ of net relevant earnings, with larger percentages applicable for those over 50. Net relevant earnings (NRE) are, broadly speaking, an individual's earnings after deduction of any business expenses. Contributions made to these plans up to the limits are fully tax-deductible and the funds in which the plans invest are free of all UK income and capital taxes.

The plans are issued on a money-purchase basis, the fund accumulated at retirement being used to provide a lifetime annuity for the planholder. The planholder need not actually retire in order to take the benefits from these plans but the benefits must be paid between the ages of 60 and 75 (earlier for some specified occupations).

The annuity paid can be in various different forms, guaranteed or not, flat rate or increasing etc. If the planholder dies before taking his annuity a lump sum can be paid, not exceeding the contributions made to the plan plus a reasonable amount of interest or bonuses. Alternatively, an annuity can be paid to the individual's widow or dependants.

Annuities can also be effected on a 'joint life basis' for the planholder and spouse, so that the annuity payments will continue until the death of the surviving spouse.

The annuity is treated as earned income when it is paid, and the planholder can elect to commute part of his annuity at retirement. This commutation permits a maximum lump sum of three times the remaining annual annuity, but limited to a £150,000 lump sum per contract.

In addition to pension benefits, such plans can provide life assurance protection. The maximum contribution which can be used to provide life cover is 5% of NRE (and any such contribution is taken into account in determining the overall contribution limit applicable to the individual).

Death benefits payable under such plans can be assigned or put in trust so that payments of benefits on death can be arranged in a way effective for inheritance tax planning.

If, in any year, an individual pays less in contributions to a plan than would be permitted, it is possible to carry forward the shortfall in contributions for up to six years. It is also possible to 'carry back' a contribution to the previous tax year (and sometimes the year before that).

(2) *Personal pension plans*

These plans are to be introduced on 1 July 1988, having been postponed from the original introduction date of 4 January 1988.

In many ways PPPs are more flexible than the Section 226 contracts which they replace. For example, employers may make contributions to an employee's PPP; an 'appropriate' PPP can be used by employees to contract out of SERPS; benefits can be taken between the ages of 50 and 75 (again, earlier for some specified occupations). Employees' contributions to PPPs are payable net of basic rate income tax under the Pension Relief at Source (PRAS) rules.

PPPs are, like Section 226 contracts, money-purchase arrangements with controls on the maximum contributions which can be made. The limits on contributions are the same as those for Section 226 contracts but, where an employer contributes to an employee's PPP, the employer's contributions must be taken into account in determining the employee's maximum permissible contributions.

The benefits provided by a PPP are, again, very similar to those available under a Section 226 plan but the tax-free cash which can be taken is a maximum of 25% of the fund, up to an overall limit of £150,000 per arrangement (ie contract) under the scheme.

FSAVC Schemes are also 'personal' pensions in that they can be effected without the consent and participation of the employer (although the employer may have to sign a certificate to confirm the employee's eligibility for membership). In spite of this, they also have similarities to Occupational Schemes in that they share the same source of tax legislation and the benefits from any FSAVC Scheme must be taken into account in determining the benefits payable under the Occupational Scheme, the maximum benefit rules applying to the aggregate benefits under the two schemes.

11.14 Moving between different types of pension arrangement

If a self-employed individual effects a PPP but then moves into employment, for example a sole trader incorporating his business, he can continue with his PPP. The same will be true with an employee who has a PPP and moves into self-employment.

In some cases, however, it is not possible to continue with the same pension plan, for example an employee who is a member of an Occupational Scheme cannot remain in that scheme if he becomes self-employed. Similarly, if a person with a PPP joins an employer's Occupational Scheme he cannot continue to pay contributions into the PPP if he has no continuing source of relevant earnings.

In those cases where a change of status affects pension planning it is usually possible for a transfer payment to be made from one scheme to another. Many companies offer such transfers on preferential terms, particularly where the individual is moving between the occupational and personal pension regimes.

Further details of pension plans and planning can be found in the *Allied Dunbar Pension Guide*.

Permanent Health Insurance:

11.15   Introduction

Permanent Health Insurance (PHI) policies are a means of providing a replacement income if an individual is unable to work through illness or disability.

Policies will usually be available to those aged between 16 and 60 and cover will usually end no later than the normal retirement date for the individual's occupation.

In the event of sickness or disability the policy will usually provide for a deferment period and payment of benefits will only commence at the end of this period. Deferment periods may be between one month and one year (usually selected by the policyholder at outset) and are valuable to the company offering the policy because they will reduce the number of short term claims they will have to meet. The longer the deferment period the cheaper the policy will be. In some cases, especially those occupations where short term illnesses are common (eg sportsmen) the company will select the period.

The benefits payable under the policy will usually be limited to approximately 75% of the individual's pre-claim earnings, often taking into account any benefits received from the State and any other policy during the period of claim. Limiting the maximum benefit in this way provides the incentive to the individual to return to work as soon as possible.

Benefits paid by such policies are usually taxable as unearned income in the individual's hands but the Inland Revenue allow a 'tax holiday' during which payments are not taxed. The tax holiday runs until benefits have been paid for a complete tax year, eg if payment of benefits commenced in May 1988, payments would not become taxable until April 1990; ie a tax holiday of 23 months in that case.

One of the most important things about PHI policies is the definition of 'disability' which is used in the policy. Under some policies a person will not be treated as being disabled if he can do any part of his former job. Others may not treat a person as disabled if he is capable of doing some other job for which he is reasonably suited, even if he is completely unable to do his previous job.

PHI plans are usually sold on a guaranteed basis so that premiums are fixed during the life of the plan. More recently some companies have produced unit-linked PHI policies under which premium rates can be reviewed in the light of actual performance of the underlying investments, expenses and morbidity experience (morbidity is the risk of a person becoming disabled).

The most flexible PHI policies will allow the level of benefit to be increased as salary increases and will also give the policyholder the option of paying a higher contribution in exchange for the disability income which will increase to offer protection against inflation during the period of disability.

Part two — The uses

In this second part of the chapter the uses of life assurance, pensions and permanent health insurance are considered with particular emphasis on the business needs of sole traders, partners and small companies.

The chapter does not consider more personal uses of life assurance but it is most important that they are not overlooked.

Life assurance is a unique product in the paying of a lump sum on the death of an individual at some unknown time in the future. As such it plays a vital role in protection of the family on the death of the breadwinner and loss of the family's income.

Although most people can see the need for life assurance on the life of the family breadwinner, it should not be forgotten that many men are only able to go out and earn an income because their wives are devoting themselves to looking after children and the family home. The death of a non-earning wife can also cause major financial difficulties such as the need for boarding school fees, a cleaner, a nanny — perhaps even the need for the surviving spouse to give up work to look after the family.

So-called 'wife assurance' should be considered in all family situations.

Life assurance is also important in inheritance tax planning, being able to provide a fund from which the liability may be met, thus preserving the deceased's estate intact.

Also not covered in this chapter is the very important use of life assurance as a means of investment, even though qualifying endowment policies and single premium savings bonds may have advantages for the individual investor and, in some cases, corporate investment.

Sole traders:

11.16   Life assurance

(1)   *Keyman assurance – loss of profits*

Although the sole trader himself will usually be the driving force behind the profitability of the business, there may be cases in which an employee is also essential to the well-being of the undertaking. Where the death of such a key person would weaken the profitability of the business or reduce its capital value as a going concern, the owner of the business should consider effecting a life policy on the life of the keyman. The status of the individual will usually satisfy the requirement for an insurable interest, providing this sum assured is reasonable in view of the keyman's value to the business.

Receipt of the policy proceeds on the death of the life assured will not normally constitute a chargeable event, and so will not trigger a tax charge on the policy, if the policy is a qualifying policy, but it is important to consider whether the policy is an asset owned by the sole trader personally or is a business asset. This will determine the ultimate tax treatment of both the premiums paid and the sums received.

If the policy is a business asset contributions paid to it, in general, will be tax-deductible provided:

(a)   the policy is a short-term assurance; and
(b)   the insurance is intended to meet the loss of profit resulting from the employee's death; and
(c)   the sole relationship between the policyholder and the life assured is that of employer and employee.

These principles were laid down in a statement in 1944 by the then Chancellor of the Exchequer Sir John Anderson. In general, the first requirement is an indication that premiums paid on a policy with a term of more than five years will not be tax-deductible.

If premiums are tax-deductible, this usually means that the policy proceeds will, in turn, be taxable as a trading receipt of the business. If the premiums do not attract tax relief, usually the proceeds will be received as a tax-free capital sum. The tax-free nature of the receipts in such cases is not guaranteed but it is normal Revenue practice. In cases of doubt it may be wise to contact the local Inspector of Taxes.

(2) *Security for loans*

If a sole trader has to borrow money for business purposes, the lender may often require assignment of a life policy on the sole trader as security. The policy should ensure that such loans are repaid on the death of the sole trader.

Premiums are unlikely to be tax-deductible as a business expense because the purpose of the plan will be to satisfy a capital liability so that the premiums are not an income expense at all.

(3) *Insurance for redundancy payments*

If a sole trader's business ceases on his death, his personal representatives are liable for making redundancy payments to eligible employees (see 10.25). The amount of any payment will depend on various factors, such as salary level and length of service, but for a sole trader employing several staff, such payments could be a significant burden on his estate.

11.17 Pensions

(1) *For the sole trader*

Pension provision for a sole trader must be through a Personal Pension Plan (PPP) or a Section 226 contract if effected prior to 1 July 1988.

As a sole trader is not an employee, Occupational Pension Schemes are not available and the question of contracting-out of SERPS does not arise.

It should be remembered that the individual can effect life assurance protection through a PPP. This can provide very cheap term assurance cover, because the premiums are tax-deductible, but paying for life cover in this way does lead to a reduction in the contributions which are going towards pension benefits.

(2) *For his employees*

For employees of a sole trader the choice is wider. The employer could establish an Occupational Scheme for his staff or, in the absence of an employer's scheme, the employees could effect PPPs for themselves.

Most sole traders will not want to assume the responsibility of establishing and running an Occupational Pension Scheme but will be able to make contributions to their employees' PPPs. Some pension providers will offer a group PPP arrangement which will be particularly suitable in these circumstances. Members of staff would still own individual plans but some aspects of the administration will be centralised, for example the collection of any employer's contributions to those plans.

If the employer does decide to set up an Occupational Scheme for his employees, a money-purchase arrangement is likely to be preferable because of the absence of long term guarantees which have to be met by the employer.

Employees should consider whether contracting-out of SERPS will be beneficial to them. This can be effected in a variety of ways: the employer may offer contracting-out under the main Occupational Scheme; those in a contracted in Occupational Scheme may be able to contract out of SERPS by means of a FSAVC Scheme (or a PPP in the restricted form described at 11.12); or the PPPs taken out by those not in the Occupational Scheme can be used to contract out on an individual basis.

If the sole trader's spouse is employed in the business, he or she is like any other employee as far as pension planning opportunities are concerned but, of course, may be treated more favourably by the employer.

(3)   *For the sole trader's spouse*

If the spouse is not employed in the business, consideration should be given as to whether this could be done, especially if the sole trader's wife is not otherwise employed.

The salary paid by the sole trader is deductible at his top rate of tax and, if it is less than the wife's earned income relief and the lower rate for National Insurance contributions, no income tax or National Insurance contributions will have to be made by either husband or wife in respect of that salary. Of course, it must be possible to justify the employment and the salary being paid by reference to the duties undertaken by the wife.

Once the wife is employed in this way, she could contribute to a PPP, or an Occupational Scheme could be set up for her by her husband. Although the Occupational Scheme may be a little more expensive to run and, if it is an insurance company scheme, may have higher minimum contribution levels, it will usually offer the chance to provide higher pension benefits for the wife than would a PPP, where the contribution is limited to a percentage of a salary.

In order to obtain the benefit of tax relief through PPP contributions, the wife should earn more than her tax allowances but this could lead to payment of National Insurance. In such cases, it may be better for the husband, as employer, to make the PPP contributions for her.

11.18   Permanent Health Insurance

(1)   *For the sole trader*

It will often be the case that if the sole trader is not able to work, the business will soon become unprofitable. Although state benefits do exist (the sickness and invalidity benefits) they are designed more to avoid poverty than to maintain an individual's standard of living. Accordingly, a PHI policy is one of the first things which the sole trader should consider.

(2)   *For his employees*

Employees of a sole trader will usually be entitled to the same state benefits (with the addition of Statutory Sick Pay) but may be treated more favourably under the terms of their contract of employment.

If the employer has undertaken to maintain the full, or a proportion of, salary during periods of sickness, he should consider effecting a PHI policy on the life of the employee, so as to 're-insure' the liability for continuing salary. Benefit received from the policy by the employer would be taxable as a trading receipt but normally deductible as a trading expense when paid to the employee. There would be no 'tax holiday' on the payments in these circumstances.

Even if the employer has not agreed to maintain salary payments beyond that required by statute, he may still consider effecting a PHI policy on key employees to maintain the profitability of the business during their absence from work.

Partners:

11.19   Life assurance

The majority of the uses of life assurance applicable to sole traders also apply to partners. Perhaps the main difference with partnerships is that they are more likely to involve key people and that consideration should be given to the future of the partnership on the death of one of the partners.

Quite apart from loss of the earning potential of a deceased partner, the surviving partners may,subject to the provisions of the Partnership

Deed, be faced with having to pay the beneficiaries the value of the deceased's partnership share. For a partnership which has made no provision, this burden can be acute and might necessitate expensive borrowing or even the sale of vital partnership assets.

Life assurance can help in these circumstances. The partners can set up an arrangement so that each of them has life cover which will be paid to the survivors on his death. The survivors then have the funds to pay the deceased partner's share to his heirs, without affecting other aspects of the viability of the business.

This partnership assurance arrangement may be achieved by each partner owning a life assurance policy on the life of every other partner but this can be unwieldy and expensive where there are more than three or four partners. An alternative is for each partner to effect a policy on his own life and write it in trust for the benefit of the other partners.

Both sorts of arrangement should be accompanied by a cross-option agreement by which the surviving partners can compel the personal representatives of the deceased to sell the deceased's partnership share to them and vice versa. The cross-option agreement can also contain further provisions to deal with the valuation of the partnership share, time for payment, the destination of surplus policy proceeds and payment of additional capital, should the policy proceeds be insufficient.

11.20   Pensions

(1) *For the partners*

Again, the pension planning routes available to partners are the same as those available to the sole trader, ie a PPP from 1 July 1988 or a Section 226 contract before that time.

The life cover which can be provided under such pension arrangements can be extremely useful for partnership assurance planning as it provides tax relief on the life cover contributions, at the individual's top rate of income tax.

However, these plans are term assurances which must end no later than the individual's 75th birthday although most life companies will give favourable consideration to a partner applying for a new life policy on the termination of life cover under a pension scheme with that same office.

(2) *For their employees*

For partnership employees the position is, again, the same as for employees of a sole trader and the comments made there also apply to spouses of the partners who are employed by the partnership.

11.21   Permanent Health Insurance

Once again, partners are in much the same position as sole traders when considering PHI policies. A partnership may be better placed to absorb the loss of profits resulting from a partner's long term absence through injury or illness but a PHI policy can secure the position still further. A policy could be taken out by each partner for his own benefit with the Partnership Deed providing for a corresponding reduction in that partner's share of profits for the period of absence. Alternatively, policies could be owned by all the partners as partnership assets so as to replace the income at the partnership level. The former method has the advantage of the availability of a tax holiday and of putting this provision into the hands of each individual.

Companies:

11.22   Life assurance

(1) *Keyman assurance*

Keyman assurance is particularly important for small companies where, for example, the Managing Director, Sales Director etc may be fundamental to the profitability and continuance of the business.

Small companies effecting keyman policies will usually not be able to obtain tax relief on the premiums but will not be taxed on the proceeds. This is because the keyman being insured will usually have a material interest in the company so that the relationship between the life assured and the policyholder will not be only that of employee and employer (11.16(1)).

In the absence of such an interest in the company on the part of the keyman, deductibility of premiums might be achieved if the policy is a short term assurance. A policy of this nature might be appropriate in the early days of the company's existence (for example, where it is expected that the company will grow sufficiently over the next five years so as to absorb the loss of the keyman after that time).

(2)   *Loan protection and repayment*

A form of keyman assurance might also be appropriate where the company is obtaining a loan and the lender requires a life policy on a key executive by way of additional security.

Even where the lender has not required a life policy as security for a loan, life assurance has a key role to play in respect of company borrowings. Although the company will usually be the borrower, it is common for lenders to require a personal guarantee from one or more directors to ensure repayment of any loan (1.3).

By having to give a personal guarantee the director is losing one of the main benefits of trading through a company — that of limited personal liability.

Bearing in mind that the death of a key person in the company organisation may well precipitate profitability difficulties and so make a calling in of the loan more likely, this is another good reason to effect life assurance on the lives of key individuals. Receipt of the policy proceeds will enable the company to repay its borrowings and so free the personal estate of the guarantor from the potential liability.

Repayment of loans should also be considered in respect of any company overdraft which could be called in on the death of a key person and in relation to directors' loan accounts where the director's estate may require repayment on the director's death.

(3)   *Key shareholder assurance*

Another aspect of small companies which needs to be considered is that of transfer of shares on the death of one of the shareholders. In many cases small companies will not be declaring dividends on the shares, but those involved in the running of the company will be drawing benefits by way of salary and director's fees. On the death of a director, those inheriting the deceased's shares may find that they have a minority shareholding in the company. The shares may be producing no dividends and may be insufficient to enable the new shareholder to become a director. In such a case the shares may be virtually unsaleable except to the other shareholders who may be able to use their position to depress the value of the shares.

Although in exceptional cases minority shareholders may have some rights against an oppressive majority under company law (5.63), the problem can be tackled by life assurance arrangements in at least two specific ways.

The company could effect life policies on the individual shareholders so that, on the death of a shareholder, it will receive a capital sum in order to buy the shares from the deceased's heirs. It has only been possible for companies to buy their own shares since 1982. An agreement can be entered into between the shareholders and the company itself in which various questions can be addressed, for example, options can be given to both sides to require a sale or purchase of the shares and to determine the method of calculating a fair price for them.

However, the deceased's personal representatives may have difficulty in enforcing their option to require the company to buy the deceased's shares in some circumstances, eg where the purchase price is to come out of the company's capital. In addition, there are various legal procedures to be gone through before an agreement to buy a company's own shares can be set up and further clearances from the Inland Revenue need to be obtained when the purchase is made to ensure there are no adverse tax consequences.

An alternative and relatively simple method of arranging a share purchase scheme is to establish an arrangement similar to that used for partnership assurance (11.19). In this way each shareholder would effect a policy on the life of each of the others, or each would effect a policy on his own life and put it in trust for the benefit of the other shareholders. The life policies will be accompanied by a cross-option agreement which would enable both the deceased's personal representatives and the surviving shareholders to enforce the sale and purchase of the deceased's shares and would tackle such questions as valuation of the shares etc.

11.23   Pensions

(1)   *For the directors and other top executives*

The directors of the company may plan for their own pension benefits through an Occupational Scheme or a PPP. In most cases the directors and key executives will join a company Occupational Scheme as this will enable them to maximise their pension benefits in a tax-efficient way.

PPPs with direct contributions from the company, will also be efficient for the purposes of income tax and National Insurance contributions, but the limit on the PPP contributions which can be made will usually favour the choice of an Occupational Scheme.

Life assurance protection can be provided under either type of scheme. Usu:.!!y it is possible to provide a higher sum assured under a PPP (where the maximum life cover contribution is 5% of net relevant earnings) than under an Occupational Scheme where the maximum sum assured is four times' salary. Despite this, the Occupational Scheme will often be preferable as the provision of life assurance under the PPP will reduce the maximum amount which can be paid towards the pension benefits.

(2) *For employees*

For other employees the choices are very much the same as for the employees of sole traders and partners. If the company does not want to make pension provision for its staff, they will be able to plan for themselves by effecting PPPs (or Section 226 contracts before July 1988). The company may choose to make contributions to its employees' PPPs. A group PPP arrangement could be 'sponsored' by the company if it wishes to indicate a greater commitment to the provision of pensions for its employees.

(3) *For spouses of the directors*

The comments made in 11.17 apply equally to employment of, and pensions for, spouses of directors and top executives of small companies.

11.24   Permanent Health Insurance

As with sole traders and partnerships, the smaller the company the more vulnerable it will be to the long term absence of a key individual. The company may effect PHI policies on its directors and top executives either to enable the company to maintain payment of salary or to cushion the company itself from the possible loss of income due to the absence of the key person. The question of whether premiums paid on such a policy are tax deductible for the company is not entirely clear.

Despite the long term nature of the policy it seems likely that premiums paid by a company on a PHI policy on an employee, to enable the company to maintain payment of salary to the employee during a period of disability, should be tax-deductible. Certainly it would appear that the receipt of payment by the company from the policy would be taxable (although matched by tax relief on the payment of the salary). In cases of doubt, companies should consult their local Inspector of Taxes.

12 The business and the outsider

Part A Contract law

12.1 Introduction

Contracts are concluded between individuals every day, when shopping, when borrowing money, when eating out in a restaurant or buying a car. Small wonder, then, that a business will conclude many contracts during the course of its life. As the stakes are usually much higher in business contracts it can be useful to be aware of the basics of contract law.

12.2 Components of a contract

Not all agreements are binding. A legally binding contract has to contain at least three elements, viz:

(1) an intention to create legal relations
(2) a valid offer and acceptance
(3) consideration.

These are expanded on in turn below. It is important to note that if any is absent, there is no contract.

12.3 Intention to create legal relations

If A and B agree to meet in a public house one evening for a drink there may well be an agreement to do so, but the parties would be surprised if you told them that if either failed to show up, the other could sue for damages for breach of contract. In fact their agreement could not be sued upon. This is because the parties, in all likelihood, had not contemplated that there would be any legal consequences if their agreement were broken. In other words, there was no intention to create legal relations.

12.4   Presumptions about legal enforceability

There exist legal presumptions about intention to create legal relations. First, in relation to *social and domestic* arrangements it is *presumed* an agreement is *not* legally binding. As to arrangements in a *commercial* context it is *presumed* that the agreement *is* legally binding. Most contracts concluded by businesses will, therefore, be presumed to be legally binding.

One notable exception is a collective agreement between a firm and a trade union, which is governed by a special rule. Under statute it is provided that in relation to collective agreements entered into after 1974, and before 1971, there is a presumption that a collective agreement is not legally enforceable unless it is in writing, and it contains a provision which states that the parties intend that the agreement shall be enforceable. (The reverse applied between 1971 and 1974.)

Finally, the presumptions about intention to create legal relations are rebuttable. Even an agreement between two businesses (which would ordinarily be a binding contract) could be expressed to be 'binding in honour only' and not legally binding. Such expressions are rare. In business life you mostly need the certainty and security that comes from a binding contract.

12.5   Offer and acceptance

Every contract must have both an offer and an acceptance to be binding. The rules about this are more involved than you would think.

12.6   Offers and invitations to treat distinguished

An offer must be distinguished from an 'invitation to treat'. An invitation to treat is *not* an offer but is instead, an invitation to make an offer; and a purported acceptance by another party of an invitation to treat will be construed in itself as an offer, which, in turn, has to be accepted. Some examples of the distinction between offers and acceptances are as follows:

(1) Advertisements for sale may commonly (though not always) be construed as invitations to treat.
(2) The display of goods in a shop window or on shelves in a shop or supermarket may itself not amount to an offer, but may be, instead, an invitation to treat.

12.7 Termination of offers

An offer may be revoked at any time before acceptance unless an option has been granted. But withdrawal of an offer must be *communicated* to an offeree and, to be effective, notification of withdrawal must actually *reach* the offeree before he has accepted; otherwise it will not be valid. An offer can terminate through lapse of time, either because the terms of the offer expressly say so, or by implication after a reasonable time. Where the proposed contract is personal to the offeror, death of the offeror will cause the offer to lapse. A counter offer by an offeree may terminate an offer (12.8). If the offer is made subject to a condition, which fails, the offer will thereby lapse.

12.8 Acceptance

As stated, an offer must be accepted. An anomalous rule applies about the manner of acceptance. Normally, communications related to contract formation must be *actually received* to be effective. Thus, if you want to withdraw an offer, it is not enough simply to decide to do it, or to post a letter; your communication of your decision must actually be received by the other party. But in the case of acceptance only, a special rule has grown up called the 'postal rule' whereby a posted acceptance in response to a posted offer is valid from the time of *posting, not* receipt. This can have strange results. Thus:

Example

A offers to B in writing by post to sell him his car. B receives the offer on 1 October. B ponders, but writes back, accepting the offer on 8 October. On 15 October, having heard nothing from B, A writes to B withdrawing the offer and, on the same day, concludes a sale with C. B's letter of acceptance arrives at A's house on 21 October having been delayed in the post through no fault of B. There was a binding contract between A and B and A was not in a position to sell to C.

On the other hand, the rule does not apply:

(1) where the letter of acceptance is not properly addressed or stamped;
(2) where the terms of the offer expressly or impliedly indicate actual communication is necessary;
(3) where other forms of communication are used by both parties, ie telephone, telex and facsimile equipment, where a party communicating may not be able to rely on a communication unless it has been properly received by the other.

An acceptance must be unqualified, or it may be construed as a counter offer. A counter offer terminates an offer. Thus:

Example

A offers to sell his car to B for £3,000. B says 'I accept at £2,500'. A then sells to C, who has offered to buy at £2,750. B, unaware of the sale to C, telephones A later to say, '£3,000 will be fine after all. I take it the car is now mine'. But B's earlier 'acceptance' was a counter offer. This terminated A's offer and B is not in a position later to revive A's original offer. The sale between A and C is valid.

12.9   Offers, counter offers and acceptances illustrated in business contracts

The above rules can be illustrated in the context of the use of standard written terms and conditions. Sometimes a buyer and a seller of goods each have their own terms and conditions of contracting, probably printed on invoices and orders. These may often conflict. For example, a buyer's terms might say 'the buyer shall be entitled to one month's grace in payment of his account'; a seller's terms might say 'payment must be made within seven days of delivery'. Or, a buyer's terms might say 'the price to be paid for the goods is fixed no matter what increase there may be in the price of raw materials'; and the seller's terms might say 'the seller may vary the price to be paid for the goods upon giving notice thereof due to increase in the price of raw materials.' What happens when such terms conflict?

The answer can be found using the principles in 12.5–12.8. Thus, if you order goods from a supplier under your own conditions of purchase, that will be an offer to him to contract on those conditions. If that order is not accepted unconditionally by the supplier, but, instead, upon the basis of the supplier's own conditions, there will be no contract. The introduction of the seller's conditions would be a counter offer and would be effective to reject your own conditions. No contract can be formed at this stage unless you accept that counter offer. If nothing further is said, but you take delivery, then you may have accepted that counter offer by conduct. To avoid that, you would have to respond to the counter offer before taking the goods, saying that you only want to contract on your own conditions, and so on.

This so-called battle of forms sounds intriguing, but it is usually lost by accident. Although it is important to bear in mind that each case turns on its own facts, two cases illustrate the above propositions.

In *BRS v Arthur V Crutchley Ltd* (1967) the sellers delivered some whisky to the buyers for storage. The seller's driver handed the buyer's foreman a delivery note incorporating the seller's conditions of carriage. This note was stamped by the buyer's foreman: 'Received under the [buyer's] conditions'. It was held that the buyer's action amounted to a counter offer which the sellers accepted by handing over the goods. The contract therefore incorporated the buyer's, and not the seller's conditions.

In *Butler Machine Tool Co v Ex-Cell-O Corporation (England) Ltd* (1979) the sellers offered to sell a machine tool to the buyers for £75,000. The sellers' offer was subject to their conditions which provided that they would 'prevail over any terms and conditions in the buyer's order'. The conditions of the sellers also included a price variation clause. The buyers replied by placing an order for the machine in question but their order was subject to their *own* conditions which were materially different from the sellers' conditions and which, in particular, contained no price variation clause. The sellers completed and signed an acknowledgement of receipt of the buyers' order. It was held, in the circumstances, that the buyers' conditions prevailed. The sellers had made an offer which had been responded to by the buyers not by an acceptance but by a counter offer which had, in turn, been accepted by the sellers.

12.10 Consideration

Consideration is a difficult concept, even for lawyers. It can perhaps be described as the value or price that you have to give to the other party to pay for what the other party is giving you. Any promise must be paid for in money or money's worth or, alternatively, something of value in the eyes of the promisor. Thus if A's grandmother promises him that he will receive £5 on his birthday, this will not be a promise supported by consideration because A has given nothing in return for it. It will be a gift.

On the other hand, although there must be consideration which the law regards as sufficient, the law will not inquire too closely into its adequacy (eg cases of a 'peppercorn rent').

You can pay for a promise and make it enforceable by giving money in return for it, or promising to do something for it, or transferring something to the promisor in money or money's worth, or doing something for the promisor that you are not obliged to do already, or forbearing from doing something which you are entitled to do.

Most contracts entered into by firms involve a promise to pay a price for delivery of goods or services or other commodity and, in return, a promise to provide those goods and services or commodity, and so, consideration will ordinarily be present.

Finally, contracts under seal are binding even if they would otherwise fail for lack of consideration.

12.11   Privity

Another rule that must be observed in contract law is that there must be privity of contract. This means that only those parties to a contract (or 'privy' to it) can, ordinarily, sue on it. Thus if A promises B that A will pay C £100, C cannot enforce this promise since he is not 'privy' to the contract in question. (C's action might also fail here on the ground that he has not given consideration (12.10)). The contract would, however, be enforceable by B as against A as long as B has given consideration to A.

12.12   Terms of the contract

Contract terms are either express or implied. Terms may be implied either because of:

(1)   custom or commercial usage; or
(2)   statute (eg terms implied by the Sale of Goods Act 1979 as to title, fitness for purpose and quality etc (12.31)); or
(3)   by the courts.

12.13   Terms implied by the courts

These may be either:

(1)   to give business efficacy to the contract; or
(2)   to fill in a term omitted by the parties that would be to an 'officious bystander' perfectly obvious that it ought to have been inserted.

A different, perhaps more flexible, approach to the implication of terms can be found in non traditional contract areas such as employment law (10.10). Otherwise, the courts are fairly circumspect about implying terms; it is not a court's job to rewrite a bargain for the parties. Generally, an express term overrides an implied term.

12.14   Excluding terms

At common law it is permissible, within limits, to contract out of liability for breach of contract or tort (although the courts tend to construe excluding terms quite narrowly, and against the person relying on them). Obviously it is wise to try and limit your exposure to liability (especially for consequential loss) as far as you can.

But this is now qualified by the Unfair Contract Terms Act 1977 which applies, in the main, to business liability. Under the Act

(1) Under s 2(1) it is not possible to exclude or restrict liability in negligence for death or personal injury and, in other cases of loss or damage due to negligence, the excluding term will only be enforceable if reasonable.
(2) Under s 3, which applies to contracts

    (a)   between a business and a consumer or
    (b)   between two businesses as long as one deals on the written standard terms of business of the other

it is not possible to exclude or restrict liability for breach of contract unless the excluding term satisfies the test of reasonableness.

Also caught by the test of reasonableness are indemnity clauses in contracts so that, under s 4, a consumer cannot be made to indemnify another for negligence or breach of contract unless the term satisfies the test of reasonableness. (Curiously though, s 4 does not apply to any contract other than one between a business and a consumer (unlike s 3 which is wider)).

What is reasonable for the purposes of the test of reasonableness will depend on the facts of each case. Factors could include the strength of bargaining position of the parties, availability of an alternative contract without the excluding term, whether any goods supplied were produced to the special order of a customer and whether there is any trade usage with regard to the term and so forth.

The controls about exclusions of contract liablity in s 3 do not apply to contracts between two businesses where standard written terms of one party are not employed. In that case, the parties are free to exclude liability for breach of contract (subject to extreme examples) within the framework of the common law.

Finally, the Act says that a manufacturer of goods cannot, in a guarantee of goods ordinarily supplied for private use or consumption, exclude liability for loss or damage arising from consumer use of the goods and arising from negligence of the manufacturer or distributor (12.51 (product liability of manufacturer)).

There are special applications of the Unfair Contract Terms Act 1977 to contracts for the sale of goods and these are discussed at 12.35.

Any exclusion clause, even if it survives the Unfair Contract Terms Act, must be incorporated in the contract before it is effective. Thus, if standard terms are used, it is imperative that your own terms are not superseded by those of the person you are contracting with (see 12.9). In any event (and particularly in the case of use of notices and statements on tickets) excluding terms which are not sufficiently brought to the notice of the other contracting party, may not bind the other party.

12.15 Conditions, warranties and other terms

The law draws a distinction between conditions and warranties. A condition is a major term, breach of which entitles the innocent party to terminate (as well as to claim damages). A warranty is a more minor term collateral to the main purpose of the contract, breach of which entitles an innocent party to damages only. Whether a term is a condition or warranty is a question of construction of the contract. Use of the words 'condition' or 'warranty' is not conclusive (although it will be very persuasive). For a stipulation may be a condition although called a warranty in the contract and *vice versa*. This is because the courts, exceptionally, have power to remove an inappropriate label that the parties placed upon a particular term.

The courts may also find that some terms cannot, in truth, be characterised as either conditions or warranties. These are so-called 'innominate' terms. A party's remedies on breach of such terms (ie whether the injured party may claim damages only, or whether he may withdraw from the contract as well) depend on how drastic the consequences of the breach are to him.

Oddly, the meaning of the terms 'condition' and 'warranty' is transposed in the case of insurance contracts. There, in general, breach of *warranty* allows the injured party (the insurance company) to repudiate the contract whereas, breach of a mere condition, allows the insurance company only to sue for damages (chapter 13).

12.16 Vitiating elements

Contracts may be affected by the presence of:

(1) mistake
(2) misrepresentation
(3) duress and undue influence.

Generally, it is thought mistake makes a contract *void*. Misrepresentation and duress and undue influence make a contract *voidable*. In the former the contract has no effect whatsoever and does not exist. In the case of the latter the contract remains on foot until it is avoided by the injured party. The injured party's option to avoid may be lost in certain circumstances (12.18).

12.17 Mistake

The law rarely allows a contract to be unravelled because of an alleged mistake. Thus, many people may enter into a bargain not quite appreciating the extent or nature of their obligations. In that sense, they may be mistaken. But contract law relies on certainty and only exceptionally will mistake be allowed to operate to set aside the contract. There are said to be three types of mistake.

Common mistake

This is where both parties share the same assumption, which turns out to be wrong. Generally, the courts will only set aside the contract if the parties are mistaken as to a *fundamental* aspect of the subject matter of the contract (eg both parties contract for the salvage of a sunken ship, but, unbeknown to them, it never existed).

Mutual mistake

This is where both parties are mistaken, but they are at cross purposes, ie A thinks he is contracting about X and B thinks he is contracting about Y. Occasionally the picture may be *so* confused that it is impossible to tell what the parties are contracting about and, if so, there will be no contract.

Unilateral mistake

Here, one party only is mistaken. Ordinarily this is unlikely to affect the contract. If you are subjectively mistaken about the terms of a contract but you nonetheless *appear* to wish to contract, the other party may assume you want to be bound and there will be a contract. The exceptions to this are where;

(1) the other party knows of your mistake and is taking advantage of it or
(2) the other party contributes to your mistake.

Occasionally, the courts can order rectification of a written contract that, because of a mistake in its drawing up, does not represent the actual intention of the parties.

12.18 Misrepresentation

A representation which induces a contract may affect a contract if it turns out to be wrong, ie is a misrepresentation. Generally, there has to be a positive misrepresentation for liability for misrepresentation to lie. Silence generally does not amount to a misrepresentation and there is in general no duty to disclose to the other party. However this has exceptions. First, there are certain contracts of the utmost good faith (*uberrimae fidei*) where full disclosure is required. Such is the case in insurance contracts (chapter 13). Second, even in general contracts, there are qualifications to the rule that silence does not amount to misrepresentation. Thus, if you begin to represent, you must paint the whole picture and not just part. Otherwise this would be misleading. And if a representation is made before the contract, this must be revised for the benefit of the other party before the contract is concluded if circumstances have changed which make the original representation misleading.

A misrepresentation can be fraudulent, negligent or innocent. All types of misrepresentation allow rescission at the instance of the injured party. But the right to rescind may be lost if a 'bar' to rescission operates, ie if:

(1)   you have affirmed the contract after learning the truth
(2)   too long a time has elapsed
(3)   *restitutio in integrum* (ie restoring both parties to their former positions in full) is impossible
(4)   third party rights would be prejudiced

Also, under the Misrepresentation Act 1967, a court has discretion to declare that the contract should continue and award damages in lieu of rescission.

Damages are available:

(1)   for fraudulent misrepresentation at common law
(2)   for negligent mis-statement at common law
(3)   for negligent misrepresentation under the Misrepresentation Act 1967 and
(4)   even for innocent misrepresentation under the Misrepresentation Act 1967, if damages are awarded at the discretion of the court in lieu of rescission (see above).

The Misrepresentation Act 1967, s 3, provides that a contract term which excludes liability for misrepresentation is of no effect unless it satisfies the requirement of reasonableness (a similar test to that which applies to terms excluding liability for breach of contract (12.14)).

12.19   Duress and undue influence

A contract may be avoided by reason of *duress* if illegitimate pressure is applied to a contracting party to induce him to contract. For long, the law recognised only physical duress, ie threats to the person. 'Economic duress' is now recognised too. But the test is quite strict and is only rarely satisfied.There is a distinction between economic duress and hard bargaining; only the former may affect a contract (although contrast the rules in some consumer legislation: see eg 12.46).

It may not be possible to avoid a contract for duress if you have affirmed the contract thereafter.

Undue influence can set aside a contract only where there is a special relationship between the parties, often, but not necessarily a fiduciary one. This can include solicitor and client, doctor and patient, parent and child, but the list is not exhaustive. In such cases there is a *presumption* of undue influence. That is why, if such a relationship ever exists between you and the other party to a proposed contract, you should get the other party to seek independent advice.

12.20   Termination of contracts

A contract may come to an end by various means, viz:

(1)   breach of contract
(2)   effluxion of time
(3)   agreement
(4)   frustration.

12.21   Breach of contract

A contract may come to an end through breach of contract, but only if:

(1)   the breach is repudiatory in nature, ie shows that one party has shown an intention no longer to be bound by the essential terms of the contract, and
(2)   that breach of contract is 'accepted' by the injured party, ie responded to by an election to terminate.

Thus, contract law applies what is known as the 'elective' theory of termination, that is to say, a contract must end by the election of the injured party who, in law, accepts the breach of the guilty party as ending the contract and treats himself as thereby discharged. Thus, if A, who is an employer of B, unilaterally reduces B's salary by 50%, B is not necessarily discharged from the contract. B, however, may discharge and release himself from the contract by accepting A's breach.

Breach of contract leads to the availability of remedies on the part of the injured party such as, principally, damages for breach of contract whether or not the breach is repudiatory, and these are not prejudiced by the injured party's election to terminate the contract.

If, however, the injured party wants to seek some sort of order from the court by way of specific performance, or an order obliging the guilty party to carry out his obligations, the injured party *has* to keep the contract alive and *not* terminate it. A good example would be a conveyancing transaction. If a seller of a house refused to convey it, it would not be in the interests of the injured party (the buyer) to terminate the contract and seek to put the relationship at an end if he wants the house, rather than seeking damages alone. The injured party should, in that case, keep the contract alive and seek specific performance of the contract.

12.22 By effluxion of time

If, for example, the parties have entered into a fixed term contract expressed to expire on a specific date, when that date comes around, the contract will expire by effluxion of time. This rule is modified in employment contracts for unfair dismissal and redundancy purposes (10.18, 10.25).

12.23 By agreement

The parties to a contract can at any time, notwithstanding continuing obligations to each other, terminate their agreement by mutual consent. This arrangement will be binding because it will have consideration, as each party is giving up continuing obligations to the other. That mutual release of obligations can amount to consideration.

12.24 Frustration

Frustration is a doctrine which can terminate a contract *automatically* by operation of law, irrespective of the will of either party. The doctrine means that if the parties have entered into a contract upon a certain assumption about the way it will be carried out, if that assumption is thwarted, the courts may exceptionally say that the contract is frustrated and has thereby come to an end.

Examples in decided cases have been where a contract for the sale of goods has become impossible because of the outbreak of war rendering delivery impossible or, in the case of a contract for personal services, where one party has become incapacitated through illness for a very long time, or where, in a contract to stage a concert or theatre production, the theatre has burned down (and no alternative venue is possible).

For frustration to operate, the basis of the contract must have been thwarted. It is no defence to breach of contract for a person trying to relieve himself of responsibilities under the contract to say that it has been frustrated because it is simply more difficult and onerous to perform. Thus, in cases arising from the Suez War in the 1950s, where contracts for the delivery of goods had to be diverted via a longer and more expensive route via the Cape, as opposed to going through the Suez Canal, contracts were held not to be frustrated as they *could* be completed, albeit more expensively. It simply meant that carriers were put to very much more trouble than they had anticipated.

Sometimes, if frustration has occurred, the Law Reform (Frustrated Contracts) Act 1943 can re-allocate the loss and inconvenience to the parties that has arisen thereby.

12.25   Remedies

Breach of contract leads to various remedies, namely:

(1)   a declaration of breach of contract
(2)   damages for breach of contract
(3)   specific performance

12.26   Declaration

A declaration is a judgment of the court declaratory of the parties' positions. It could state, for example, that a party was in breach or that a contract subsists, where there is doubt about this. It is not a common remedy and is rarely of use without more.

12.27   Damages

Damages in contract law

(1)   are designed to put the injured party into the position he would have been in had the contract been performed;
(2)   should be in the reasonable contemplation of the parties as would be likely to arise from the ordinary course of things or from special circumstances that the parties were aware of or ought to have been aware of (like loss of a sub-sale for example).

These rules, as they apply to sale of goods contracts are discussed again at 12.42.

The injured party must take reasonable steps to mitigate his loss and he cannot recover avoidable loss. Thus, for example, a wrongfully dismissed employee has to take reasonable steps to get another job (see 10.26) and a disappointed buyer of goods has to take reasonable steps to find a replacement contract.

Damages calculated on the basis of speculating what would have happened had the contract been performed, ie 'loss of bargain' are sometimes referred to as 'expectation damages'. Occasionally, too, where there is no quantifiable damage for loss of bargain a court may also award what are known as 'reliance damages', ie expenses that have to be thrown away by the injured party as a result of the breach that must have been contemplated by the parties would be incurred under the contract.

Finally, sometimes parties put 'liquidated damages' or 'penalty' clauses in their contracts (12.44). You have to be very careful here. If you have provided say, that if a machine is delivered late, there shall be payable £1,000 per week until it is installed, this *may* not be enforceable. It will be enforceable if it is a genuine pre-estimate of the buyer's loss for late delivery. If so, it will fix in advance the amount of damages due; and, normally, in that case, the buyer will not be able to sue for any more even if it turns out that estimate was wrong. But if it is a penalty in the legal sense of the word it will not be enforceable. Some perfectly enforceable liquidated damages clauses are called 'penalties' in contracts and some clauses claiming to be 'liquidated damages' clauses are really penalties in law. A court can assess what the effect of the clause really is; but it is best to avoid the use of the term 'penalty' if you are including a liquidated damages clause, as the word does have pejorative overtones.

12.28   Specific performance

Sometimes, instead of damages, specific performance may be obtained. Thus, if a buyer and seller of a house contract for the sale of a house, damages may be inadequate for the buyer if the seller refuses to convey. An order for specific performance, ie compelling the seller to convey to the buyer, may be given by the court. As discussed above (12.21) for specific performance to be granted, the contract must still be alive and not terminated by the injured party. Specific performance can occasionally be granted in cases of sales of things as well as real property, such as sales of machines and other *specific* items.

Specific performance is discretionary and will not be granted in cases of hardship, or where it is impracticable or in cases where personal services are the subject to the contract. Thus, only exceptionally will a court order specific performance of a contract of employment or contract for services (chapter 10).

An injunction to restrain a breach of contract may also be available and this may also indirectly have the effect in some cases of an order for specific peformance.

12.29   Illegality and unenforceability

Finally, some contracts may be unenforceable because they are *illegal*. These would include contracts to supply the enemy in wartime, to defraud the Revenue and to commit a breach of the law.

Certain contracts may not be enforceable by reasons of public policy because they are in *restraint of trade*. Thus certain restrictive covenants entered into by employees with their employer (10.11, 10.14), and by sellers of businesses with buyers of businesses not to compete with their former employer or with the former business as the case may be, may be unenforceable and void if contrary to public policy. They will be unenforceable if the covenants are too wide and go too far beyond what is necessary for the protection of the business interests of the party in whose favour the covenant is drawn and beyond what is reasonable in the circumstances. Firms should take specific legal advice upon the drawing up of these sorts of agreements as the issue of their enforceability can be very delicately balanced.

Part B Sale of goods

12.30   Introduction

In general, the rules relating to the sale of goods can be found in the law of contract (see Part A). But there are additional rules for this type of contract that have to be observed.

The implied terms in the paragraphs which follow govern all contracts for the sale of goods save in relation to the implied terms as to merchantable quality and fitness for purpose (12.33),which apply only in relation to goods supplied in the course of a business and not otherwise.

Some of the implied terms are conditions and some warranties. The difference between conditions and warranties has been discussed generally at 12.15. The Sale of Goods Act 1979 repeats that whether a stipulation in a contract is a condition or a warranty (breach of the former giving rise to a right to reject the goods (ie repudiate), the latter giving rise to damages), is a question of construction of the contract.

12.31   Title and quiet possession

(1)   Under section 12 of the Sale of Goods Act 1979 there is an implied *condition* on the part of the seller that he has a right to sell the goods.

(2)   There is an implied *warranty* that the goods are free from any charge or encumbrance not disclosed to the buyer before the contract is made.

(3)   There is an implied *warranty* that the buyer will enjoy quiet possession of the goods except so far as it may be disturbed by the owner or other person entitled to the benefit of any charge or encumbrance that the buyer knew about before the sale.

12.32   Conformity with description

Under section 13 of the Sale of Goods Act 1979 where there is a contract for the sale of goods by description there is an implied *condition* that the goods will correspond with the description.

If the sale is by sample as well as description (ie if you are sent a sample to inspect to see if you want to contract for the purchase of the real thing) then it is not sufficient if the bulk of the goods corresponds with the sample if the goods do not also correspond with the description.

What is a sale by description is a question of fact in each case. It will usually mean an active description by the seller, say in a letter or a catalogue or even an oral statement. A sale of goods is not prevented from being a sale by description simply because, having been displayed for sale, the goods are selected by the buyer.

12.33   Merchantable quality and fitness for purpose

(1)   Under section 14 of the Sale of Goods Act 1979 there is an implied *condition* that where a seller sells goods *in the course of a business* the goods supplied under the contract are of merchantable quality. However this does not apply in the case of defects specifically drawn to the buyer's attention before the contract is made. Nor does it apply in favour of a buyer who examines the goods before the contract is made as to defects which his examination ought to reveal to him.

Goods are of merchantable quality under the Sale of Goods Act 1979 if they are as fit for the purpose or purposes for which goods of that kind are commonly bought as is reasonable to expect having regard to any description applied to them, the price and all the circumstances.

(2)   Where a seller sells goods *in the course of a business* and the buyer expressly or impliedly makes known to the seller any particular purpose for which the goods are being bought, there is an implied *condition* that the goods supplied under the contract are reasonably fit for the purpose in question. This applies whether or not this is a purpose for which goods of that sort are commonly supplied. However, this does not apply where the circumstances

indicate that the buyer does not rely on the skill and judgement of the seller or that it is unreasonable for him to rely on the seller's skill and judgement.

12.34   Sales by sample

Under section 15 of the Sale of Goods Act 1979, in a contract for sale of goods by sample there is an implied *condition*

(1)   that the bulk will correspond with the sample in quality
(2)   that the buyer will have a reasonable opportunity of comparing the bulk with the sample
(3)   that the goods will be free from any defect which renders them unmerchantable and which would not be apparent on reasonable examination of the sample in question.

12.35   Exclusion of liability in contracts for the sale of goods

As in the general law of contract, the law governing exclusion clauses in contracts for the sale of goods is affected by the Unfair Contract Terms Act 1977.

Under the Unfair Contract Terms Act 1977, in contracts other than with consumers it is possible to exclude liability for:

(1)   Liability for non-conformity with description (12.32)
(2)   Non-merchantable quality of goods (12.33)
(3)   Liability for goods being unfit for the particular purpose for which the purchaser requires them (12.33)
(4)   Non-conformity with sample (12.34)

provided that the contract term which excludes liability satisfies the test of reasonableness.

It is not, however, possible to exclude liability for breach of those terms if you are dealing with a consumer. Any such excluding term would be void.

Also, it is not possible to exclude liability for breach of the terms relating to title and quiet possession under s 12 of the Sale of Goods Act 1979 (12.31) at all, whether you are dealing with a business or a consumer. Again, any such excluding term would be void.

The Consumer Protection (Restrictions on Statements) Order 1976 (an order made under the Fair Trading Act 1973: 12.48) makes it an offence in the course of sale to *consumers* to apply terms which are void under the above principles.

As discussed at 12.14, liability to a third party in negligence resulting in death or personal injury cannot be excluded and liability for other damage caused by negligence can only be excluded insofar as the term excluding liability is reasonable. When one party deals as a consumer or the other party deals on the other's standard terms of business, liability for breach of contract generally cannot be excluded by a business seller unless the term excluding liability is reasonable (12.14).

The Unfair Contract Terms Act 1977 does not cover certain contracts for the international sale of goods (12.49).

12.36   Other rules in sales of goods

The Sale of Goods Act 1979 lays down other rules governing the contract for sale of goods, many of which can be modified by express agreement between the parties. If any of the rules imposed on you by statute are found to be inconvenient, this may emphasise the need for you to draw up your own conditions of sale (12.44). However, the following rules apply unless you modify them in your own conditions.

12.37   Time

Whether a stipulation as to time is of the essence of the contract (ie is an important term, a condition) depends on the intention of the parties. You can specifically provide in your conditions when time is important. Otherwise, the Sale of Goods Act 1979 provides that time for payment is not of the essence unless otherwise agreed. But time for delivery in commercial transactions will often be regarded as of the essence in the absence of a contrary intent.

12.38   Passing of property

'Property' is synonymous with 'ownership' or 'title'. The single expression 'property' is used hereafter, but it can be taken to mean ownership or title as well. 'Title' is the expression used as an alternative to 'property' at 12.43. In a contract for unascertained goods the property in them does not pass unless and until they are ascertained (ie allocated to the contract (eg packeted, labelled or earmarked) with the consent of the parties).

In a contract for specific or ascertained goods, the property passes when the parties intend it to pass. *Unless the parties agree differently*, the following are the rules for determining that intention:

(1) In an unconditional contract for specific goods in a deliverable state property passes when the contract is made and it is immaterial whether the time for payment and/or delivery is postponed.

(2) In a contract for specific goods where the seller has to do something to put them into a deliverable state, property passes when he has done so and the buyer has notice that it has been done.

(3) In a contract for specific goods in a deliverable state but where the seller has to do something to ascertain the price (such as measuring or calculating weight or bulk or size), property passes when he has done so and the buyer has notice.

(4) When goods are delivered or are on approval or on sale or return property passes when the buyer signifies his approval or acceptance or adopts the transaction or retains the goods beyond the fixed time for return of the goods or, if no time is stipulated, beyond a reasonable time without indicating rejection.

(5) In a contract for unascertained goods or future goods by description property passes when goods of that description in a deliverable state are unconditionally appropriated to the contract by either party with the consent (express or implied) of the other.

The rules about when title to goods passes may be altered by consent. For example the parties often impliedly agree that ownership does not pass until the goods are paid for. This is what happens in relation to smaller consumer purchases in shops. A seller also often stipulates that ownership does not pass until the price has been paid in full in commercial contracts (see the discussion on reservation of title at 12.43). In short, the whole issue is subject to the intention of the parties.

12.39 Risk

Risk usually follows passing of property. So a buyer stands the risk of accidental loss to the goods as soon as property passes (12.38) even though he may not be in possession of them. This may be altered by consent (12.43), so that a seller can transfer risk and possession but retain property, for example.

12.40 Delivery

It is the duty of the seller to deliver goods and of the buyer to accept and pay for them in accordance with the contract. Delivery involves passing of possession of the goods from one person to another and is distinct from the passing of property in the goods (see above).

Whether delivery is to be by collection by the buyer from the seller or physical delivery by the seller to the buyer depends on the contract.In the absence of agreement, the Sale of Goods Act 1979 assumes delivery is by collection by the buyer from the seller. This is often negatived so that the seller takes on the job of delivery.

Delivery usually involves transfer direct to the seller but you can agree otherwise. For example the seller may deliver to someone having authority to receive the goods like a dyer or finisher of textiles who may be treating the goods before they reach the purchaser on the purchaser's behalf.

If there is short delivery the buyer may accept the goods at the contract rate or reject them. If there is over delivery the buyer may accept only the correct amount or accept all of the goods at the contract rate or reject all of the goods. If the goods are mixed with other (non contract) goods the buyer may accept only the right goods and reject the rest or reject all of the goods.

12.41 Acceptance

The buyer accepts the goods when he intimates this to the seller or when, after delivery, he does any act in relation to the goods which is inconsistent with the seller's ownership (like selling them to someone else), or if after a reasonable time he retains the goods without intimating to the seller he has rejected them. If goods which have not previously been examined by the buyer are delivered he has a reasonable opportunity of examining to see that they conform with the contract requirements. Until that time has elapsed he will not be deemed to have accepted them.

12.42 Remedies

A *seller's* remedy for breach of contract is an action for the price or an action for damages for non-acceptance. In the latter case, the measure of damages is the estimated loss directly and naturally resulting in the ordinary course of events from the buyer's breach under the principles at 12.27.

Where there is an available market the measure of damages is usually the difference between the contract price and the market value when the goods ought to have been accepted or if no time is fixed, when the buyer refused to accept.

Special damages are also recoverable where the law allows this (eg unusual loss in the contemplation of the parties: 12.27). The principles of mitigation of loss (12.27) apply.

If the seller is still in possession of the goods he may have a lien on them (ie a right to withhold until the price is paid). Sometimes he may have the right of stopping the goods in transit if the buyer has become insolvent. Advice should always be taken in this area, though, as a mistake could lead to legal action by a buyer.

The remedies of the *buyer* are recovery of the price on a total failure of consideration, rejection of the goods for breach of condition, and damages for non-delivery. The measure of damages is the loss directly and naturally arising in the ordinary course of events from the seller's breach under the principles at 12.27. This will usually be the difference between the contract price and the market price at the date of the seller's breach.

Special damages may be recovered where there is consequential loss in the contemplation of the parties (see above). If delivery is delayed, the measure of damages is the difference between the value of goods when they should have been delivered and their value at the time of actual delivery.

Specific performance is also available but only in the case of specific or ascertained goods (12.28).

As can be seen, the above is a specialised application of the rules set out in relation to contracts generally in Part A.

12.43   Reservation of title clauses

It is for the parties to agree when property and risk in the goods passes. Otherwise, risk in the goods passes when property is transferred and property is often transferred upon delivery, or even earlier (12.38).

However, those imposed rules can be altered by contract if appropriate. One problem in recent times has been the all too common insolvency of purchasing companies who, at the time of failure, have not yet paid for goods delivered to them by a selling firm. If property has passed upon delivery by the seller (or even earlier), the seller has no further claim to the goods. The goods become part of the buyer's property. As such they can be sold on or seized by a receiver.

Accordingly, if a buyer becomes insolvent before a seller has been paid, the seller is at considerable risk. In those circumstances, a seller will only be an unsecured creditor of the buyer and cannot reclaim the goods. If he is an unsecured creditor, he will in practice, rarely be paid, or if he is paid, will only be paid a small proportion of his debt.

In *Aluminium Industries BV* v *Romalpa Aluminium Ltd* (1976) (the 'Romalpa' case) a seller purported to reserve property or title to goods that had been sold pending receipt in full by the seller of payment from the buyer. Until such time the goods were to be treated as the property of the seller and all proceeds of sale of the goods in the possession of the buyer would also be treated as being the property of the seller. The court gave effect to this clause.

Nowadays it is common for conditions of trading to contain a 'Romalpa' or reservation of title (property) clause which purports to reserve title in goods sold to a buyer until payment in full has been received by the seller.

Such clauses are generally regarded as valid but it is important to take advice upon the exact wording of such a clause. In particular, the following points have to be noted:

(1) Both legal and beneficial title in the goods must be reserved, not simply beneficial title.
(2) It will only be possible to reserve title to goods which maintain their original identity. Thus, if you are a supplier of glue which becomes incorporated into a chair by reason of application of the glue to various bits of wood, your product may lose its identity. Your reservation of title clause will probably not work.
(3) It should be possible to reserve title to proceeds of sale if your goods are sold on your behalf by the buyer whilst a reservation of title clause in respect of the goods is still in force. This sounds inconsistent, but can operate if the reservation of title clause is properly worded. However, in practical terms, it is very unlikely that you will be able to claim priority over such proceeds of sale, bearing in mind that the company will not usually have put these proceeds of sale into a separate bank account or have separately identified them for you.

Therefore, in practice, a reservation of title clause, assuming it is properly drafted, may operate so as to allow you to recover specific ascertained goods from your buyer that have not changed their identity in respect of which money has not been received. In practice, intense and swift negotiations with a liquidator or a receiver are necessary when your buyer becomes insolvent in order that you can rapidly take possession of the goods which you maintain are still yours and which have not been paid for. Slightly different rules may apply when an administrator is appointed under the Insolvency Act 1986 who has certain powers of sale over goods which are subject to a retention of title clause (chapter 5).

Finally, it is to be stressed once more that this is a complicated legal matter and your conditions of trading should really be drafted by a lawyer. The next section deals with conditions of trading generally.

12.44 Conditions of trading

Many of the rules in the Sale of Goods Act 1979 can be modified by contract and there are other reasons why you might wish to have your own conditions of trading, for example, to insert further terms into the contract in your favour (such as a *Romalpa* clause, discussed at 12.43). Common terms in conditions of trading of a *seller* can include the following. The emphasis could be changed if the terms are for use by a purchaser.

(1) that the purchaser is contracting in the course of his business
(2) that variations of conditions are not applicable unless authorised by a senior officer of the seller
(3) that certain warranties and conditions are excluded (subject to the Unfair Contract Terms Act 1977; 12.14, 12.35)
(4) that the buyer has inspected or is deemed to have inspected the items to be purchased
(5) that title does not pass unless certain circumstances are satisfied and that, until then, title is reserved (12.43)
(6) that liability for consequential loss is excluded (subject to the Unfair Contract Terms Act 1977)
(7) that payment terms are as laid down in the contract
(8) that cancellation is expressly not permissible
(9) that the seller reserves the right to correct clerical errors
(10) that risk passes to the purchaser upon departure of goods from the seller's premises
(11) that drawings and designs and intellectual property in relation to production of goods remain with the seller
(12) that acceptance of the goods denotes acceptance by the buyer of goods in a satisfactory condition (subject to the Unfair Contract Terms Act 1977)
(13) that an arbitration clause applies (optional)
(14) that the contract shall be governed by English Law (essential if you contract with a foreign company)
(15) possibly, that a liquidated damages clause regulates certain losses (but see 12.27).

As discussed, the above examples are slanted towards the seller. Conditions of trading can be slanted towards a seller *or* a buyer and you may wish to have two sets. Thus if you are a manufacturer and seller of goods you will want to have seller orientated conditions for the sale of your goods and buyer orientated conditions for when you are buying your raw materials.

Of course, other contracting parties may have thought of this too and, unfortunately there will, from time to time, be a clash between your own conditions and those of your contracting party. In that case, it is important that you win 'the battle of forms' by making sure your own conditions prevail in the interchange of orders, confirmations of orders, invoices and delivery notes that often ensues. These rules are set out at 12.9.

Alternatively you can, if there is time, negotiate a special contract with the other party, incorporating items from both sets of terms, ie a compromise. It is important to note, however, that certain provisions of the Unfair Contract Terms Act 1977 which prevent unreasonable exclusion clauses only apply to contracts between businesses and consumers or between businesses where written *standard* terms are employed (12.14, 12.35). A specifically negotiated contract may not be such a standard form contract and if between two businesses, outside the protection of that part of the Act.

12.45   Credit sale, conditional sale, and hire purchase agreements

Certain goods are sold on credit. The most common of these contracts are:

(1)   *A Credit Sale Agreement*

This is a sale of goods by instalments. The money is not payable forthwith but property in the goods passes to the buyer straightaway. Thus if there is default in repayment of any instalments there is no automatic right for the seller to get his goods back (but this may be altered by agreement: 12.43). He can only sue and get a financial remedy.

(2)   *A Conditional Sale Agreement*

This is where goods remain the seller's until they are paid for in full by the buyer. The seller can therefore regain possession if there is default in payment.

(3)   *A Hire Purchase Agreement*

This is where a supplier hires goods on payment of a number of agreed instalments but has also, coupled therewith, an option to buy at the end of the period of hire for a nominal sum.

12.46   Consumer credit

It is not within the scope of this book to discuss credit and security at length. But if you want to sell goods or give services on credit to individuals you may have to be aware of the Consumer Credit Act 1974. This Act regulates personal credit agreements (ie agreements with individuals, including partnerships, but not companies) where the credit does not exceed £15,000 (excluding interest which is called a 'charge' for credit).

If you are a seller of goods on credit who is covered by the Consumer Credit Act you *must* get a *licence* from the Director General of Fair Trading. This requirement covers not only creditors but also credit brokers such as retailers who have arrangements to introduce customers requiring credit to a particular finance company. Activity and lending by unlicensed creditors is a criminal offence. The Director General of Fair Trading also controls advertisements by credit dealers and also statements by dealers describing the terms on which they offer credit.

Agreements controlled by the Act may be subject to rules requiring certain information to be given to a debtor and copies of agreements to be given to a debtor, and requiring contracts to conform to a certain type, size and colour of print and to give details of rights and duties of either party.

There may be a statutory right of cancellation over a limited period in favour of a debtor where an agreement is concluded otherwise than at the trade premises of a creditor. During the credit period there are rules inhibiting summary termination for default without notice and restraining a creditor applying for an enforcement order by the court before certain procedures are followed.

In hire purchase and conditional sale agreements covered by the Act there is an implied right for the debtor to terminate the agreement on notice, return the goods, pay off arrears and relieve himself of liability for future payments if the agreement becomes too much for him. There is control over penal (12.27) minimum payment clauses on termination.

Finally, a court may have powers to reopen certain agreements which are 'extortionate', ie if they require debtors to make exorbitant payments or contravene fair dealing. This includes evaluating such an agreement against prevailing interest rates, considerations of the debtor's age, experience and financial pressures, and the basic price of the goods charged.

12.47   Implied terms in other contracts

Under the Supply of Goods (Implied Terms) Act 1973 and the Supply of Goods and Services Act 1982 the implied terms in sale of goods contracts apply more or less to other contracts, for example to hire purchase and hire and contracts to supply work or materials respectively. Exclusion of such terms is controlled by the Unfair Contract Terms Act 1977.

In certain contracts for the supply of services the Supply of Goods and Services Act 1982 implies that services will be supplied with reasonable care and skill, within a reasonable time and for a reasonable charge, unless such is modified by the parties.

12.48   Other examples of consumer legislation

(1) Under the *Unsolicited Goods and Services Act 1971* (as amended) it is an offence to send unsolicited goods to other parties and as a result, those persons to whom goods are sent may decline to pay for those goods and, after a certain minimum period of time, may keep the goods as if they had full title to them. There are also provisions dealing with the rife problem of unsolicited order forms for entries in telex and other directories. Unless such forms comply with the Act there may be criminal liability for the sender and claims for subscriptions may be unenforceable.

(2) Under the *Fair Trading Act 1973* it is possible for the Director General of Fair Trading to issue codes of practice under which bodies or trade associations are encouraged to operate their own arbitration systems in relation to consumer complaints. Several orders have been made under this Act. Further, under the Fair Trading Act 1973 it is possible for action to be taken in relation to an undesirable trade practice or other undesirable conduct prejudicial to consumers.

Under the Consumer Protection (Restriction on Statements) Order 1976, an order made under the Fair Trading Act 1973, it is an offence to supply goods to consumers by the use of notices, advertisements or statements containing void exclusion clauses under the Unfair Contract Terms Act 1977 (12.35). It is this order which also prohibits suppliers from making statements about a consumer's rights about merchantable quality and fitness for use, etc without at the same time stating that a consumer's statutory rights are not affected.

(3) Under the *Trade Descriptions Act 1968* it is an offence to:

(a)   apply a false trade description to any goods; or
(b)   supply or offer to supply any goods to which a false trade description is applied.

(4) Under the *Consumer Protection Act 1987* it is also an offence to make a misleading indication of the price at which goods, services, accommodation or facilities are available.

12.49   International sales of goods

Special rules apply in relation to imports and exports (not all of which can be set out here).

There are particular types of contracts in relation to international sales of goods, including fob and cif contracts.

Under an fob contract, the seller's duty is to place the goods free on board a ship nominated by the seller. That is, the seller is responsible for costs up to loading but excluding freight and insurance. Property and risk usually pass on shipment.

Under a cif contract, the price includes cost, insurance and freight. The seller's duty is not only to ship the goods but also to obtain bills of lading and policies of insurance and to transfer these documents to the buyer. He usually does so against payment by the buyer.

Export and Import Licences are usually required and your local Chamber of Commerce can assist in giving you information in that area.

There is a specialised mode of securing payment applicable to international contracts for the protection of both parties where either is unsure of the creditworthiness of the other. This is through the system of banker's commercial credits.

Under this system a buyer instructs his bank to open a credit with a bank in the seller's favour which the bank then agrees to do. But the buyer says to his bank that the seller is only allowed to draw on the credit on presentation of the usual selling documents, viz the seller's invoice, bill of lading and (in cif contracts) the insurance policy or certificate.

Export credit guarantees, which may also, in effect, insure a seller against failure by a buyer to pay may be available from the Government's Export Credits Guarantee Department.

Finally it is prudent to specify in your conditions of trading that English law will apply (12.44).

12.50   EEC law

Distribution, patent licensing, know how, manufacturing and other agreements within the EEC, particularly of an exclusive nature, are subject to EEC competition law rules which regulate how far parties can restrict competition within the Common Market. Specific advice is necessary on your conditions of trading in this regard to make sure you do not infringe EEC law.

Part C Product liability

12.51 Introduction

It is important to note that a manufacturer of goods may be liable to other persons or companies for harm or damage caused by him irrespective of his obligations to a direct purchaser of those goods under a contract.

Contractually, the framework is usually that a manufacturer manufactures goods and sells them to a retailer. A contract is concluded between the manufacturer and the retailer. When the retailer sells to a third party who is often (but not always), the ultimate consumer of the goods, a further contract is concluded between the retailer and the consumer. Contractually, if a defective product causes damage or loss this consumer will be able to sue the retailer for breach of contract. If this is well founded, the retailer may be able to mount individual separate action claiming breach of the retailer's contract with the manufacturer.

The consumer may be able to sue the retailer under the general law of contract (see Part A) or under the implied terms in a contract for the sale of goods (see Part B). But the multiplicity of actions that results through this contractual ladder is cumbersome and expensive. It would be simpler if the consumer could sue the person responsible, ie the manufacturer, direct. To require the consumer to sue the retailer and the retailer to sue the manufacturer requires two actions where, arguably, one would do. But the consumer cannot sue the manufacturer direct in contract because of the doctrine of privity of contract (12.11).

Occasionally there can be a direct link between the consumer and the manufacturer if the manufacturer issues a *guarantee*. But such guarantees are often exclusionary (subject to the Unfair Contract Terms Act 1977) (12.14) and can be of limited value.

12.52 Liability in tort to third parties

A tort is a civil wrong inflicted on another causing him harm which can make you liable to that party, irrespective of whether you have a contract with him. You can be liable in tort to another for accidents to your employees and visitors (and under the Occupier's Liability Act 1984), for interfering with another's goods (eg wrongful detention) for dealing wrongfully with another's goods (ie conversion), sometimes for allowing dangerous matter or things to emanate from your land (eg discharge of waste from your factory) and also for negligent misstatements or negligent advice. In this section we look in detail at potential liability for defective products.

The law of tort opens up the possibility of a manufacturer's liability directly to third parties (even someone who has not bought, but has nonetheless used, the products) at large particularly under the tort of *negligence*. Under the tort of negligence, a person may be liable to another where:

(1) a duty of care is owed by one person to another person
(2) that duty is broken; and
(3) harm or damage is suffered by the person to whom the duty is owed.

There have been many attempts to define the terms under which a duty may be owed to a third party. But, in short, a person will be liable in negligence to another if it is reasonably foreseeable that his actions will cause damage to another.

It may be reasonably foreseeable for a manufacturer to be liable to an ultimate consumer of products supplied by a manufacturer if the products are defective. A duty of care may therefore be owed by the manufacturer of such products to a third party who is a purchaser of those products or whom it is contemplated may consume those products even if not a purchaser. A manufacturer may be liable in negligence if:

(1) he has failed to exercise reasonable care in the production of the products
(2) the defect in question is unlikely to be discoverable by any reasonably foreseeable subsequent examination.

The extent of recovery of damages in this area is complex, particularly in the area of economic loss, where recovery is more difficult. Damages arising from consumer injury are more straightforward.

12.53 Product liability

It is therefore most important to seek to take out insurance cover for product liability arising from these principles (chapter 13). Of course, we have seen cases in the courts (such as cases alleging liability for defective drugs) where the task of the ultimate consumer of products in finding a manufacturer liable is extremely difficult. A product liability case can be hard to prove and can go on for many years. Nonetheless, the risk is there for a manufacturer, and insurance should be taken out (chapter 13). This is all the more important should goods be exported and even manufactured in foreign countries, such as the United States, where product liability laws can be even stricter than in this country. Further and very specific advice should be taken in these circumstances.

There is also legislation governing dangerous and defective goods, the most important of which is the Consumer Protection Act 1987 which considerably widens the possibility of liability for defective products.

12.54 The Consumer Protection Act 1987

This came into force on 1 March 1987 and was intended to implement the product liability directive of the EEC.

It imposes civil liability for damage caused by a defective product. A product is defined as 'any goods or electricity' and includes a product which is part of another product whether by virtue of being a component part or raw material. The importance of this significant new statutory liability is that it can impose liability without the need for proof of negligence (contrast the common law, discussed at 12.52).

Liability is imposed on:

(1) the producer of the product
(2) any person who by putting his name on the product or using a trademark or other distinguishing mark in relation to the product has held himself out to be the producer of the product
(3) any person who has imported the product into a member state of the EEC from a place outside the EEC in order in the course of any business to supply it to another.

Such a person is directly liable to any person who suffers damage in respect thereof. A defect is defined under the Act as occurring where the safety of the product is not such as persons generally are entitled to expect.

There is no liability for loss of or damage to *property*:

(1) which is not intended for private use;
(2) in respect of any loss or damage to property below £275.

There are defences under the Act including where:

(1) The defect is attributable to compliance with any requirement imposed by or under any enactment or with any EEC obligation.
(2) The person proceeded against did not at any time supply the product to another.
(3) The only supply of the product to another person by the person proceeded against was otherwise than in the course of business.
(4) The defect did not exist in the product at the time of supply.

(5)   The state of scientific and technical knowledge at the time of supply was not such that a producer of products of the same sort as the product in question might be expected to have discovered the defect if it had existed in his products while they were under his control.

(6)   The defect constituted a defect in a product (the ultimate product) in which the product in question formed part and was a defect wholly attributable to the design of the ultimate product, or to compliance by the producer of the product in question with instructions given by the producer of the ultimate product.

It is not possible to contract out of liability under the Act.

12.55   Consumer safety

There are provisions in the Consumer Protection Act 1987 governing consumer safety. Under these, it is an offence to supply goods if they fail to comply with the 'general safety requirement'. Goods fail to comply with the general safety requirement if they are not reasonably safe having regard to all the circumstances including:

(1)   the manner in which, and purpose for which, the goods are being marketed, the get up of the goods, the use of any mark in relation to the goods, and any instructions or warnings given in relation to them

(2)   any published standards of safety in relation to those sort of goods

(3)   any means by which it would have been reasonable (taking into account the cost, likelihood, and extent of any improvement) for the goods to have been made safer.

13   General insurance

by Gill Clark, Eagle Star Insurance

13.1   The need for insurance cover

All businesses, whether large or small, have to take risk. It is essential to recognise the uncertain nature of risk. Can you appreciate the financial loss which may be incurred as a result of, for example, an extensive factory fire, or a burglary? Adequate insurance cover is a fundamental requirement to ensure the continuation of your business in the event of a loss.

13.2   Protection

It is also important to recognise at this early stage that not all risks can be insured but, in return for a known premium, insurance provides for the uncertainty of most losses in your business environment to be transferred to the insurers who arrange cover for thousands of businesses.

You therefore stand to benefit from insuring the risks to which your business is subject since insurance can protect your business interests by allowing you to continue with your business plans and concentrate on production. There is then no need to make contingency plans or tie up capital in the form of reserves to cater for the possibility of a risk actually occurring and causing a loss which could not otherwise be withstood by your business. Finally, insurance can also free the businessman from a lot of the worries which are incurred in the running of the business.

13.3   Compulsory insurance requirements

Although arranging insurance is primarily a voluntary move, governments have legislated to make some forms of insurance compulsory. The compulsory insurance requirements are a result of the following:

Employers' Liability (Compulsory Insurance) Act 1969

This Act makes it compulsory for an employer to insure against his legal liability for bodily injury or disease sustained by employees arising out of and in the course of their employment. Evidence of this policy has to be provided in the form of an insurance certificate which must be displayed in a prominent position on the premises.

The Road Traffic Act 1930

This Act (now incorporated in the 1972 Road Traffic Act) introduced compulsory insurance for the owner of a vehicle for his legal liability for death or bodily injury to a third party. There is no legal obligation to insure against damage to one's vehicles but most companies when quoting 'third party' not only include injury to other people but also damage to their property.

EEC Motor Insurance Directive

With effect from 31 December 1988, all motor policies will have to provide liability cover for damage to third party property. This is in respect of the 84/85 EEC Motor Insurance Directive.

Under the Directive a limit of indemnity of £250,000 will only apply for damage to third party property arising from one accident or series of accidents arising from one cause. This third party property cover is already provided by most insurers.

Statutory examination of engineering plant

By law, many items of plant and machinery such as boilers, excavators, cranes, air and steam pressure vessels, lifts and lifting machinery must be inspected and certified by a qualified person. These examinations are largely in response to the requirements of the Factories Act, the Health and Safety at Work Act, and associated legislation.

These services provided by some of the major insurers are sometimes part of a wider policy cover or are on a fee only basis.

13.4   The insurance intermediary

It is possible to purchase insurance in two ways: direct from the insurance company or through an insurance intermediary. As a commercial buyer of insurance, it is recommended that your insurance requirements be arranged through an insurance intermediary to assist you in identifying the risks which confront your business. The variations in policy wording offered by the different insurers will further add to the complexity of arranging insurance cover.

The insurance intermediaries understand the market and know the various types of cover that can be provided, the most competitive premium rates and the best claims services available.

Insurance intermediaries can be classified as follows:

Insurance agent

An insurance agent, consultant, financial adviser or appointed representative works on a part-time basis and does not profess to have such a wide knowledge of the whole general insurance market as the insurance broker. He often works in another professional field and can introduce insurance in the course of his main business activity.

Insurance broker

A broker is a full-time intermediary and is expected to have a wide knowledge of the insurance market.

Until recently, anyone could describe themselves as an insurance broker. The Insurance Brokers (Registration) Act 1977 created The Insurance Brokers Registration Council (IBRC) in order to govern the registration and regulation of insurance brokers. To be registered as a broker, an individual must:

(i)   have an approved qualification or
(ii) have been employed by an insurance broker or an agent for at least two years or
(iii) have been employed by an insurance company for five years.

The insurance broker, by definition, may be an individual or firm whose full-time occupation is the placing of insurance with companies. Only Lloyd's brokers can place insurance at Lloyd's and write 'and at Lloyd's' after their names.

From 1 December 1981 it has been illegal for any individual to describe himself as a broker without having registered under the Insurance Brokers Act.

The broker acts as an agent for the insured but sometimes has the authority from insurance companies to issue cover for certain classes of insurance. The broker's advice is mainly free since the broker receives remuneration from the insurance company and you therefore do not pay more for using the service of an intermediary than going direct to the insurance company itself.

13.5 Types of cover available

There are many areas of your business which will need some form of insurance cover from physical property to liability and indemnity insurances.

13.6 Property insurance

The physical assets of your business, that is the buildings, stock and machinery need to be protected from damage.

This can take many different forms:

(a) *Fire Policy*
A standard fire policy is used for almost all businesses and provides compensation as a result of damage to the property insured. The fire policy also covers damage caused by lightning and explosion. The latter is limited to explosion of domestic boilers only.

The protection offered by a fire policy may not be enough, so insurers provide cover for a number of additional risks for a comparatively small extra premium. These additional risks, known as 'special perils', provide an extension to the basic policy. They include any of the following: storm, flood, burst pipes, impact, riot and malicious damage and earthquake.

The policy can be taken out on an 'all risks' basis. In addition to fire and special perils, it includes accidental damage or loss not specifically excluded.

(b) *Theft Policy*
This provides compensation in the event of the loss of the property insured by theft. It also includes theft damage to buildings. A more detailed description of your stock is necessary, as it is usually this which is attractive to thieves. Commercial theft policies usually require evidence of entry to or exit from your premises by forcible and violent means.

(c) *Goods in Transit Insurance*
Every business depends upon the movement of goods and documents and as insurance is not provided for business effects under a motor policy, goods in transit insurance is a necessary protection.

An 'all risks' policy will be issued if your business owns a small fleet of vehicles. The policy will probably specify the number of vehicles, with individual limits for each vehicle.

If your business owns a large fleet of vehicles, you would be well advised to insure it on 'a declaration basis' whereby the insurance is based on the maximum number of vehicles in operation at the inception date of the policy. There is usually a limit per vehicle. Any adjustment in the premium rate is made at each renewal when the total number of vehicles is again declared.

A problem arises, however, when your goods are sent via a contracted haulier. If the goods are lost or damaged while in the care of the carrier, compensation may not automatically be forthcoming as the carrier may be able to prove that he is not liable or, alternatively, can rely on contract conditions to avoid liability.

Various conditions of carriage exist, most notably those resulting from the Road Haulage Association's Standard Conditions of 1967 and 1982. A maximum limit of £800 per metric ton is set to cover a carrier's liability. This being the case, it is therefore well advisable that you insure your own goods under an 'all risks' policy as a carrier's policy ultimately protects the carrier rather than your business.

For goods transported by rail, the liability accepted by the rail authorities is slightly wider than that of the haulage carriers. Even so, additional insurance cover can be arranged at a low premium, thus enabling any loss or damage to be dealt with by the insurance company and not directly with the rail authorities.

The Post Office sets various limits of liability but, as with the above, independent insurance cover can be arranged.

(d) *Money Insurance*
This provides compensation to your business in the event of money being stolen either from your premises or while being carried to or from the bank. There are various limits which can be arranged.

(e) *Engineering Insurance*
An engineering policy provides cover for damage to machinery and can also cover explosion of steam boilers and pressure plant. Cover for electrical and mechanical breakdown is also available for most machinery including computers.

Most engineering policies will provide cover for business interruption/loss of profits as a result of the above.

Most insurers will provide inspection services as many forms of inspection are compulsory by law. An engineering policy will therefore cover damage to or breakdown of specific items of plant and machinery, inspection services and legal liability for injury or damage caused by plant and machinery.

13.7   Liability insurances

The running of a business means legal responsibilities in respect of employees, the public and customers. It is therefore extremely important that all businesses have adequate insurance protection for legal liabilities which may arise. Insurance companies therefore provide employers', public and product liability insurances to provide protection against this.

(a)   *Employers' Liability Insurance Policy*
This is a statutory requirement under the Employers' Liability (Compulsory Insurance) Act 1969 which came into force on 1 January 1972. All employers must take out insurance against liability for bodily injury or disease sustained by employees arising out of and in the course of their employment in the UK. An insurance certificate has to be displayed to provide evidence of the insurance being in force.

An employers' liability policy protects you, as an employer, against:

(i)   your own personal negligence
(ii)   failure to provide suitable and safe plant, a safe place to work and competent staff
(iii)   the personal negligence of employees and their negligence in carrying out their duties
(iv)   breach of statutory duty as defined in the 1969 Act for the health and safety of employees (re Health and Safety at Work Act 1974)

The Act stipulates a minimum indemnity of £2 million in respect of claims relating to employees arising out of any one occurrence. Many insurers provide an unlimited indemnity for this class of business. Solicitors' costs and opponents' costs are also covered.

Employers' liability insurance thus provides cover against damages which your business may have to pay for bodily injury or illness sustained by an employee and the costs of defending an action under the Health and Safety at Work Act 1974.

(b)   *Public Liability Insurance Policy*
This insurance, unlike employers' liability insurance, is not compulsory by law, but public liability claims carry the same financial threat to your business.

Public liability insurance provides cover for legal action against you for accidental bodily injury to third parties and accidental loss of or damage to third party property arising through the negligence of your employees. Loss of or damage to any property which is being worked upon is excluded. A few insurers will consider offering this cover. However, the cost of repair or replacement of the actual work being undertaken by yourself will be excluded.

A public liability claim can arise through the negligence of you or your employees, if for example;

(i)   customers or other members of the public are injured whilst visiting your premises
(ii)   fire spreads to a neighbouring building.

The policy has a limit of indemnity which applies in respect of any one claim or a series of claims arising from one source. In view of the increasing awards made by the courts, you should ensure that your policy provides an adequate limit of indemnity, probably at least £1 million.

(c) *Product Liability Insurance Policy*
A public liability policy will provide protection for accidental injury, loss or damage caused by the actions of yourself or your employees. It will not, however, provide cover for injury, loss or damage caused by goods which you manufacture, supply or repair.

Product liability insurance provides for protection of your legal liability and there have been some important statutory developments:

(d) *Consumer Protection Act/EEC Product Directive*
The Consumer Protection Act 1987 (12.54) was passed by Parliament prior to the last General Election in 1987. Part 1 of the Act brings into law the European Community Directive on Liability for Defective Products which could have a far-reaching effect on the product liability market.

Under the directive, member states are required to introduce laws imposing 'no fault liability' on producers of defective products that cause injury or damage. A claimant will no longer have to prove that you have been negligent in manufacturing the product, only that the product is itself defective and has caused injury or damage.

Product liability cover is available as an extension to a public liability policy.

(e) *Professional Indemnity Insurance*
This type of insurance provides cover for liability arising from professional negligence. This may apply not only to the professions such as doctors and solicitors but also to anyone working in an advisory capacity.

Professional negligence can result if you or your employees give defective advice which results in others suffering, either by acting upon your advice or misconstruing the meaning of the advice. Professional indemnity insurance can be provided to meet the cost of any award against you. Not all insurers are prepared to offer this cover.

13.8 Motor insurance policies

Any motor vehicles which you use must be insured for third party liability. All vehicles driven, however, must meet the requirements of the 1930 Road Traffic Act (now incorporated into the 1972 Road Traffic Act), to provide an indemnity against liability at law for death or bodily injury. This is the minimum legal requirement and is commonly referred to as RTA cover. Normally an insurance company will provide third party cover also to include damage to property. A further addition is where damage to your own vehicle itself from fire and theft is included, a 'third party fire and theft' policy.

Finally, the most common form of cover is the comprehensive policy which includes accidental damage to your own vehicle.

Motor insurance is divided into: (a) commercial vehicles; (b) private cars; (c) motorcycles.

In a business, if you have a number of vehicles, these can be insured as part of a motor fleet policy.

A motor fleet policy covers all vehicles owned or operated by your business and can also include hired or loaned vehicles, whether they be private cars, goods carrying vehicles or motorcycles.

Comprehensive cover is essential for the small to medium-sized firms who do not have the facilities and resources to repair their own vehicles.

If the damage is so severe as to make the vehicle uneconomical to repair, the insurers will consider the vehicle to be a 'total loss' and settlement will be made on the current market value of the vehicle.

An excess may be applied in which case you will be liable for the first amount of any claim. This is usually in the region of £50 to £250. The excess is usually applicable to young drivers under the age of 25, or as a result of the past driving record of particular drivers.

You can agree to pay a voluntary excess in return for a reduced premium. Other factors such as the vehicle type, the location of your business and past claims experience are taken into account when assessing the premium.

13.9 Business interruption insurance

The physical assets of your business will be protected by material damage insurance but is is quite possible to go out of business following a loss where adequate insurance of physical assets exists. As a result the earning capacity of your business should also be protected in the form of a business interruption/consequential loss policy. However, for a payment to be made, a material damage policy must exist covering the same perils and liability must have been admitted under that policy.

Business interruption insurance is designed to protect your net profit and to meet continuing payments for fixed overheads if insured damage has occurred at your premises resulting from occurrences against which you are insured.

The essential features to be taken into consideration when arranging a business interruption policy are as follows:

Maximum indemnity period

You will need to assess how long it will take to get your business running normally again and also make sure that your cover will allow enough time for rebuilding or re-equiping your business premises and restoring trade to the level it was at before the loss.

This is incorporated into the Policy as the 'maximum indemnity period'.

Cover under the policy will cease at the end of the period and thus it is important that the indemnity period selected is more than adequate. Obviously, any estimation of the maximum indemnity period requires in-depth calculations and usually either your insurers or insurance intermediary will help in selecting the correct time period.

Careful consideration should also be given to the nature of your business, the machinery used and location of your staff. A serious interruption, for example, may force staff to leave, machinery may not be available and stock may not be readily replaced. The maximum indemnity period should take account of all these factors so that the possibility of inadequate cover is minimised.

Sum insured

As with all policies of insurance, the sum insured has to be correct as under-insurance may well mean that you will receive only partial payment in the event of a loss.

Gross profit for insurance purposes is not the figure shown in your trading and profit and loss accounts but is calculated according to a definition stated in your policy. Particular attention should also be paid to the future expectations of your business. Thus the sum insured should take into account real growth and inflation.

Most policies are now arranged on a 'declaration linked' basis where there is no sum insured. Instead, you must estimate the gross profit which you expect to earn during the period of insurance. As a result, the premium is calculated on this estimated gross profit and is altered at the end of each period of insurance when the actual gross profit is known. An allowance is made for future expansion.

Your business may, of course, be affected by losses outside your premises and therefore most business interruption policies are capable of being extended, the most common being:

(i)   Denial of access — if neighbouring premises are damaged by an insured peril you may be prevented from entering your premises, thus resulting in a loss of earnings.
(ii) Failure of public utilities — if access or trade is prevented as a result of insured damage at the premises of the gas, water, or electricity supply authority.

Other extensions exist and vary from insurer to insurer depending on your type of business.

Loss of book debts insurance

Any business which allows credit for the payment of goods or services relies on its accounting records for the collection of monies due. If these records are destroyed, by fire for example, money owed to you may never be collected.

Cover for debts in this way is possible by book debts insurance. This does not provide insurance protection against bad debts. Cover is for fire, explosion, aircraft and riot and optional additional perils. The sum insured should represent the maximum amount of debts outstanding at any one time.

13.10   Other insurances to consider

Fidelity insurance

This type of insurance is centred around fraud or dishonesty on the part of your employees. Cover is provided in respect of loss of money or goods belonging to or held in trust by yourself, caused directly by an act of fraud or dishonesty committed by an employee.

As a condition of the policy, fraud or dishonesty has to be perpetrated and discovered during the period for which the risk is on cover, but occasionally a discovery period of one to two years after the expiry date of the time period is provided.

In considering the risk, the insurers will wish to know what precautions you have taken to deter such fraud and dishonesty, the frequency of internal and external audits, and the number of employees. Cover is then provided on an annual basis.

Obviously the financial impact of fraud from within can pose a serious threat to your business, particularly if, as is often the case, the fraud has continued and remained undiscovered for a long period of time. Fidelity insurance should thus be considered as a viable insurance option.

Credit insurance

This protects your business against bad trade debts and covers the risk that if you sell goods, the purchaser may not pay for them as a result of insolvency.

For foreign transactions, the government has set up the Export Credits Guarantee Department, primarily to assist exporting companies against the risk of not being paid.

Premiums are charged on a turnover basis or are adjustable according to the amount of debt outstanding at regular intervals.

Legal expenses insurance

The public in general are becoming more litigation conscious and thus there is an even greater likelihood that at some time or other your business may become involved in legal action.

Protection is available in the form of legal expenses insurance. For example, costs may be incurred as a result of legal actions brought about by an aggrieved employee who considers that he or she has been unfairly dismissed. The insurance cover provides financial support to defend or pursue legal rights. The cover extends to include the solicitor's fees and expenses along with any court costs and opponent's costs if appropriate.

13.11   Type of policies available

The policy of insurance issued by your insurance company will state what risks are covered by the policy, the premium cost, the name of the insured and the period of time over which the cover applies.

13.12   Single risk policies

Single policies such as a fire policy or a burglary policy, are usually more appropriate to the very large organisation. There will thus be one policy for fire, one for consequential loss and for various other single risks. The organisation which is large enough financially may opt to retain several risks through self-insurance.

The disadvantage of a single policy is: that the system of one premium and one renewal for each risk insured proves costly from the administrative point of view.

13.13   Package/Combined policies

Obviously the single policy will not appeal to the smaller business such as shops and offices. For smaller manufacturing or distribution businesses, insurance companies can arrange a combined policy. This incorporates separate sections for fire, consequential loss, liability, burglary, money etc. The wordings would be the same as if separate policies were issued but the business has the advantage of one policy and one renewal premium. There are, however, usually maximum limits on the premium for this type of policy.

Package policies are also available covering a wider range of classes of business including property, loss of earnings, money and legal liability cover. The package policy is capable of covering almost all of your insurance needs. You select from all the options available the combination which you require. Various benefits therefore accrue:

(1)   Simplified rating structure
(2)   Only one proposal form to complete
(3)   Only one premium and renewal.

The package policy is therefore flexible in accommodating your changing business needs. These package policies are ideally suited to shops, hotels and offices.

14 Key rates and allowances — 1987/88

(Companies year to 31 March 1988)

Chapter

INCOME TAX

2

Taxable Income	Slice	Rate	Total Tax
£	£	%	£
17,900	17,900	27	4,833
20,400	2,500	40	5,833
25,400	5,000	45	8,083
33,300	7,900	50	12,033
41,200	7,900	55	16,378
Over 41,200		60	

Income Tax Allowances

Personal allowance — married	£3,795
single	£2,425
Wife's earnings allowance — maximum	£2,425
Additional personal relief for children	£1,370
Age allowance — married (Age 80 £4,845)	£4,675
single (Age 80 £3,070)	£2,960
income limit	£9,800

COMPANIES

4

Full corporation tax rate	35%
Small companies rate	27%
Advance corporation tax rate	27/73rds

CAPITAL GAINS TAX

6

Rate	30%
Annual exemption (individuals etc)	£6,600

INHERITANCE TAX

7

Band £	Death rate %
0—90,000	Nil
90,001—140,000	30
140,001—220,000	40
220,001—330,000	50
330,001 upwards	60

Annual exemption £3,000

VAT

8

Rate 15%
Registration threshold from 18 March 1987 £21,300

15 Glossary

Tax and law glossary

The following is a selection of terms which are explained in more detail where indicated.

ACAS	Advisory Conciliation and Arbitration Service
Ad valorem duties	Duties which are charged as a percentage of the subject matter — particularly stamp duty
Administrator	An officer appointed by the court who takes charge of the company's affairs on insolvency and one of whose aims is to secure the survival of the company (5.69)
Advance corporation tax	Tax payable by companies on dividend payments, etc, which is offset against the full (mainstream) corporation tax liability (4.8)
Articles of association	The regulations of the company governing procedure of the company and its operation from day to day and the members' relationship between themselves (5.28)
Back duty	Under-assessed tax for previous years, normally due to evasion
Basic rate tax	Income tax at twenty-seven per cent for 1987–88 (2.1)
Business Expansion Scheme	Government scheme for encouraging investment in smaller companies by giving tax relief on money subscribed (4.25)
Capital — authorised or nominal	The limit of capital to which the company can go to in issuing new shares without passing a resolution to raise its capital

— issued or allotted	The amount of shares actually issued by the company to its members
— paid up	The amount of issued or allotted share capital paid up by the members
Capital duty	duty paid on issue of shares at the rate of £1 per £100 or part thereof
Class rights	Rights attaching to different classes of shares in the Articles (5.32)
Close companies	Companies closely controlled by generally no more than five shareholders and their associates (4.21)
Condition	In contract law, a term of the contract of such importance that breach would entitle the injured party to repudiate (12.15)
Constructive dismissal	In employment law, an employee initiated dismissal in response to an employer's repudiatory conduct
Continuous employment	In employment law, employment continuous under a contract of employment for the purposes of the EP(C)A (10.16)
CRE	Commission for Racial Equality
Debenture	In company law, a document evidencing a loan to a company (5.19), usually containing a charge on the company's property
Domicile	The country which you regard as your natural home. If you go abroad, it is the place of abode, to which you intend to return
Earned income	Income derived from an individual's personal, mental or physical labour and some pensions
Employee	A person who works under a contract of employment or apprenticeship (see EP(C)A, s 153(1)) (10.7)
EOC	Equal Opportunities Commission
Ex gratia	Without liability. Often used in settlements of, for example, employment cases (10.28)
Fidelity	In employment law, a duty of faithfulness or loyalty (10.11)
Fiduciary duties	Duties attaching to the office of a director analogous to those of a trustee and involving a duty not to

	let his own position conflict with that of the company and to be trustee of the company's assets (5.52)
Floating charge	A charge other than a fixed charge and one which companies may grant to lenders and which is not attached to a specific asset or assets but attaches only to a class of asset or assets (5.20)
Frustration	A doctrine in contract law which brings a contract automatically to an end by operation of law without the need for action by either party (10.18, 12.24)
General Commissioners	Lay people appointed to hear tax appeals
Higher rate tax	Income tax at the higher rates, currently forty to sixty per cent (2.4)
Indexation allowance	Capital gains tax relief for inflation (6.9)
Industrial tribunal	A body set up to hear statutory employment rights such as unfair dismissal, redundancy and the like (10.23)
Interest in possession	Entitlement to receive the income of a settlement (7.20)
Liquidator	An officer who presides over and administers the dissolution of a company
Mainstream corporation tax	A company's main corporation tax liability based on its accounts (4.10)
Memorandum of association	A constitutional document of a company setting out its name, office, objects clause, statement of limited liability and capital and which can be altered only in limited ways (5.8)
Ordinary residence (individual)	Residing in a country in the ordinary course of your life
Private company	A company which may not offer its shares to the public and which is not a public company (1.11 and 5.3)
Privity	A rule in contract law that only a party to a contract may sue under it
Public company	A company which uses the suffix 'plc' and which has a minimum share capital of £50,000, a quarter of

	which is paid up and which observes certain additional requirements under the Companies Act 1985 (1.11 and 5.2)
Resolution	A decision of a company at a general meeting or at a board of directors meeting
Receiver	An officer appointed by the court or by debenture holder to take charge of the company's affairs and realise its assets. Often he will be an administrative receiver under the Insolvency Act 1986, if a receiver and manager
Rights issue	An issue of shares to all shareholders *pro rata* with their existing shareholdings
Romalpa Clause	A reservation of title clause in conditions of trading of a company (12.43)
SMP	Statutory maternity pay, a maternity benefit administered by the employer, similarly to SSP (below)
Specific performance	An order, in contract law, for the enforcement of the obligations of a defaulting party under a contract (12.28, 10.26)
SSP	Statutory sick pay, a payment administered by the employer replacing state sickness benefit for 28 weeks of sickness, the cost of which is deducted from an employer's national insurance contributions
Stamp duty	Duty payable at $\frac{1}{2}$% on transfers of shares and differing rates on transfers of property by companies (5.22)
Table A	Table A of the Companies (A–F) Regulations 1985 (SI 1985 No 805) or Table A of an earlier Companies Act as the context requires (5.8)
Tort	A civil wrong committed against another party, eg negligence or trespass
Ultra vires	A doctrine in company law that a company must keep within its registered objects. It is tempered by

	certain statutory protection in favour of third parties.
Unfair dismissal	A dismissal contrary to the EP(C)A (10.17)
Unfair prejudice	In company law, the basis of a petition by a minority shareholder under s 459 of the Companies Act 1985
Warranty	In contract law, a term breach of which will entitle the injured party to sue for damages but not to repudiate (12.15) (contrast a condition and contrast also insurance law below)
Worker	An employee or another person who provides or executes personal services for another under a contract
Wrongful dismissal	A dismissal in breach of contract at common law

Insurance glossary

When it comes to arranging insurance or making a claim, the following may be a basic guide to explaining some of the insurance terms which may be used:

Average	If the sum insured is inadequate the insurers will only receive a premium for a proportion of the risk and not for the entire risk. If a claim is made, any claims settlement will take this under-insurance into account by applying the condition of average — the policyholder will have to share in the loss by making a contribution to the loss proportioned to the amount of under insurance.
Certificate of insurance	This is usually required when insurance cover is compulsory by law as in the case of Employers' Liability Insurance & Motor Insurance.
Claim forms	The standard forms used by insurers to collect all the information per-

	taining to the loss and to provide assistance in assessing claims.
Contribution	Right of an insurer to call upon others liable to the same insured, to share in the cost of an indemnity payment. For example, if the same property is insured with two different insurers.
Cover note	Provides evidence that the insurance cover is in force before the policy document has been issued. If a loss occurs during the period the cover is in force, the insurers are liable under the terms of their standard policy.
Endorsement	An alteration in the wording of a policy is made by issuing what is termed an 'endorsement slip' and should be attached to the policy concerned.
Excess	The policy wording excludes the first £ x of loss. This may be compulsory or voluntary.
Indemnity	Exact financial compensation sufficient to place the insured in the same financial position after a loss as he enjoyed immediately before it occurred.
Index-linking	The sum insured rises in line with a pre-determined index. It is designed to combat the effects of inflation producing under-insurance.
Insured Perils	Those named in the policy as insured — fire, explosion etc.
Material fact	Any fact which would influence the insurer in accepting the risk and in fixing the premium terms and conditions of the contract. This should be disclosed at the proposal stage.
Operative clause	States the conditions under which the policy operates.
Premium	Contribution to the fund or price which an insured pays for the insurance cover.
Proposal form	Document issued by the insurers to record the information which the

underwriter requires in order to assess the nature of the risk being proposed.

Reinstatement
A means by which indemnity can be provided; referring to property insurance where an insurer undertakes to restore or rebuild property damaged by an insured peril.

Reinstatement of sum insured
Where partial losses have been paid the insurers will usually deduct the amount of the loss from the sum insured. If reinstatement applies, the sum insured is automatically reinstated free of charge. This applies to certain types of insurance only.

Schedule
Part of the policy which records the details of the particular contract.

Sum insured
Maximum liability of the insurer and the amount upon which the premium is based. It is not the amount which the insurers promise to pay in the event of loss.

Under-insurance
The sum insured is not equal to the value at risk. Under-insurance results in the insured paying too low a premium for the nature of the risk involved.

Utmost good faith
(uberrimae fides)
Positive duty to voluntarily disclose, accurately and fully, all facts material to the risk being proposed, whether asked for or not.

Warranty
In insurance contracts, fundamental conditions at the root of the contract a breach of which will render the contract null and void. (Contrast the meaning of this term in general contract law.)

Index